Education Now

Education Now

How Rethinking America's Past
Can Change Its Future

PAUL THEOBALD

Paradigm Publishers
Boulder • London

Copyright © 2009 Paradigm Publishers

Published in the United States by Paradigm Publishers, 3360 Mitchell Lane, Suite E, Boulder, CO 80301 USA.

Paradigm Publishers is the trade name of Birkenkamp & Company, LLC, Dean Birkenkamp, President and Publisher.

Library of Congress Cataloging-in-Publication Data

Theobald, Paul, 1956–
  Education now : how rethinking America's past can change its future / Paul Theobald.
      p. cm.
  Includes bibliographical references and index.
  ISBN 978-1-59451-623-8 (hardcover : alk. paper)
  ISBN 978-1-59451-624-5 (paperback : alk. paper)
  1. Education—Aims and objectives—United States. 2. Education—Economic aspects—United States. 3. Education—Political aspects—United States. I. Title.
  LA209.T43 2009
  370.973—dc22

                                                                                        2008024754

Printed and bound in the United States of America on acid-free paper that meets the standards of the American National Standard for Permanence of Paper for Printed Library Materials.

Designed and typeset by Straight Creek Bookmakers.

13 12 11 10 09   1 2 3 4 5

For my father and mother, Gil and Page Theobald,

from whom I learned all-too-slowly about the satisfaction inherent in work done well

📖

Contents

Preface

This is a book about the impact of a complex web of interrelated assumptions. Happily for the reader, however, anything of merit herein rests on merely one such assumption. Those willing to entertain the plausibility of this assumption should read on. Those unwilling can save themselves a good deal of time by stopping here. The assumption is this: the parameters of what constitutes an American culture—be it called a feverish consumer culture, a freedom-loving culture, a star-struck culture—whatever it may fairly be called and whatever it actually is, is determined by the assumptions embedded in decisions made about how to cultivate an economy, how to govern a mass society, and how to educate a nation's youth. In other words, culture is not something that develops on its own accord irrespective of larger political, economic, and educational arrangements. Quite the opposite. Culture develops squarely within the parameters created by these arrangements. In effect, culture is partly a self-fulfilling prophecy. We assume people are "wired" to live a certain way, so we adjust our political, economic, and educational systems to accommodate this; and lo and behold, a culture develops that matches the assumptions embedded in our political, economic, and educational thinking.

Cultural adjustments, cultural correctives—whatever one might wish to call a change in the way we are with one another or the way we are with others around the globe—will come about only at the time most Americans are willing to throw out current assumptions and adopt new ones. Thus, as I say, this is a book about assumptions.

There is one further point to consider before pushing on. The interrelated nature of the assumptions that feed our political, economic, and educational theory means that we can't seek to change one realm and ignore the others. The liberal revolutions and the ascendancy of capitalism in the eighteenth and nineteenth centuries were the result of simultaneous and whole-scale changes in political, economic, and educational thinking. Nothing less would have loosened the grip of 1,000 years of feudal tradition. Nothing less can successfully generate change of the sort that will have an impact on the character and quality of our culture today. The "game plan" for this book, therefore, is to first identify the popular assumptions of the past, contrast them with those that were rejected, and trace the impact of the decision to select one set of assumptions over another to our current cultural conditions. The second task is then to resurrect the rejected assumptions of the past—those that would have created a different future than what we now know—and project what they could do for us today. The first task represents the larger intellectual endeavor and is accomplished in Chapters 1 through 3—though this represents more than half of the book. The second task, a shorter one, is accomplished in Chapters 4 through 6.

I should say, finally, that in attempting to write this book my intellectual debt is probably greatest to the profoundly beautiful work of Charles Taylor and Wendell Berry, but I owe much to many others. I do want to take full credit for the book's shortcomings, however. With that in mind, I'd like to relay the story of Corregio when he was brought to see Raphael's *St. Cecilia* in 1515. His first words, so the story goes, were "I too am a painter." Citing this as he acknowledged his wonder at the great writers who preceded him, Montesquieu wrote, with Corregio, "And I too am a painter." So, in my turn, I wish to add, with humility, "I too can paint."

Acknowledgments

I need to say a word here about a few individuals who don't know me at all. Anything of merit in this book leans heavily on their insightful analysis of the circumstances that define the twenty-first century world. In this group I put the Canadian philosopher Charles Taylor; the former World Bank economist Herman Daly; and the Kentucky farmer, essayist, poet, and novelist, Wendell Berry. Among the many important lessons learned from these individuals is that it is possible to write about complex ideas with clarity. Though I am no match for any of them in that regard, I have done my best to apply their lessons in this work.

Crystallizing emerging conceptions about the interconnectedness of political, economic, and educational thinking was a product of numerous conversations with individuals I know well. That is a much larger group, and I want to let them know here that I am not only in debt to them intellectually, but I am also grateful for their friendship. I would not be who I am, nor would this book be what it is, without their influence on my thinking. For that, my sincere thanks go out to Bob Bilby, Craig and Aimee Howley, John Goodlad, Ron Rochon, Clif Tanabe, Dale Snauwaert, Dennis Jensen, Alan DeYoung, Jim Knotwell, Jim Anderson, Tim Sharer, Todd Dinkelman, Larry Cozad, Barb Black, Michael Corbett, Ed Mills, Larry Rogers, Michael Johnson, Jeanne Surface, Jim Curtiss, John Siskar, and Tim Glander.

Last, sincere thanks to my ever patient wife, Maureen. This book would not have been written at all without her tactful, well-placed urging. I have never known an individual with a greater or more heartfelt longing for justice and equity in this world. It is that characteristic I wish most for our children.

Introduction

A Tale of Two Schools

See if you recognize this school. It is an enormous new-looking building, perhaps a mere decade old. Its length seems to take up an entire block. At its center is a circle drive large enough to accommodate 20 sitting buses at the start and end of each school day. The exterior consists of sand-colored brick with narrow windows that look dark from the outside. There is a substantial play area in the back of the building, though neighbors can't tell you the last time they saw students playing in this area during the school day. A large parking lot on one end of the building contains the cars of roughly 80 percent of the faculty and staff. The rest must find spaces on the streets nearby. A few more than 800 schoolchildren, kindergarten through grade eight, enter this building Monday through Friday, nine months a year.

What these students find when they enter is a businesslike, purposefully created step-it-up atmosphere that promptly moves them to the places they are supposed to be at during designated hours. The curricular and instructional regimen is set in stone. Reading and mathematics dominate the school day, with periodic breaks for science and social studies. Extraneous classes—art, music, and physical education—have been cut to a bare minimum, perhaps one such class period over an entire week. The atmosphere is not unfriendly, but neither is it marked by informal interchange or conversation. There isn't time. Should a kindergarten student dawdle at snack time, the uneaten portion will be taken away. Every working professional in the building has come to understand that the school's test scores must be elevated in order to maintain the security of their jobs and the reputation of the school. There is no margin for error.

Those eighth graders who graduate from this school will more than likely move across town to a high school of similar-looking construction, though it is flanked by spacious practice fields, storage buildings, and a track and football stadium. The academic career of most of the students coming from the K–8 building has been decided to one degree or another. Some are moving into geometry, others into algebra, still others into algebra part one, and for a poor few there is consumer mathematics. The science curriculum is not as varied, though "tracked" variations exist. It is much the same with language arts. Students who have performed at similar levels in the K–8 building will be attending high school classes with others at that level.

The step-it-up atmosphere of the K–8 building exists only in certain corners of the high school. Those students who have been earmarked as "college-bound" by prior test scores will make their way toward "advanced placement" (AP) classes. Many will enroll in college courses before graduating from high school. These students will compete against one another for the "top of the class," hoping to improve their status as college applicants.

Because the school doesn't function this way for all students, because it has created a curricular track for the non-college bound students, the very feel of large portions of the high school is anything but "step-it-up." In fact, it is quite the opposite and may best be described as "laid back." It is marked by little effort at improving academic performance. Part of this laid-back atmosphere is created by student resistance to having lost out in the race for the top of the class and to being labeled, informally, as second-rate high school students.

Politicians and business leaders rail at this laid-back high school atmosphere. They want every student to be surrounded by the step-it-up atmosphere. They want every student engaged in an academic competition to be the best in the class. They rail in vain, however. For the past century the American high school has been too tightly connected to the economic role an individual will play with his or her life after graduation. The school's prediction in that regard dominates the curricular and instructional experience each student receives. Like it or not, the array of economic opportunities that awaits our high school graduates ranges from that which requires a postsecondary education to that which requires skills mastered merely at the eighth grade. As long as we continue to look at America's public school graduates as fodder for the economy, some students will be shuffled into interesting, influential jobs while others will take up boring, uninteresting jobs. As long this remains true, a laid-back atmosphere will dominate the school experience, especially as students get closer and closer to its end.

This book will go a long way toward explaining how these circumstances came to be, and it will suggest some things that might be done to change them. In the process, hopefully, the reader will see that what passes now for school reform, be it stepped up testing, school-to-school comparisons, teacher salaries tied to student tests, vouchers, charter schools, direct instruction, phonics, you name it—none of it will have an appreciable impact on the status quo. What schools must do is examine and modify the purposes for which they exist. Change those, and you can change the nation's educational performance. By way of a partial explanation, let's have a look at another school.

Picture again the K–8 building described at the outset. Focus your gaze on the southwest corner. In a wing consisting of two restrooms and eight classrooms, a school within a school exists. Eight teachers and a handful of collaborating "specialists" (special education, art, physical education, and music teachers) and teacher aides make up this school's curricular and instructional labor force. Their students number about 200 and take up roughly one-quarter of the available classroom space in a building built for 800. Roughly 25 students are assigned to each of the eight rooms, one grade to each room, encompassing, therefore, grades one through eight.

Each day is well planned by the entire teaching team, though in this school, unlike its large counterpart described earlier, no two days are alike. The amount of time spent on reading will vary from student to student, as will the materials used for reading instruction. It is much the same for all school subjects, and the teachers work to ensure that there is no status hierarchy among those subjects. The student who excels in art receives the same accolades as the student who excels in mathematics.

Teachers encourage one another to experiment with creative approaches to curriculum and instruction. They discuss what works, what doesn't, and why. Students and teachers frequently leave the building to study science in the school's garden or to conduct surveys in the school's neighborhood. Each grade-level class makes one substantial contribution to the school's community each year. The first graders might canvass a neighborhood, accompanied by eighth graders, parent volunteers, and teacher aides, to conduct fire alarm tests. For their part, eighth graders might petition the city for the removal of abandoned homes that present a safety risk in the neighborhood. The next eighth-grade class might petition for the creation of an urban farm on lots previously occupied by abandoned homes—creating a school-orchestrated food supply for needy families in the neighborhood.

When students are in a classroom, there is a pronounced mixing of ages and grades. Older children help younger ones learn traditional school subjects and, in the process, add depth to their own understanding. There is no "step-it-up" atmosphere in this school. Although everything is undertaken with earnestness, smiles and laughter are frequent. It is a pleasant place, and both teachers and students are happy to be there. What is more, parents are happy that their children are there.

The pronounced difference between this school and the first one stems most significantly from a difference related to purpose. No one would argue with the proposition that an education ought to enable an individual to live well. But many will argue that it is overly simplistic to suggest that our public schools should function near-exclusively to outfit youth for an eventual occupational destiny. There is an economic dimension to human life, to be sure, but it is not the only one. In fact, as history has proved again and again, without a political dimension in the lives of individuals, the doors to economic opportunity may easily remain closed.

The school-within-a-school functioned on the assumption that an education ought to prepare individuals to be citizens as well as economic actors, and that changed everything. Changing everything meant that all children had a much better chance to shine, to demonstrate their strengths, to work on their weaknesses absent the stigma that comes with formal and informal labels. Using a world filled with curricular resources just outside the school door, student engagement can be heightened, learning increased, and in-depth understanding reached far more frequently.

Of course politicians and business leaders cannot envision, and therefore will not readily countenance, any shift in the near-exclusively economic ends of the current public educational system. They fear that such a shift would mean fewer AP classes, fewer ninth graders taking geometry, fewer twelfth graders taking calculus—and thus America's global economic standing would markedly diminish. In their eyes, fewer AP classes would mean fewer scientists whose work might otherwise keep America's economy at the top of the international heap. This is pure speculation, mind you, for there is no evidence whatsoever to suggest that it is true. And consider the case of many of America's great twentieth-century scientists. Not only did they miss out on AP classes altogether, but many spent their first eight years in a one-room school utilizing whatever textbooks might be on hand. Yet still they moved on to college, calculus, and advanced sciences.

Pursuing an educational end that is speculation at best, and empty and damaging at worst, we have made the first school described here the dominant educational experience in this country. Given a choice, the vast majority of America's parents would rather send their children to the second school. Why, then, is it so difficult to make the second school the nation's dominant educational experience? We know it happens in pockets here and there, but it cannot seem to break out and become the norm instead of the exception.

The first three chapters of this book attempt to answer this question. The American public is generally unaware of the degree to which the great life questions that face all people—how they will govern themselves, how they will meet their needs, and how they will educate their youth—are all intertwined; the answer to one question drives the answers to the others. A society can make the educational question the primary one, and indeed philosophers as far back as Plato have made that case, but it has seldom become a reality. Or a society can make the political question the primary one, as was the case in the feudal states of the Middle Ages. Or societies can make the economic question the primary one, as is the case with most modern democracies in the world today—the United States included. Elevating the economic dimension to life meant that certain political and educational choices became predictable. For example, the political system needed to keep people free to pursue their economic goals. Ours does that. And the educational system needed to prepare individuals for their economic role. Ours does that, too.

After describing in these first chapters how these circumstances came to be, I lay out the ways in which change might be made to happen across all three realms: politics, economics, and education. For a central theme of this book is that changing one sphere requires change in all three. Nothing less will work, or so I will argue. Given this, I will go to some length to expose the interconnectedness of America's political, economic, and educational theory. We will start at the beginning, at the point of America's birth. Working through our political options near the end of the eighteenth century, we will see that our decisions hinged on what we believed life to be at its very essence. Although our ideas about this changed to some degree over time, we are currently wedded to the assumption that life is one prolonged economic struggle; thus our political, economic, and educational institutions look and feel the way they do.

A few words need to be said about terminology—starting with my use of the words *political* and *economic*. Throughout this book I will use these terms in a philosophic, rather than technical, manner. Technically, *politics* refers to decisionmaking while *economics* refers to systems of production and distribution. Philosophically, the words refer to human proclivities, the desire within people to play a role in decisionmaking or the desire to play a role in the production and distribution of goods and services.

An example may be helpful. I will sometimes ask a classroom full of young adults what the group would do if they found themselves alone on a large island. Someone will inevitably suggest that they would start out in search of food or shelter. Occasionally a student will suggest that the group would sit down and make some decisions about who would do what, when, and where. The first response is an example of the economic proclivity within humankind; the second represents the political one.

Another term that might require some explanation is the use of the word *liberal*, for its proper use is slowly disappearing from the vocabulary of the American public. Liberalism is a political perspective that calls for decisionmaking premised on freedom, human dignity, rationality, and representative democracy. In the strictest sense, the two largest political parties in the United States are both liberal. But the public relations campaigns of Ronald Reagan and the first George Bush transformed the term into a synonym for permissiveness and inefficiency in government, thus creating great potential for confusion when Americans come across the term used to describe policy premised on the conviction that freedom—or liberty, from which the term liberal was derived—is among the highest of human values. I have tried to minimize the use of the word in the interest of minimizing confusion, though at times its use could not be avoided.

A final word has to do with the use of gender terminology. Like others who are aware of the historical subordination of women and its lingering effects, I consciously try to avoid use of male pronouns to convey something ostensibly universal. But the fact that many, indeed most, of the individuals I cite in this book freely did so creates a dilemma for which I have no adequate solution. In the interest of clarity, however, I have decided to adopt the traditional patriarchal usage when discussing authors writing pre-mid-twentieth century and refrain from this usage elsewhere.

Plato wrote *The Republic* as an argument for the best sort of governmental arrangements possible. The book, however, is mostly about education. I should warn the reader that in a similar fashion, this is a book about the best sort of educational arrangements possible, though large parts of it are devoted to politics and economics. It is my firm belief that these three realms of human experience—politics, economics, and education—are intimately and inescapably linked. To change one, we must change them all. This book is an effort to move in that direction.

CHAPTER 1

While Publius Sleeps

Publius, I'm quite certain, requires an introduction these days, for it is hardly a household name. Actually, John Jay, James Madison, and Alexander Hamilton selected it as an author's pseudonym for the essays they wrote in defense of the Constitution created in Philadelphia during the summer of 1787. The essays were published in New York newspapers (New York was then the U.S. capital) as the nation debated the merits of adopting a totally new government. Collectively they became known as the *Federalist Papers,* after being published in two volumes early in 1788. Ever since that time they have served as the nation's intellectual mainstay in defense of the Constitution. In fact, the *Federalist Papers* have even been cited by Supreme Court justices as a rationale for judicial opinions.

Using pseudonyms for what we might today call "op-ed pieces" was common in the eighteenth century. For one, it protected the author from charges of libel. For another, it presented an interesting vehicle for adding another layer of meaning to an essay, a kind of intellectual exclamation point. Much of the national debate over the proposed U.S. Constitution took place in the newspapers of the nation—a significant development to which we will return later—and most of it was authored by individuals taking names reminiscent of the days of the Roman Republic. If the pro-Constitution arguments were published by Publius, the anti-Constitution arguments were written by Cato, Brutus, and Agrippa. Make no mistake about it: having thrown off the shackles of monarchical rule, Americans were going to set up something quite different. But what? The only time-tested nonmonarchical examples provided by history were the Greek and Roman republics, thus the widespread use of Roman pseudonyms.[1]

To keep this nation-building experience in proper perspective, however, we need to recall that the Philadelphia convention was not our first go at creating a government. Our first try was called the Articles of Confederation, a list of principles and procedures that all states in the union agreed to abide by and uphold. Actually, this is not totally accurate, for the official title was the Articles of Confederation and Perpetual Union. Historians dropped the "perpetual union" part because after just six years we decided to throw out the Articles as a basis for governmental arrangements. So much for perpetual.

Described in its simplest terms, the Articles of Confederation called for domestic issues to be considered and resolved within the various states, whereas foreign affairs were to be handled by a national Congress. Those who dutifully read their school history books know that the national Congress of the Confederation almost immediately had a difficult time coercing certain states to pay back their Revolutionary War debts. As a consequence, or so the story goes, delegates met in Philadelphia during the summer of 1787 to create a new form of government. This, it turns out, is not quite accurate either. The delegates met in Philadelphia for the expressed purpose of searching for ways to amend the Articles of Confederation—not to throw them out. But throw them out they did. Actually, almost everything that took place at the Philadelphia convention was questionable from a legal standpoint. And the legal questions were never particularly well answered. For instance, changes to the Articles, according to law, were to be made only with the unanimous consent of all the states. The delegates at Philadelphia decided their new Constitution would be ratified if they could manage to get nine of thirteen states to support it. From where did the authority for this decision come? On top of this, changes to the Articles were to be decided in the seated legislatures of the various states. The Philadelphia delegates decided that the issue of ratifying the Constitution would be settled by separate state constitutional conventions rather than the seated legislatures. From where did authority for this decision come?

Most of the extralegalities surrounding the Philadelphia convention are overlooked—they are certainly not a part of the sanitized (some would say falsified) history in the schoolbooks our children read. But perhaps these were small sins when the larger context is considered, since history (up to that point) afforded few examples of a switch in governmental organization that was so widely debated and, in the end, so popularly decided. If the conundrum of wishing to establish a republic premised on the rule of law could only be accomplished by breaking the law, so be it. Few argued that the hypocrisy inherent in the ratification of the U.S. Constitution would set it up for eventual failure, though some did.[2]

For now we need to recognize that setting up a new government requires some shared assumptions on a few simple questions. I suppose, in fairness to trained philosophers and other academicians, I should preface this discussion by saying that these questions are not really "simple." There are a good many caveats, contingencies, if/thens, and yes/buts that surround them. Having said that, however, I believe that the essential thrust of each question is straightforward and uncomplicated enough. So I will push on. Is human life, essentially, one prolonged period of economic activity? Or, said another way, is life essentially an individual endeavor? Before we attempt an answer, let's look at an alternative question. Is human life essentially a sustained period of shared existence with others? Or, said another way, is life essentially a social endeavor?

Any reasonable person will of course respond that life is both an individual and a social undertaking and that it has economic and political dimensions (political in the sense that we must establish rules related to how we will live social and economic lives). And this is true enough. It may even be self-evident, to use a phrase made popular by Thomas Jefferson. But let me refer back to the original question. Is life *essentially* an individual or social experience? Is it *essentially* about economics or politics? This may seem like splitting hairs, but what life is, at bottom, makes a big difference if you happen to be hard about the business of creating a new government.

As it happened, 1787 was an auspicious time in the history of Western political thought, and it is instructive to examine that history in order to make sense of the assumptions undergirding Publius's essays and the Constitution itself. We should remember, though, that first and foremost in the minds of the framers was the ubiquitous assumption that government is the greatest of all threats to freedom. A hard-won military victory over the government of George III seemed like ample proof of this assumption to the former colonials. So ruling out monarchy, the framers debated the choice of governmental options with an eye toward checking the self-aggrandizing tendency of governments. But what were the options, and on what assumptions were they based?

As our founders cast about in Philadelphia for some kind of governmental recipe to replace the monarchical traditions of Europe, ancient Greek and Roman examples loomed fairly large. But these examples came with a serious defect. They were followed by an extended period of famine, disorder, and recurring plagues known as the Dark Age. To many this meant that these ancient republics were a failure and that their essential features were to be avoided, not emulated. In general, if you were of the opinion that the Constitution drafted in Philadelphia put too much authority in a distant, centralized, and therefore dangerously powerful government, you concentrated on what was good about the classical world, especially the tendency toward small, autonomous, though federated, states. If you were pro-Constitution, you concentrated on dismissing the small ancient republics as places defined by constant squabbling, political disorder, and a potentially disastrous inability to defend themselves from large imperial powers.

It turns out the American stage was not the first on which the debate regarding the wisdom of a large, strong national government versus a weak federal government binding small, fairly autonomous states took place. One of the giants of eighteenth-century political theory, the Frenchman Charles de Secondat Montesquieu, argued that republics needed to be small in order to be effectively self-governed. David Hume of Scotland challenged Montesquieu's arguments about the necessity of small republics, even going so far as to suggest that the opposite was true—that large republics with highly centralized authority were more likely to succeed than small ones. In a paper entitled "The Idea of the Perfect Commonwealth," published in 1752, Hume argued that small size and the proximity of the government to the people will invite aggressive, turbulent debate, thus breaking down governmental efficiency. Allow a large state to take republican form and it would much more efficiently deal with the problem of faction formation that haunted Madison and Hamilton. Wrote Hume,

> In a large government, which is modeled with masterly skill, there is compass and room enough to refine the democracy, from the lower people, who may be admitted into the first elections or first concoction of the commonwealth, to the higher magistrates, who direct all the movements. At the same time, the parts are so distant and remote, that it is very difficult, either by intrigue, prejudice, or passion to hurry them into any measures against the public interest.[3]

Here was a scholarly argument that legitimated a strong central government. And all signs point to the fact that Madison, at least, knew it well: "Extend the sphere, and you take in a greater variety of parties and interests; you make it less probable that a majority of the whole will have a common motive to invade the rights of other citizens; or if such a common motive exists, it will be more difficult for all who feel it to discover their own strengths and to act in unison with each other."[4] College students reading Locke's *Second Treatise* are often struck by the familiar ring to some of his phrases—for their resonance with Jefferson's phrases in the *Declaration of Independence* are striking. The same can be said, however, for the phraseology of Hume's "Idea of the Perfect Commonwealth" showing up in Madison's Federalist #10.

But Hume brings us to the eighteenth century, almost to the American Revolution itself—and that is too big a leap for us. "Modern" political theory, that which provided the steam for the destruction of feudalism and the largest source of accessible ideas for our struggling founding fathers, really came to fruition in the seventeenth century—and even at that, much of it rested on a few powerful ideas that date back further still, to the sixteenth century. To fully come to grips with how our current political circumstances came to be, we must look at these ideas in some detail.

The End of Feudalism and the Advent of Modern Political Theory

A myriad of political, economic, and religious developments in England during the 1640s and 1650s came together in such a way as to create a truly unprecedented historical moment. It was during these years that a kind of precursor to the dilemma faced by our founding fathers occurred. England, our "mother country," found itself without a king and consequently saddled with the same burden that faced our founding fathers a little over a century later. That is, it had to either set up a new system of governance or reproduce the old one. This moment served as the birth of most modern political theories, from reactionary to radical. In fact, the choices made at this critical point in time continue to shape the course of history in virtually all Western democracies, and for this reason we will explore this moment in some detail. Perhaps the best way to describe the events preceding, during, and after the English Civil War of the 1640s is to say that given these developments—economic, social, religious, and political—the old monarchical system no longer seemed to work.

First, the economic climate of England between 1540 and 1640 can accurately be described as a period of unprecedented inflation. The price of wheat and other agricultural commodities rose repeatedly throughout the 100-year period, a circumstance that some historians contend triggered the development of a kind of agrarian capitalism. The rising prices were a strong incentive for increasing production among those fortunate enough to own their own holdings. "Enclosure" was the most common method, and since twenty-first-century citizens are generally unfamiliar with what this was, some explanation is required.

Most rural areas had strips of land that belonged to no one but were held in common for the use of the entire neighborhood. Rules and regulations related to the use of the "commons" evolved out of the deep feudal past. In some cases these tracts of land were used for crop production, but more frequently they were used for grazing of livestock. As textile production in England intensified—partially due to expanding trade networks made possible by technological innovations in navigation and in shipbuilding—the demand for wool skyrocketed, turning sheep husbandry into an extremely profitable niche market.[5]

Even when wool demand ebbed during the eighteenth century, the pressure to enclose commons continued unabated—perhaps even intensified—as England's farmers shouldered the burden of feeding the growing urban industrial centers. The act of enclosure devastated the rural poor who relied on the use of the commons to make their slender ends meet, forcing many to move to cities in search of paid employment. In fact, it is likely that enclosure and the rural depopulation and urbanization it created was the main influence on the development of truly radical political ideas in the sixteenth and seventeenth centuries. Today we sometimes hear talk of "restoring the commons," for in retrospect it is easy to see how the removal of the commons was coincident with the removal of a political dimension in the lives of average citizens.[6] While the commons lasted, everyone in the neighborhood had a say in how the commons would be kept and in who would play key stewardship roles related to its maintenance. As the victims of enclosure drifted into England's industrial cities, however, they lacked even the vote—a reform measure that didn't arrive until the late nineteenth century.[7]

From time to time there was significant royal opposition to enclosure, though kings were not particularly successful at stopping it. Parliament, dominated by landholders who stood to gain from it, predictably passed legislation to ease the enclosure process. The first such bill was passed in 1621. In 1633, however, when Charles I grew upset with Parliament and disbanded it for a period of years, he came down hard on enclosers, fining some 600 of them. This action only served to generate greater levels of antipathy between the Parliament and the crown, antipathy that would ultimately end in civil war.

Because enclosures were generally tied to the intensification of wool production, they were often "hedged in" with vegetation that produced a kind of fence—or actual stone fences were built, though these were much more costly. This practice led to naming certain rural opponents of enclosure "Levelers," for they often made clandestine trips to enclosures to level hedges or stone fences out of protest. The term would in turn come to name a group of political protesters who sought to level the political and economic playing field, so to speak, by demanding a voice for commoners in the decisions that affected them. The Levelers would attract prominent members of the rural gentry and the urban merchant class and become a major political voice during the civil war years of the 1640s.

Agriculture, however, was not the only occupation that underwent significant changes as a result of whole-scale expansion efforts. Coal mining increased dramatically so that by the eve of the Civil War, England produced three times as much coal as the rest of Europe combined. It was used to fuel the burgeoning industrial centers, but it also enabled greater levels of iron and steel production, which in turn worked as a catalyst for a large range of industrial manufacturing operations that increasingly displaced small-scale craftsmen: everything from cannon and musket production to sugar-refining, paper production, soap-making, and glass-making—and the list could go on and on.

The social fabric of English society was severely strained by a century of steady inflation and the headlong rush toward industrial development. Put simply, it was not a good time to be poor. Rural tenant farmers were displaced in large numbers, becoming urban dwellers too often unemployed or underemployed. As late as 1820, the Duchess of Sutherland carried out a massive enclosure, dispossessing 15,000 tenants from over 794,000 acres. The farmers were replaced by 131,000 sheep. Evicted families were given approximately two acres of marginal land on which to live.[8] Unable to feed themselves from unproductive land, they drifted, living as paupers. Those who found work, underpaid to start, continued to lose ground in terms of their ability to meet basic needs as inflation continued unabated. England experimented steadily with workhouses for the poor, mostly dispossessed rural dwellers. Emigration to North America, while attractive, was simply not an option for the poorest in England. With so many on the verge of starvation, child labor became a prominent fixture in industrial cities and on intensified farming operations.

It is quite likely that the amount of starvation throughout England between 1540 and 1640 rivaled the worst medieval shortage periods.[9] Parliament answered with what became known as the Poor Laws (1531 to start, and many later variations all the way into the twentieth century). The law essentially created a tax in each parish to be collected for poor relief, but that relief was often hard to obtain as local parishes varied considerably in terms of their determinations regarding who was eligible.[10] The nineteenth-century historian Thomas Carlyle was the first to point out the connection between widespread enclosure and the development of Poor Laws.

Deteriorating economic circumstances triggered outbreaks of protest and violence. In Northhamptonshire in 1607 a Leveler gathering turned violent. There were tenant farmer revolts in southwestern England during the late 1620s, and antienclosure riots all across England during the first years of the 1640s. The homes of the wealthy were sometimes entered and plundered by "masterless men," a common seventeenth-century phrase. Wagons carrying foodstuffs destined for urban centers were often stopped and forcibly emptied by groups of such men. Writing in 1642, Lionel Cranfield, Earl of Middlesex, remarked that "the countenances of men are so altered, especially of the mean and middle rank of men, that the turning of a straw would set a whole county in a flame and occasion the plundering of any man's house or goods."[11]

Had this kind of social unrest been confined to the rural poor—and to England's countryside—it may be that the great political drama of the 1640s and 1650s would have never unfolded. England had endured peasant revolts earlier in its medieval past.[12] With so many victims of enclosure ending up in the cities, however, particularly in London, the scale and potential consequence of rebellion increased dramatically. And the threat of urban protest was further augmented by the fact that many of England's wealthiest merchants, bankers, insurance dealers, and the like also lived in urban areas and were also disaffected by the policies of Charles I. To fully appreciate the role played by England's new merchant class in the ensuing drama, however, we must look briefly at profoundly new developments in the English religious scene.

It is not uncommon to hear the English Civil War referred to as the "Puritan revolution," though such a label tends to obscure the effect of new forms of industrial and agricultural activity and the resulting social and political consequences. Because the seventeenth-century religious scene was so dramatically different from what we know today, it requires a little description.

The first thing to keep in mind is that the Church of England was *the* state church. As a result, every Englishman was a member, and every Englishmen was required to attend Sunday services at the local parish. In fact, individuals were subject to fines for missing a service. On top of this, all were required to tithe— that is, each family had to give one-tenth of its earnings to the pastor of the local church. Over time, the church became virtually indistinguishable from a formal governmental agency, with taxing ability and a court system. It became the holder of public records in much the same way county courthouses function in the United States today. If vagrants required flogging, it happened in the churchyard. If an individual was to be fined, it was assessed by a church official. Writing in 1653, an ex-army officer complained of the way local pastors brought parishioners "to their courts for working on holidays or marrying without a license or upon groundless suspicion of unchastity. Many such poor pretenses [were given] merely to drain the people's purses."[13] In a way that is particularly difficult for us to comprehend from our historical vantage point, justice was a religious affair.

Ministerial appointments were a matter of political patronage, and with few exceptions, local pastors had tight familial connections to the landed aristocracy. In this way the interests of both the church and state became interlocked. And in the days before newspaper, radio, and television, the local church was the sole source of information about the world. The king was free to direct the topic of sermons and did so on many occasions. James I directed the clergy to preach against the "the insolency of our women" in 1620, and Charles directed them to preach in 1626 that refusing to support the crown financially was a sin. The tight connection between church and state meant that the government was able to exercise considerable control over what the people of England heard from the pulpit, and presumably, therefore, what they talked about. In this way the church became an indispensable ideological agent for the crown. As political reformers grew more bold in the seventeenth century and talked openly about a separation of church and state, it was an argument every bit as much about the freedom to engage different ideas as it was about the freedom to worship as one pleased, an argument relevant to our nation's founders and to us today.

By the mid-sixteenth century, "Puritan" theology emerged as a highly desirable alternative to what many saw as a corrupt state church. Puritans were those who embraced the theology of John Calvin and others—particularly John Knox and his Presbyterian teachings that gradually moved south from Scotland. They rejected the heavy emphasis on sacraments and ritual in the Church of England, for it had retained many components of the Catholic faith, including a highly ritualized liturgy. In its place Puritans called for more preaching—with messages uncontrolled by united church-state interests.

Puritans believed that God determined who was saved and who was not prior to a person's birth. The anxiety inherent in this doctrine of "predestination" led Puritans to acquire outward signs that might indicate God's selection of those who were on their way to eternal salvation. There was a heavy emphasis placed on improving God's earth through persistent work—and, as a consequence, they rejected the custom of observing so many "holy days." Like Catholic nations, England observed over 100 holy days in honor of various saints—and any Englishmen who worked on these days was subject to a fine of some consequence—a practice that infuriated Puritans.

Historians since R. H. Tawney in the first years of the twentieth century have generally agreed that the Puritan work ethic coincided—and significantly aided—the rise of capitalism in England, and later in the United States.[14] Part of this was due to the emphasis on industriousness that was preached incessantly from Presbyterian pulpits. The slowly developing "Protestant work ethic" would eventually lead to the creation of workhouses and farms for the able-bodied poor. To a far greater degree than the world had quite possibly ever known, Calvinist and Lutheran theology turned protestant Christianity into an individualized religion.[15] Calvinism in particular lifted salvation up for the taking—provided one was willing to produce the effort and industry required to show the rest of the world that you were one of the elect.

Much of the Puritan story is familiar enough. Elizabeth mercilessly persecuted Puritans throughout the 1590s, prompting many to emigrate to what became "New England." The reign of both James and Charles brought greater toleration and thus significant growth in Puritan ranks—especially in the growing urban centers. Many Puritan leaders found their way into the House of Commons, and because the Church of England was virtually indistinguishable from royal authority, antipathy between the crown and Parliament grew. This was just one more outward sign that the system was crumbling.

Civil war broke out in 1642 between the crown's forces and the New Model Army of Parliament under the command of Oliver Cromwell. There was tumult and disorder throughout much of the decade, which ultimately led to Charles's capture in 1647 and his execution in 1649. Parliament abolished the monarchy and the House of Lords, in effect creating a kind of republic or English Free State. But what was the new government to look like? How would it function? What would its relationship be to the Church of England? There were many questions to be answered. And there were many with varied answers to the questions. The circumstances of the 1640s and 1650s were the source of a veritable explosion in the production of quite diverse political theories. The choices made at this pivotal "moment" in history had a deep impact on the choices made in Philadelphia in the summer of 1787 and thus continue to affect daily life in the United States during the twenty-first century.

One crucial idea that took hold during the 1640s was first articulated almost a century earlier by an obscure English scholar named Sir Thomas Smith. Born in 1513 to parents of minor gentry status, Smith attended Cambridge and eventually became an accomplished classics scholar. His keen intellectual abilities soon brought him into governmental service as a Member of Parliament and as Elizabeth's ambassador to France. Smith wrote two books, both published shortly after his death. The first, *A Discourse of the Commonweal of This Realm of England*, was actually more of a treatise on economics than politics, and we will therefore revisit it in the next chapter.[16] But in it Smith set in motion a political idea that would have far-reaching consequences.

Thomas Smith conceived of the state as "a multitude of free men collected together by common accord and covenants among themselves." This idea was a sharp break with feudal conceptions of statehood. Far from being a collection of free individuals, a state was thought to be nothing more than the personal rule of a monarch tied to physical, geographic boundaries. Similar views characterized the state as a collection of corporate bodies or communities, or it was thought to be an expression of God's will. A sixteenth-century French political philosopher, Jean Bodin, serves as a nice contemporary contrast to Smith. Said Bodin, "A group of families bound together by mutual trust forms a corporate association or community, and a group of corporate associations and communities bound together by a sovereign power forms a commonwealth."[17]

With Smith and Bodin in the sixteenth century, we see the start of an English-French contrast in terms of what constitutes a state, a contrast we can follow through time and into the political ideas of the Englishman Locke and the Frenchman Montesquieu—two heavyweights in terms of their impact on the founding fathers in 1787. It should be apparent, meanwhile, that a state composed of free-acting individuals driven, as Thomas Smith thought, by self-interested greed and avarice, would suggest a political system predicated on unfettering human ambition, curbing it only when it comes into conflict with the ambitions of others. The assumption undergirding such a governmental system is that life is essentially an economic and individual undertaking. In contrast, in a state composed of corporate bodies and communities, the political system would more likely be geared toward improving the well-being of the communities that compose it, not self-interested individuals. The assumption underlying this governmental system is that life is essentially a social and therefore political endeavor.

Thomas Hobbes was the first to offer a well-conceived plan for governmental arrangements based on the idea that a state was a collection of self-interested individuals. Hobbes was born in 1588, the son of a minor clergyman of few means. Hobbes was nevertheless educated at Oxford and thereafter spent virtually his entire life defending the aristocracy of which he was not a part. Whatever else may be said of Thomas Hobbes, he was indisputably a brilliant man. Friend to Galileo, professional associate of Descartes, personal secretary for a time to Francis Bacon, Hobbes knew and was a part of the seventeenth-century's intelligentsia.

In 1640 he wrote *The Elements of Law,* a staunch defense of absolutism. It was initially circulated merely as a manuscript until being published a decade later. Even informal manuscript circulation, however, was enough to label him a monarchist, and late in 1640, after Charles finally reconvened the Parliament he had dismissed back in 1629, Hobbes fled to France in fear for his safety. While there he composed his two most influential works. The first, *De Cive,* was a defense of the monarchy against the charges of Parliament. The second, *Leviathan,* published in 1651, was a remake of *De Cive* that essentially accepted regicide and therefore legitimated the rule of Oliver Cromwell, but its arguments were intended to invest Cromwell with the same sovereign power that once belonged to the now dead Charles I.

One might think that Hobbes's devotion to the monarchy would have relegated him to the margins of political theory. But this has not been the case. One reason for this is that Hobbes made persuasive arguments about man in the "state of nature," portraying humans as individualistic and selfish. The state of nature became a popular Enlightenment construction, often used as the first step in trying to identify how governmental operations would have evolved if they hadn't been usurped by the power of lords and kings. And Hobbes picked up on Thomas Smith's conception of the state as "a multitude of free men collected together" and advanced it to an acceptable concept in the seventeenth century. But more important still, Hobbes set in motion a popular view about man's motives and inclinations—and thereby his suitableness for playing political roles. Hobbes believed that men were born free and equal in the state of nature, but rather than this fact being a wellspring for political democracy, he interpreted it as a condition that demands an authoritarian power. Because men were free and equal, they would inevitably compete for dominion over one another. Said Hobbes in *De Cive*, "All society is either for gain or glory: not so much for love of our fellows, as for love of ourselves." And since all have the freedom to compete for gain, the state of nature is in effect a state of "all men against all men."[18] Because this condition produces fear among all, all come together in civil society and create that government—give consent to that government—which can through the rule of law remove fear and guarantee order. The catch regarding consent is that, according to Hobbes, once it is given it cannot be taken back. If it could, this would reintroduce the likelihood of self-interested men once again seeking dominion over one another, thus reinserting fear into civil society.

Hobbes's great contributions were (1) to lend popularity and force to the idea of a state being a collection of individuals, and (2) to argue that men by nature are too selfish, too concerned with their own gain, to play any kind of a political role in civil society. In Hobbesian political theory, the best sort of government is created by minimizing citizen participation within it. Although John Locke would reject the authoritarian and monarchical elements of what Hobbes had to say, he would nevertheless provide a softer sort of intellectual second to these Hobbesian contributions. We can see Hobbes, too, in James Madison's classic defense of the Constitution: "If men were angels, no government would be necessary." And in Hamilton: "Why has government been instituted at all? Because the passions of men will not conform to the dictates of reason and justice without constraint."[19]

Before turning to Locke's work, however, we should situate Hobbes among other political theorists who saw a chance to restructure English society in the wake of Cromwell's military victory over royal forces. Robert Filmer looms fairly large among them. Like Hobbes, Filmer was a monarchist, but one who possessed little tolerance for Hobbes's anticlerical bent. Filmer was the first of eighteen children, the son of parents from landed gentry. As the eldest son, through the feudal practice of primogeniture (which limited one's ability to distribute land holdings to the eldest son, thus preserving the size of feudal estates), Filmer inherited at least four manors and hundreds of acres. He was educated at Cambridge but came back to his estates in Kent after graduation and participated mainly in local political affairs. During the late 1630s, as anti-Charles sentiment was growing, Filmer wrote *Patriarcha: A Defense of the Natural Power of Kings Against the Unnatural Liberty of the People,* and as a manuscript, it was distributed around the County of Kent. Perhaps due to the political volatility of the era, Filmer refused to have the manuscript published. Whether this is why or not, it may have been a very good decision, for the work inevitably dubbed him as a staunch royalist. As it was, when Parliamentary forces took control of Kent in 1643, Filmer was imprisoned for a time.

Because there were several manuscript copies floating around, *Patriarcha* eventually found its way into print in 1680, after Filmer's death. Its sophisticated legitimation of the monarchy became quite useful to those who decided, after Cromwell's death, that the monarchy needed to be restored. The arguments of *Patriarcha* rested on firm belief in the absolute veracity of the Bible, a starting point that played well with royalists true to the Church of England, but also with many Puritans.

Filmer argued that human society descended from Adam—and since God created Adam first, he had authority over all who came later. All men were born unto fathers and all were consequently subject to their authority. Filmer would hear nothing of the increasingly popular idea that all men were born free and equal. Quite the contrary, Filmer argued that all men are naturally subject to authority at birth. He especially attacked the growing belief that a government is legitimated by the consent of the governed. Filmer claimed that a person is born into a particular society quite arbitrarily and the matter of "consent" doesn't enter into it. There is no choice in the matter, just as one has no choice about being born subject to the authority of one's father. As a descendant of Adam, who had dominion over all who came after, the king has dominion over all in his kingdom. All owe their allegiance to the king and always have. For Filmer there is no such thing as a prepolitical "state of nature" where man roamed with no allegiances and under no authority.

As noted earlier, *Patriarcha* found a receptive audience among supporters of the Restoration, for it served as a legitimating defense of a monarchy at a time when much antimonarchical sentiment lingered. It therefore became a target for those who continued to oppose the idea of a return to monarchy, John Locke in particular. Locke found exceptionally egregious the way Filmer's doctrines were expounded in England's churches—crystallizing in his mind the dire need for separating church and state. In the introduction to the *Second Treatise of*

Government, Locke stated, "I should not speak so plainly of a gentleman, long since past answering, had not the pulpit, of recent years, publicly owned his doctrine and made it the current divinity of the times."[20] In fact, Locke devoted the entire *First Treatise of Government* to a step-by-step refutation of Filmer's arguments. This cleared the way to establish two critical points made in the *Second Treatise*: men were born free and equal, and no government was legitimate that lacked the consent of the governed.

It is interesting that Locke took such pains to refute Filmer and said so little about Hobbes, the other great monarchist of the age, especially since Hobbes is still recognized as one of England's greatest political philosophers. But Locke didn't respond to Hobbes because he was not at all popular in the last half of the seventeenth century, even among conservative royalists. In fact, in 1666 the House of Commons decided that it was Hobbes's atheism that had caused the fire and plague that scorched London that year. He narrowly avoided imprisonment for this dubious charge. Another reason Locke didn't respond to Hobbes is because Hobbesian thought meshed well with Locke's basic premises. Locke argued, for instance, like Hobbes, that human nature mitigated against an active political role for commoners. Said Locke, "appetites and aversions" would inevitably "carry men to the overturning of all morality."[21] Like Hobbes, Locke argued that men were born free and equal, and that governments *do* require the consent of the governed. But Hobbes used these rather radical premises to argue on behalf of a monarchy; Locke did something close to the opposite.

By the 1650s, however, far more egalitarian and democratic proposals were abundant—and these no doubt were a major obstacle for Hobbes as he tried to sell England on re-creating authoritarian power. For instance, James Harrington published *Oceana* in 1656, dedicating it to Cromwell. *Oceana* was a thinly veiled story about an island republic that utilized a division of governmental powers to achieve an egalitarian commonwealth. Gerrard Winstanley published *The Law of Freedom* in 1651, also dedicated to Cromwell. It too was a blueprint for remaking a new political system for England. Winstanley went considerably beyond Harrington in suggesting the possibility of an increasingly collectivist society buttressed by a sound, life-long educational system.

Within the political thought of Harrington and Winstanley it is possible to discern the genesis of an English alternative to a trajectory begun by Hobbes but completed more acceptably and more thoroughly by Locke. This Hobbes-Locke trajectory would clear the way for the advent of a commercialist/mercantilist economy by empowering England's business interests at the expense of small freeholders and laborers, and to some degree at the expense as well of those among the landed aristocracy who were not able to adequately diversify their revenue streams through commercial investment. Abolishing the House of Lords as Cromwell's army gained the upper hand militarily served as a kind of precursor, a sign that England was moving in a direction that ultimately culminated in 1911 when the

House of Lords was rendered powerless by the Liberal leadership of David Lloyd George and Herbert Asquith. To be sure, the lords reclaimed their authority for a time after the Restoration, but that time was limited by the power of democratic ideas spread ceaselessly throughout England during the 1640s and 1650s. The alternative trajectory, of which Harrington and Winstanley were a part, may be described as a postfeudal agrarian open society, and although it seems culturally out of step from our vantage point today, it was nevertheless a real alternative for England in the 1650s and the United States in the 1780s.

James Harrington was born in 1611 to parents of minor gentry status. He attended Oxford but left before graduation. Thereafter he traveled in Europe extensively and returned to his familial home in Rand, living a quiet single life. At some point, perhaps through family connections, he reportedly became a personal attendant to Charles I, though there is some historical confusion over this. Some accounts hold that he was deeply saddened by Charles's execution (some even say he was on the execution stand when it occurred) and became a recluse for the next seven years of his life. Whatever the facts are, it is true that little is known about his life before 1656 when he published *Oceana*, a decidedly antimonarchical piece of political theory. In fact, the work was considered so radical that Harrington was imprisoned for a time after the Restoration of Charles II. He died in 1666.

Harrington leaned heavily on Machiavelli as he created his tale of the island republic of Oceana. From the outset it is clear that Harrington had deep admiration for the Greek and Roman republics, as well as sixteenth-century republican Venice. But he found shortcomings in each that led to his unique prescriptions for what England might become. In Harrington's estimation, republics that relied too heavily on urban-commercialist enterprise were necessarily weak, while republics that emphasized rural population growth and agrarian economics were much stronger. Harrington asserted that the owner-operator of a land holding is a far superior citizen soldier then the wage laborer living in the city. Further, for Harrington, the fact of land ownership, over and above the inequity in urban living conditions, creates a more orderly, rational public square—thus also adding stability to the republic. "Commonwealths upon which city life hath the stronger influence, as Athens, have seldom or never been quiet, but at best are found to have injured their own business by overdoing it," but where a republic "consisteth of a country, the plough in the hands of the owner findeth him a better calling, and produceth the most innocent and steady genius of a commonwealth, such is that of Oceana."[22]

In other words, Harrington was a kind of Thomas Jefferson of the 1650s—an advocate for a much more democratic agrarian future in England—just as Jefferson sought for the United States. Harrington, however, laid out a political system and certain key public policies designed to create that kind of future. He offered them to Cromwell in the hope that he might adopt them. Without question, Harrington favored a much wider distribution of land ownership than that which then existed in England.[23] He promised to create this circumstance by adhering to Oceana's "agrarian law," a series of restrictions on primogeniture, dowries, and land sales. These restrictions were designed to open up land owner-ship for those industrious enough to make it happen. Harrington believed that by dramatically increasing this population, Oceana (England) would also dra-matically increase the stability of the commonwealth. His political system placed authority in a national assembly composed of two houses. The higher house was for the wealthiest land owners, and its function was to debate ideas related to the well-being of the commonwealth. The function of the lower, popular house was to choose from among those ideas passed along by the higher house, and to do so without much debate. Harrington believed this system would capture the best long-term vision for the republic and check it against the immediate reali-ties and circumstances faced by the majority of the population. The quiet, or passive, popular legislative body reveals the pervasiveness of the feudal notion that elites possess the wisdom necessary to rule, while it similarly reveals the increasingly popular notion that the people must be connected to government in some fashion. If in analyzing the possibility of an open society Madison and Hamilton took anything from Harrington, it was, regrettably, that the people could legitimately be kept at arm's length while the real decisionmaking took place among the wealthy and well-born.

In an attempt to explain why James Harrington remains a rather obscure politi-cal theorist today it is often said that he predicted badly—that the future he envi-sioned never came into being. Why, therefore, should students engage the political theory of James Harrington? But such a take on this question misses the point. While it is true that in the years after his death England reembraced monarchical power, moved substantially toward a more or less permanent professional army, and made its first steps toward a commercially oriented, government-finance-driven economy—all of which were antithetical to Harrington—these develop-ments do not prove him wrong. England's future unfolded after Harrington's death according to decisions made in the policy arena—decisions made in accord with a vision for England's future quite different from Harrington's. All of this is to say, of course, that the world would look very different today if decisions had been made consonant with Harrington's description of Oceana.

The same can be said for our next political theorist, the even more radical Gerrard Winstanley. Born in Lancashire in the north of England in 1609, he was influential on the English political scene during the late 1640s and early 1650s, not so much for what he wrote as for what he did.[24] For Winstanley collected a group of individuals who became known as the "diggers" and lived according to principles he laid out, digging and planting crops on poor, unenclosed common lands. He defended the actions of the diggers with brilliant essays and pamphlets—many of which have been saved. In 1651—the same year Hobbes published *Leviathan* for

Cromwell's benefit, Winstanley published *The Law of Freedom,* also dedicated to Cromwell, laying out a blueprint for an education-based agrarian republic. Needless to say, the plan was rejected by Cromwell, England moved in a completely different direction, and Winstanley removed himself from public life—scarcely to be heard from again.

But the digger story is intriguing, and the short-lived movement has served for more than 300 years as an untapped possibility for radicals (there is some academic speculation about the similarities between Winstanley and Marx, for example[25]) and as a warning to conservatives of what can happen when policies too disproportionately favor those with property.

Winstanley was the son of a Lancashire clothier and may have attended grammar school as a boy. In 1630 his father used connections to apprentice Gerrard to a London tailor by the name of Sarah Gater. Gater was a widow who inherited a significant library from her first husband who had died in 1624. Winstanley had access to this library as a result of this apprenticeship, a circumstance that clearly aided his intellectual development, though in the corpus of his works (all published in the four years between 1648 and 1652) he makes virtually no reference to other books. Winstanley became a free citizen of London in 1638, at which point he opened his own retail clothing shop. But the timing of this venture was not good and by the outbreak of Civil War in 1642, Winstanley was near bankruptcy. Finally, in November of 1643, he and his wife left his London home and shop, paid his creditors as far as his assets permitted, and moved to near Cobham in Surrey. Describing these circumstances five years later, Winstanley claimed, "I was beaten out both of estate and trade, and forced to accept the good will of friends crediting of me, to live a country life."[26]

Winstanley apparently herded cattle for neighbors, and scholars assumed these were years that cut close to the bone for Winstanley—that he and his wife were as poor as Winstanley's pamphlets would lead one to believe. Recent scholarship, however, suggests that he was likely not destitute; he had inherited property in the Cobham vicinity from his father-in-law, a London surgeon. In fact, it appears as if the "cattle herding" was actually a small but lucrative cattle business.[27] Regardless, the breakdown of traditional English society during the Civil War seems to have had a profound effect on Winstanley. The collapse of the Church of England after Parliament's execution of Archbishop of Canterbury William Laud meant that the mechanisms of civil restraint were considerably loosened or absent altogether. Press operators, for perhaps the first time in history, did not have to worry about ecclesiastical censorship. Radical ideas were distributed far and wide; many condemned the landed aristocracy, the established church, and the monarchy they supported.

Despite his lack of a college education, Winstanley was a gifted writer, and he joined the nationwide fervor as a pamphleteer. In the spring of 1649, however, with Cromwell's victory secure, the House of Lords abolished, the king executed, and on the heels of yet another extremely poor fall harvest, Winstanley and a small group of followers settled on St. George's Hill—a little-used commons outside of London—to "dig" the earth, plant crops, build homes, and share the earth as a "common treasury." Winstanley claimed that through a vision God had instructed him to lead this venture:

> I have now obeyed the command of the Spirit that bid me declare this all abroad, I have declared it, and I will declare it by word of mouth, I have now declared it by my pen. And when the Lord doth show me the place and manner, how he will have us that are called common people, to manure and work upon the common lands, I will go forth and declare it in my action.[28]

This he indeed did. But his actions incensed property owners in the area, especially as the population of Winstanley's digger colony grew from about a dozen to fifty or sixty. And rumors spread of digger colonies springing up elsewhere in England. In fact, a colony was started on wasteland near Wellingborough, shortly after Winstanley's was established on St. George's Hill, and there is evidence of still other efforts in Buckinghamshire, Hertfordshire, Middlesex, and Kent. The Wellingborough diggers prepared and published a declaration stating that "rich men's hearts are hardened; they will not give us if we beg at their doors. If we steal, the law will end our lives, divers of the poor are starved to death already, and it were better for us who are living to die by the sword"[29]—evidence that not all digger communities embraced Winstanley's pledge of nonviolence.

When the property owners around St. George's Hill appealed to Cromwell to have the diggers removed, he sent his leading general, Lord Fairfax, to speak with Winstanley. Surprisingly (especially considering Winstanley refused to remove his hat in his presence), Fairfax was congenial and not overly worried about the symbolism of Winstanley's experiment. So local opponents of the community took matters into their own hands. They brought legal suits against the diggers and harassed them with dubious trespass charges. Worse, they orchestrated physical harassment after dark, and pledged as they were to nonviolence, the diggers on St. George's Hill suffered from numerous beatings.

After a tumultuous four months or so, the diggers moved away from St. George's Hill and resettled near Little Heath in Cobham, also on little-used common land. There was apparently less immediate agitation over the actions of the diggers at Cobham, and as a result they were able to construct more secure dwellings and last in that location for about eight months (making Winstanley's period of "action," as he put it, almost exactly one year in duration). By all accounts it was a minister of the residual Church of England, such as it was in 1650, that dealt the final blow to the digger experiment. His name was Plat, and Winstanley described his actions at Cobham Heath:

Thereupon at the command of Parson Plat, they set fire to six houses, and burned them down, and burned likewise some of their householdstuffe … throwing their beds, stooles, and householdstuffe, up and down the Common, not pitying the cries of many little children, and their frightened mothers. The poor diggers being thus suddenly cast out of their houses by fire, both they, their wives and children were forced to lie upon the open common all night: yet the rage of Parson Plat and his company rested not here, but in the night time, some of them came again upon the Commons, while the diggers were quiet, some of them in bed, and said, we have authority from our master, that is Mr. Plat, to kill you and burn the rest of your goods."[30]

Not much is known about Winstanley's life after the digger experiment.[31] There is some question about whether the corn chandler by the name of Gerrard Winstanley who died a Quaker in 1676 in London was in fact England's leading digger or another by the same name. But in November 1651 he put the finishing touches on his greatest work, *The Law of Freedom in a Platform or True Magistracy Restored*. In a lengthy preface addressed to Cromwell he told him rather bluntly, "The crown of honor cannot be yours, neither can those victories be called victories on your part, till the land and freedoms won be possessed by them who adventured person and purse for them."[32]

Winstanley was deeply moved by the extent of England's rural poverty—the starvation and ill-health resulting from enclosure, dispossession, failed harvests, and the burden of "freequartering" both armies at various points throughout the Civil War. The collapse of royal power and the established church gave him great hope that the resources of England might be more equitably distributed. Said Winstanley, "Rich men receive all they have from the labourer's hand, and what they give, they give away other men's labours, not their own. Therefore they are not righteous actors in the earth."[33] He envisioned a democratic commonwealth that rested on elementary education, apprenticeships, and formalized adult study groups designed especially as an avenue for policy surveillance. Unlike Hobbes and later Locke, Winstanley believed that all men should play a political role beyond the selection of representatives. They had to exercise their voice lest decisions be made to the benefit of the few at the cost of the many.[34]

The period of England's Civil War was the genesis for a full range of political theory—from something as conservative and religiously oriented as Filmer's *Patriarcha* to something as radical and anticlerical as Winstanley's *The Law of Freedom*. But at the core of virtually all theories—all conceptions of how to replace the old feudal order—was the question of property. Winstanley's take on this was the idea that the earth was a kind of natural treasury, a birthright, and that everyone born into English society had a right "to free enjoyment of the earth." He was far from alone in this. In fact, this was a view shared by many Levelers in Parliament during the Civil War, and by many in Cromwell's New Model Army. The records of the Putney Debates in late 1647 provide a rare glimpse of just how radical rank-and-file soldiers had become and just how much anxiety this caused for army leaders, including Cromwell. The debates were held in Putney Church, where army radicals offered Cromwell a written constitution—*An Agreement of the People for a Firm and Present Peace, Upon Grounds of Common-Right and Freedom*—a document that was debated for a period of several days. The soldiers called for an extended franchise, for greater political autonomy at the local level, for an abolition of tithes, for religious toleration, and perhaps most controversial, for a wider distribution of property as a natural right of free-born persons.

Cromwell and his articulate son-in-law, Henry Ireton, steadfastly refused to entertain the idea that property might constitute a natural right—for this idea had the power to completely transform the English political, economic, and social scene. It is possible that the implications of this idea alone led to Cromwell's purge of the radicals within his army and the gradual silencing of Leveler ideas within the ranks. Every time he turned around, even while among his soldiers, Oliver Cromwell received advice about what to make of England. And in the end he rejected Hobbes, Harrington, Winstanley, and his New Model soldiers in an effort to placate the conservative, propertied interests in England. During his years as "Lord Protector" of the Free State, and during the years that his son held the same office, the franchise was not expanded, religious freedom was not advanced appreciably, and the distribution of property was not altered. Yet even these concessions to the most powerful in English society were not enough to make the commonwealth experiment last. By 1660 the same powerful figures who had cast their lot with Parliament against the king were now ready to restore the Stuart monarchy on the theory that the devil you know is better than the devil you don't.

In short order, however, the well-known devils—this time in the persons of Charles II and later James II—were making decisions reminiscent of their executed father. The resulting discontent finally ended in 1688 with the bloodless "Glorious Revolution," the end of the Stuart kings, and the establishment of William and Mary in a constitutional monarchy that, in theory at least, gave the greatest share of governmental authority to Parliament.

But make no mistake about it: powerful ideas were unleashed during the interregnum period (1649–1660). Primary among them was the idea that rights belong to people, not property. In fact, ever since the interregnum, the idea that individuals are accorded certain inalienable rights merely by birth was available to the human imagination as a source of either hope or fear. For Winstanley, it was a source of hope; for Hobbes, a source of fear. Before the seventeenth century ended, however, John Locke would reduce the fear by converting the idea of a natural right to property into the right to compete for the acquisition of property, a far more palatable concept to the powerful in late seventeenth-century English society. In the process, he took away the primary motivating force behind the advocates of monarchical authority (protecting one's estate from the whimsical redistribution brought about, in theory at least, by a politically active nonpropertied majority) and gave the future revolutions a far greater chance of success—America's included.

It is useful to look at Cromwell's options for re-creating England with the monarchists Hobbes and Filmer on one side and the more radically democratic Harrington and Winstanley on the other. England's ultimate path can be seen as a kind of middle option—one that was derived primarily from the pen of John Locke—and one that was not articulated in time to be useful in any way to Cromwell. Locke's *Two Treatises of Government* were anonymously published in 1690—though it is clear now that they were circulating in manuscript form at least a decade earlier, but still long after the interregnum. Probably because of his extreme antimonarchical views, Locke did not claim authorship of the treatises until it was revealed in his will after his death.

John Locke was born in 1632. At age ten he watched his father, the patriarch of a modest landed estate, march off to Parliament's army where he served as a captain during the Civil War years. He went to good schools and graduated, eventually, from Oxford. He then became a philosophy professor at his alma mater while working on and obtaining a medical degree. For the rest of his life he remained an active participant in English medical sciences, acquiring significant notoriety as a scientist and a physician.

At some point during the late 1660s he left Oxford to become the personal physician of Lord Shaftesbury—a distinguished English aristocrat who supported Parliament during the Civil War years, served on Cromwell's Council of State, then switched allegiances and became an advocate of the Restoration, served as Charles II's Lord Chancellor for thirteen years, then once again became a fierce opponent of the monarchy. Shaftesbury tried desperately to prevent the succession of Charles II's brother, James II, to the throne. It is clear that Locke's close relationship with Shaftesbury brought him into England's tumultuous political scene and was probably the impetus for Locke's *Two Treatises of Government* in which he destroyed Filmer's arguments (which, as noted earlier, had been used extensively to support the Restoration) and legitimated the people's right to rebel when a government fails to work on their behalf.

The treatises were radical enough that, despite the anonymous authorship, Locke was forced to flee to Holland in 1683 and remain there until after the Glorious Revolution and the ascendancy of William and Mary to an ostensibly limited monarchy (soon enough the Georgian era would raise serious questions about the extent of these monarchical limits), at which point he returned to England. Locke's relationship to Shaftesbury appears to have been a catalyst to a wide array of financial investments—the silk trade, the slave trade, and various Caribbean explorations—all of which established Locke as a major economic player in England, complementing his growing renown as a scientist and a political philosopher. From 1696 to 1700 Locke served on England's prestigious Board of Trade, an entity designed to advise the government on economic policy. From this position Locke helped fashion what is often called the "financial revolution" that totally transformed the English economy and that later served as a model for finance-oriented American statesmen, most notably Alexander Hamilton.

Perhaps Locke's most enduring contribution is the extent to which he was able to tie thinking about government to the realm of economic activity. He begins the *Second Treatise* by rehashing his devastating critique of Sir Robert Filmer in the *First Treatise*—completely disconnecting the realm of civil government from the realm of Christian faith—and then moves into a Hobbesian-style discussion of man in a "state of nature." Locke's description of this natural "state of perfect freedom" sounds almost like Winstanley, as various scholars have noted. But whereas Locke begins by insisting with Winstanley that God gave "the World to Men in Common" he shortly thereafter breaks with him by dramatically amending this proposition. It turns out, according to Locke, that God actually "gave the earth to the use of the Industrious and Rational" among men—not to everyone. He ties the origin of property claims to labor and then lays out a theory of government designed to protect property as effectively as any monarchical system.[35]

Locke argues that man first acquired property when he went to the work of gathering acorns or apples. In doing so, they became his as long as he left "enough and as good" for others. Anticipating skeptics who might ask whether this act of mixing labor with a natural resource and thereby creating private property should actually require the mutual consent of those who lived in the vicinity of those apples and acorns, Locke replies that "if such a consent as that was necessary, man had starved, notwithstanding the Plenty God had given him."[36] In other words, Locke dismisses the skeptic with a bit of humor. If a person needed consent to gather apples, arguments would ensue, no one would agree, and all would starve. This makes humankind, and our stubbornness, the butt of a nice little joke, but it does not in any way constitute a logical or empirically based argument. In point of fact, humankind has shown itself in virtually every age to be capable of making consensual decisions related to available resources. But the skeptic is nevertheless laughed away by Locke.

All political theory must hinge on some conception of human nature, some conception of what people are, at bottom. Hobbes weighed in on this question by concluding that in a state of nature it was "all against all" for whatever they could get. Locke's conception of human nature is not that different, though he refrains from combative terminology. For Locke, at bottom, people are economic actors, because this is all his conception of a pre-political state of nature would allow. To suggest that the economic act of collecting apples was somehow subordinate to the political act of neighbors generating rules related to collecting apples would have derailed his subsequent arguments.

Locke needed to demonstrate unequivocally that man is essentially an economic animal. To feed himself he must work. Work establishes a property claim and does so without the consent of others. Further, others cannot violate this claim. Said Locke: "Thus the grass my horse has bit, the turfs my servant has cut, and the ore I have digged in any place, where I have a right to them in common with others, became my *property,* without assignation or consent of any body. The labour that was mine, removing them out of the common state they were in, hath *fixed* my property in them."[37]

With the authenticity of the property claim firmly established, he went on to explain how the advent of the money economy removed natural law limits (leaving "enough and as good" for others and avoiding spoilage). For Locke, "the invention of money, and the tacit agreement of men to put value on it, introduce [the possibility of] larger possessions." Money, which keeps "without wasting or decay," can be used to pay for labor that enables unlimited accumulation. In turn, the laborer can use money wages to acquire needed goods.[38]

According to Locke, man acquired "possessions in different proportions" through "different degrees of industry" and through "the invention of money." But the resulting discrepancies between those with and without property were not a problem for Locke. In fact, he argues that those who are industrious enough to acquire private property make a great contribution to society, even to its poorest citizens, by improving the productivity of the land well beyond what it could produce in a natural state or while it is held in common by many. This argument was intended to quiet the critics of enclosure. Said Locke: "He who appropriates land to himself by his labour, does not lessen, but increase the common stock of mankind: for the provisions serving to the support of human life, produced by one acre of inclosed and cultivated land, are ten times more than those which are yielded by an acre of land of equal richness lying waste in common."[39]

In time, as more and more land came into private hands, communities came together and determined the "bounds of their distinct territories and by laws within themselves regulated the properties of the private men in their societies, and so, by *compact* and agreement, settled the property which labour and industry began." In other words, Locke implicitly agreed with Hobbes that people enter into governed society to "enjoy their properties in peace and safety." Government, for Locke, was about enabling economic activity in the larger society by removing the contentiousness that accompanied the acquisition of property in the state of nature—and defending the larger society from the threat of foreign powers. Should the government fail at these tasks, the people possessed a natural right to rebel and replace that government with one that would not fail.[40]

I will return to Locke's governmental prescriptions in the next section of this chapter, for his views in this regard were of great significance to the American founders. But first I'd like to examine a few key pieces of Locke's theory of property. Recall his quip about the grass his horse eats and the turfs his servants cut. Locke clearly believes that the fruits of labor one pays for or owns (Locke supported slavery and invested in the slave trade) belonged to the employer or slave owner. If my servant cuts the grass, the grass becomes my property. For the effort the servant is entitled, apparently, to some kind of wage but not necessarily to a livelihood. For Locke, the employer is under no obligation to measure what a wage will purchase, or whether it will lend itself to a dignified life.

In subtle or perhaps not so subtle ways, like the offhand remark about the turfs cut by his servant, Locke cleared an intellectual path that paved the way for capitalistic enterprise. Saying this much isn't particularly controversial. In fairness, though, I should note that there is maybe more controversy surrounding Locke's legacy than any other modern philosopher. For some he legitimated the domination of the wealthy over the poor and in so doing set the table for Karl Marx's critical theorizing in the nineteenth century; for others, he correctly laid a blueprint for the later ascendancy of democracy.

Hero or villain is not particularly important. What is important, however, is to recognize the power of two far-reaching ideas that Locke solidified in the Western mind—two ideas that go a long way toward explaining why we in the United States have the governmental system that we have, and why this system has consistently proved itself incapable of solving twenty-first century problems.

The first idea is that life is essentially an economic endeavor, and only secondarily a political one. On this point even Locke's most casual readers will surely agree. The second is that the well-being of others can be gauged by the "degree of industry" they themselves display. While this is a somewhat less obvious point than the first, it is nevertheless a very difficult one to refute. Witness Locke's celebration of enclosure amidst contemporaries who wept openly at the dispossession, poverty, and starvation it caused. A major theme of this book contends that Locke was just plain wrong, dead wrong, on both counts—and thus we are adrift on an intellectual (philosophical, ideological, social) trajectory that cannot lead to a desirable future. For the appeal of these ideas to those with power (in England and in the fledgling United States) was great enough to ensure that government, at least, would function on the assumption that these ideas were 100 percent correct. Operating on this erroneous assumption, we have relegated a future to ourselves and our children marked by problems of huge proportions, problems that indeed threaten the very existence of humankind on earth. But once again, I'm pushing too far ahead. Having examined the options open to England at its auspicious moment in history, it's time now to return to those great American statesmen who hammered out a Constitution one hot eighteenth-century summer in Philadelphia.

The L-Stream and the M-Stream
(With Deference to Charles Taylor)

Charles Taylor, a leading Canadian philosopher, once argued that there were essentially two streams of philosophical thought that went into the creation of the

United States.[41] The first and clearly dominant one was the L-stream, for John Locke, often referred to as "America's philosopher." With Locke's conception of man as pre-political and therefore primarily an economic being, one whose actions would lead "to the overturning of all morality" if unrestrained, came a logic that suggested a government that focused on the orchestration of the economy, downplaying the role that citizens might play as political beings.

The second and subordinate philosophical source for our founders was the M-stream, for Montesquieu. Much more than Locke, Montesquieu provided a road map for what a nonmonarchical government might look like, even though he himself felt that limiting the monarchy was a better option. Our beloved trinity—executive, legislative, and judicial—comes straight from Montesquieu. John Locke offered a strong centralized legislative body flanked by an executive power over external affairs and an executive power for internal, domestic affairs.[42] His prescription failed to put the power-checking dynamic into the judicial system. And balancing these powers with a system of power checks germane to each part of government—executive, legislative, and judicial—this was Montesquieu's gift as well.[43] And Montesquieu's firm belief that republics should stay clear of militarist and imperial ambitions was a quite prominent philosophical value in the United States, at least prior to our war with Mexico.

But from the perspective of those who came to dominate the creation of America's Constitution, there were down sides to Montesquieu. As previously discussed, Montesquieu believed that republics should be small in size. There was nothing small about the combined thirteen colonies. And Montesquieu was far more tolerant of established religion than Hobbes or Locke, seeing an especially important role for it within limited monarchies. The historical role played by several of the colonies, that is, as an escape from religious intolerance, meant that this side of Montesquieu's thought would not be well received.

More important, Montesquieu roundly rejected Hobbes's basic premises and those similar notions advanced more acceptably by Locke. For instance, the state of nature for Montesquieu was not a state of "all against all" (Hobbes) or a state where men "would overturn all morality" (Locke). Said Montesquieu:

> Hobbes asks, If men are not naturally in a state of war, why do they always carry arms and why do they have keys to lock their doors? But one feels that what can happen to men only after the establishment of societies, which induced them to find motives for attacking others and defending themselves, is attributed to them before that establishment.[44]

Montesquieu paints quite a different picture of the state of nature, and this was the essential feature of Montesquieu's political philosophy that was so bothersome to Madison, Hamilton, and their followers who carried the day that summer in Philadelphia. Instead of individuals roaming around and exerting their strength to acquire from anyone all that they could get, Montesquieu's natural man would be quite timid, aware of his weakness, and therefore inclined to peace rather than war. In fact, he asserts that "peace would be the first law of nature." And while fear might lead them to initially flee from one another, "mutual fear would soon persuade them to approach one another."[45]

Once societies are established, war becomes an option and a necessity for those who are attacked. But the crucial point is that this is a decision made through the use of reason, not an inevitability of man's nature. In short, Montesquieu's analysis suggests that man is essentially a social and political being, and an economic being only secondarily. In fact, for Montesquieu it is the sociability of reasonable men that produces conceptions of morality and justice, not their utility for augmenting economic activity.

Montesquieu was born Charles-Louis de Secondat in 1689 into a wealthy French family. He joined the ranks of the nobility in 1716 when he inherited his name, several estates, and a regional judicial post from his childless uncle. In preparation for this inheritance Montesquieu studied law at Bordeaux, and although he eventually sold his inherited judgeship to raise revenue, laws, and especially the spirit behind their creation, remained a lifelong intellectual fascination for him. Although the vineyards on his estates enabled Montesquieu to become a noted wine merchant and manufacturer, his life never moved far from academic pursuits. With the publication of the enormously successful *Persian Letters* in 1721, he became prominent among distinguished French literary society.

Like many aristocrats of his day, Montesquieu spent three years (1728–1731) traveling throughout Europe—two of those years in England. Through his travels he saw many types of governments, and these experiences were augmented by seemingly exhaustive study of the classical regimes in Greece and Rome. In fact, his second book, *Considerations on the Causes of the Greatness of the Romans and Their Decline* (1734), has remained a pivotal work as the first sociologically oriented history of a particular society.

But perhaps Montesquieu's greatest intellectual contribution was to present to the world, through *The Spirit of the Laws* (1748), a clear typology of governmental systems that was a marked improvement over what was available in the works of Aristotle, Aquinas, and his own sixteenth-century countryman, Bodin. Montesquieu wrote about republics, limited monarchies, and despotisms, chronicling the strengths and weaknesses of each. Interestingly, he also wrote about the education appropriate to each governmental form, placing himself among a relatively small number of political theorists going back to Plato who recognized the integral relationship between choices about governance and decisions about how to educate youth. Republics, unlike monarchies and despotisms, require "the full power of education," according to Montesquieu. He noted further that the cultivation of virtue was the organizing principle of republics and that in order for this type of governmental form to be successful, it must create among the population "a continuous preference of the public interest over one's own," something that requires concerted educational effort.

Montesquieu makes no reference to the English colonies in this regard, but perhaps more than any other place on earth at this time, England's North American colonies, especially those in New England, were nearly compulsive about the creation of schools and the spread of literacy. And this is not an observation from hindsight. Consider the comments of England's conservative apologist Edmund Burke about the raucous American colonies:

> Permit me, Sir, to add another circumstance in our colonies, which contributes no mean part towards the growth and effect of this untractable spirit—*I mean their education.* In no country in the world perhaps, is the law so general a study. I have been told by an eminent bookseller, that in no branch of his business ... were so many books as those on law transported to the plantations. I hear that they have sold nearly as many of Blackstone's *Commentaries* in America as in England.[46]

Clearly Montesquieu's views about education had an impact on America's founders. Philadelphia's Benjamin Rush urged the creation of state-sponsored free schools, stating that he believed it was possible to convert schoolchildren into "republican machines." Many others concurred. Robert Coram of Delaware wrote, "In our American republics [this was written in 1791, after ratification, yet note the sentiment that the states still constituted separate republics], where government is in the hands of the people, knowledge should be universally diffused by means of public schools."[47]

Perhaps the greatest legislative accomplishment under the Articles of Confederation were the Northwest Ordinances (1785 and 1787) that laid out the terms for settlement west of the Appalachians, north of the Ohio River, and east of the Mississippi. These ordinances actively promoted the creation of schools, noting that "religion, morality, and knowledge being necessary to good government and the happiness of mankind, schools and the means of education shall forever be encouraged." Further, the ordinances created policy to be sure that this would happen, stipulating that one square mile from each township would be used "for the maintenance of public schools." This policy was amended over the years, but the basic idea nevertheless served as a catalyst for generating school finances throughout the nineteenth century, and it lingers to this day as a revenue-generating mechanism in a few states.[48]

Once again, to a greater degree than either Locke or Hobbes, Montesquieu helped the American colonists formulate a vision for what a republic might be. While the concept of free state-sponsored schools took several decades to catch on, it is worth noting that it eventually did so in the 1830s and 1840s, a point that can accurately be described—as Tocqueville's famous *Democracy in America* vividly demonstrates, as the high point of the M-stream in American consciousness.[49]

Montesquieu also popularized the relationship between the well-being of a republic and the frugality of its citizens, noting that this virtue tends to minimize the discrepancies between wealth and poverty. A further advantage of "establishing frugality in domestic life" was that it "opened the gate to public expenditures, as happened in Athens and Rome."[50] American statesmen, and here Benjamin Franklin probably serves as the best example, extolled the virtue of frugality as essential to the success of the American experiment.

Montesquieu's prescriptions for republican simplicity had a deep and profound effect on the founding generation. The fact that America's military success against England launched a fairly unprecedented governmental experiment was not lost on the former colonists, and in perusing the letters, sermons, essays, and books of the founding generation it is impossible to fail to be impressed by the earnestness they brought to the business of setting up a republic. They did not want to fail. Every suggestion was considered and debated, then used or rejected. In this process Montesquieu figured prominently, as even a brief glance at the founding era literature demonstrates.

In a 1768 sermon, Daniel Shute of Boston described "the nature of the human species." He adamantly rejected the Hobbes-Locke thesis about the state of nature. Shute believed man was "adapted to society," which in turn afforded "vastly more happiness then solitary existence could do. From the make of man, the disadvantages of a solitary, and the advantages of a social state, evidently appear."[51] Shute was not interested in entertaining theories about a presocial state of existence dominated by ceaseless and self-aggrandizing economic activity. Man at all stages had been a social, and thus political, being.

In 1774 Nathaniel Niles delivered a similar sermon in Newburyport, Massachusetts. Echoing Montesquieu's analysis of the strengths of republics, Niles asked his listeners to "imagine a state whose members are all of a free spirit." He then asked them to imagine that

> the individuals are all of one mind. They unite in the same grand pursuit, the highest good of the whole. Only suppose all members of such a state to be acquainted with the best means of promoting their general end; and we shall see them all moving in perfect concert. The good of the body will be their first aim. And in subservience to this, they will impartially regard the particular interests of individuals.[52]

Niles's sermon demonstrates the considerable tension between the individualistic orientation of the L-stream and the community focus of the M-stream. On this question, Niles shows a clear preference for Montesquieu.

It was a popular preference. Witness Robert Coram, writing in 1791: "The end of government, we are told, is public good, by which it is understood the happiness of the community." Or Samuel West, speaking before the House of Representatives of the Massachusetts Bay Colony in 1776: "It becomes me not to say what particular form of government is best for a community," but aristocracies and monarchies "are two of the most exceptionable forms of government." Note that his first measure of fit for a government was the role it would play or fail to play on behalf of a community—not an individual. Or Timothy Stone speaking in Hartford in 1792:

> Civil liberty is one of the most important blessings, the most valuable inheritance on this side of heaven. That constitution may therefore be esteemed the best, which doth most effectively secure this treasure to a community. That liberty consists of freedom from restraint, leaving each one to act as seemeth right to himself, is a most unwise mistaken apprehension. Civil liberty, consists in the being and administration of such a system of laws, as doth bind all classes of men, rulers and subjects, to unite their exertions for the promotion of virtue and public happiness.[53]

Once again, the negative freedom of the Hobbes-Locke tradition is condemned, while Montesquieu's community-oriented notion of civil liberty is affirmed. Clearly the Shutes, Corams, and Stones of the early republic were plentiful, but they were not among the nation's elite statesmen and thus were not present in Philadelphia during the summer of 1787. The leaders of that group were far less enamored with Montesquieu's idea of a republic and were much more likely to embrace the L-stream.

Since the publication of Charles Beard's *An Economic Interpretation of the Constitution of the United States* in 1913 there has been considerable scholarly controversy concerning the degree to which the 1787 Constitutional Convention and the document it eventually produced was the product of the elite upper class trying to establish much greater control over policy via a government they felt they could control as opposed to the federal government under the Articles, which, as an example, couldn't effectively handle the relatively minor tax-resisting struggle created by Daniel Shays and other west Massachusetts farmers. Beard documented the wealth and personal holdings of the convention attendees to demonstrate that they were in fact far from "average" citizens.[54] And in the subsequent essays by Publius defending the draft Constitution produced at the convention, Beard pointed out a kind of obsession with the fear of "factions," and what they might do if they possessed sufficient political power. The most often quoted passage in this regard came from the pen of James Madison: "A rage for paper money, for an abolition of debts, for an equal division of property, or for any other improper or wicked project, will be less apt to pervade the whole body of the Union than a particular member of it; in the same proportion as such a malady is more likely to taint a particular county or district, than an entire state." Shay's Rebellion looms large in these remarks. Madison's logic was that factions could not be prevented, but with sufficient power vested in a centralized government, they could be controlled.

In a society under the forms of which the stronger faction can readily unite and oppress the weaker, anarchy may as truly be said to reign as in a state of nature, where the weaker individual is not secured against the violence of the stronger; and as, in the latter state, even the stronger individuals are prompted by the uncertainty of their condition to submit to a government which may protect the weak as well as themselves; so in the former state, will the more powerful factions or parties be gradually induced, by a like motive, to wish for a government that will protect all parties, the weaker as well as the more powerful.[55]

Madison's embrace of the L-stream is obvious. Montesquieu may have been on to something with a governmental trinity, each with power checks on the other, but Montesquieu's state of nature would never do for Madison. The potential for mischief on the part of factions in a society charged with working out differences in the public square seemed too great for Madison, who believed, à la Hobbes and Locke, that "the latent causes of faction are sown in the nature of man."[56] Montesquieu's views on faction are most obvious in his *Considerations*. "As a general rule, whenever we see everyone tranquil in a state that calls itself a republic, we can be sure that liberty does not exist there." Montesquieu chastised the received wisdom about Rome. "We hear in the authors only of the dissensions [factions] that ruined Rome, without seeing that these dissensions were necessary to it, that they had always been there and always had to be." He explained further: "What is called *union* in a body politic is a very equivocal thing. The true kind of union is harmony, whereby all the parts, however opposed they may appear, cooperate for the general good of society—as dissonances in music cooperate in producing overall accord."[57]

For Montesquieu, the political community was the heart and soul of republics. Rome fell because its imperial designs made it grow beyond what he believed a republican government could handle. It necessarily evolved toward despotism, thus his warning that republics must cultivate frugality to impede any imperialistic impulse and that they must remain small to enable republican government to work. In this prescription, faction was no evil to be neutralized by, in Madison's words, "controlling its effects"[58] but was a necessary condition that allowed citizens to play a political role with their lives.

In this regard, one of Montesquieu's startling eighteenth-century insights was recognition of the role that intermediate bodies, or local associations, could play in the equitable functioning of government, be it a republic or a limited monarchy. Local associations served two purposes of particular import for Montesquieu. First, they served as the vehicle for individuals to lead fulfilled lives from a political standpoint; second, they aided in the development and implementation of policy that was sensitive to the interests of diverse groups and differing localities. When Alexis de Tocqueville toured the United States during the 1830s, he made note of the proliferation of such associations. Said Tocqueville, "In every case, at the head of any new undertaking, where in France you would find the government or in England some territorial magnate, in the United States you are sure to find an Association."[59]

Many of these associations were focused on single issues: a county wool growers' association, for example. But many others went considerably beyond single issues. In fact, the historian Christopher Clark has called the American 1840s a "communitarian moment," citing the proliferation during this decade of community-building experiments like Hopedale, Brook Farm, Fruitlands, and the Northhampton Association for Education and Industry as examples.[60]

It has only been in recent years that we have begun to understand the significance of local associations in terms of the health and well-being of democratic arrangements. Robert Putnam and his colleagues made a huge contribution toward this understanding with their longitudinal study of democracy in Italy entitled *Making Democracy Work.* Putnam set out to discover why the economy of northern Italy was prosperous and flourishing while at the same time the economy in the south of Italy was depressed and languishing. Simplified, he found in the north an abundance of local associations that vitalized discussions over policy and ultimately proved to be a stimulus to economic activity. By contrast, southern Italy was more tradition-bound, marked by the absence of such local associations and less energetic encouragement of decision-makers to respond to changing circumstances.

Several years later Putnam made another scholarly contribution of enormous significance. In *Bowling Alone: The Collapse and Revival of American Community,* he documented the dramatic collapse of American political and civic associations after 1980. The title captures a telling dynamic in our society. While the number of Americans who go bowling for entertainment has climbed, the number who go bowling in community leagues has declined precipitously; thus the title serves as a metaphor for an important trend. The end result is that coincident with decline in local associations has been significant drops in where the United States ranks on measures of democracy compared to other nations around the world. Robert Dahl's *How Democratic Is the United States Constitution?* documents our fall within the ranks of democratic nations.[61] Though Putnam doesn't put it in these terms, *Bowling Alone* essentially chronicles the ascendancy of the L-stream in American consciousness along with the complete subordination of the M-stream.

As citizens we are deemed to be economic actors, primarily, and no more is asked of us politically then to come out and vote once every two years. We apparently possess too much potential for "improper and wicked projects" to be structurally involved in governance. Faction is "sown into our nature," and thus we must leave government to those with the intellectual wherewithal to play us off against one another. But it is important to recognize that there were other options, other interpretations of man's nature, other ways to structure a governmental system. Charles Taylor's L-stream and M-stream distinction helps to clarify the options, just as Robert Putnam's work helps us understand the consequences of the choices made. With these understandings, it is much easier to envision alternatives to our current thinking about how politics, economics, and education ought to happen in the twenty-first century—the focus of the second half of this book.

Defenders of the status quo will no doubt rush to point out that Montesquieu was no democrat, and that he called for a representative system because he didn't think average citizens were capable of wrestling with tough issues related to the public good. This is true enough. But it is also true that this opinion stemmed from the fact that eighteenth-century France had no educational system capable of delivering the "full power of education," his prerequisite for the success of republics. Without it, man remained "that flexible being who adapts himself in society to the thoughts and feelings of others."[62] In America, starting from scratch as it were, many thought such an educational system could be built into the overall structure of society. Thomas Jefferson certainly believed this:

> And say, finally, whether peace is best preserved by giving energy to the government [Madison and the L-stream logic] or information to the people. The last is most certain, and the most legitimate engine of government. Educate and inform the whole mass of the people [in other words, put the M-stream into action]. Enable them to see that it is their interest to preserve peace and order and they will preserve them.[63]

The essential distinction between the L-stream and the M-stream cuts all the way back to conceptions about what constitutes a state or a commonwealth in the first place. Thomas Smith's notion of a state as "a multitude of free men collected together" was a sharp contrast to Bodin's definition of a state as "groups of corporate associations and communities." The L-stream followed Smith's conception of the state as an aggregation of individuals to a vision of society built around a view of freedom that enables material accumulation. For reasons detailed in the next two chapters, the L-stream gained sufficient force to bury the M-stream in America and thus contributed to a demise of virtue and communal solidarity. When the owners of the local factory decide to remove the plant to Mexico, or when the state department of education coerces small schools to consolidate with larger ones, very few object by saying "this will hurt the community," because the well-being of communities is not a primary criteria for policy in this country, thanks to the ascendancy of the L-stream.

It has been more than 200 years since our Constitution was adopted. Publius, its staunch defender, has long been asleep. During this time much has happened, many changes have occurred, many new technologies have been developed, and most important, many new insights about the human condition have been discovered (or, in most cases, rediscovered). Indeed, Thomas Jefferson saw the

Constitution growing outdated as early as 1816 when he noted that "laws and institutions must go hand in hand with the progress of the human mind." He hoped that the Constitution would be amended so that it could undergo changes "at stated periods," maybe once every fifty years—giving each generation the same level of independence as the one before it.[64]

As this chapter demonstrates, the assumptions undergirding the governmental system created in 1787 Philadelphia effectively detached liberty from virtue to the point that unrestrained economic activity now threatens the carrying capacity of the earth itself. A correction is needed. The L-stream requires rebalancing with the M-stream. We will take up this discussion in the final three chapters, but first we must turn to examinations of economic (Chapter 2) and educational (Chapter 3) theory that have been aligned with, and have emanated from, L-stream political theory.

CHAPTER 2

Passion and Greed

The demise of feudalism and the triumph of liberal political theory rested on the cumulative effect of many political theorists. While Locke and Montesquieu loom large in this regard, the course of history was shaped too by the minority views offered by the likes of Hobbes, Filmer, Winstanley, Harrington, and many others. The total package added up to a quite unprecedented notion: all men were entitled to freedom of every sort—civil, religious, political, intellectual, and economic.

Such a belief, ultimately, did not square well with practices like slavery or those policies and traditions that secured the subordination of women—as Mary Wollstonecraft ably pointed out in her 1792 publication *The Vindication of the Rights of Women,* and so these practices would gradually erode. Make no mistake about it; the advance of seventeenth- and eighteenth-century political theory created new possibilities in the world that few would hesitate to describe as positive—and remarkably so. But the story of human history since the liberal revolutions has been anything but onward and upward—especially if we use human misery or premature death as a gauge.[1] Why is this so?

To get to the bottom of this question we must shift our focus away from questions related to governance to the more mundane questions about how individual and societal needs came to be met in the postfeudal world. A society premised on human freedom, after all, is a very different thing than a society based on patterns of feudal authority. In fact, for thousands of years the production of food, clothing, and shelter everywhere was directed either by entrenched traditions or by authoritarian directives. Individuals were born into their economic roles, and for all intents and purposes there was no moving beyond or above one's occupational inheritance. But such a world was antithetical to the vision of freedom created by the political theorists, and this fact has had huge consequences for the course of human history—on at least two levels: one dealing with the ramifications of this new vision as it related to the notion of community and how communities function, the other related to the inevitable consequences of raising the specter of risk in the minds of men.

First, community. It didn't take long for individuals to view community as a potential obstacle to the free play of human freedom. Here the example of enclosure works as well as any. The aspiring encloser wants to use his freedom to maximize his income by purchasing the neighborhood commons. The farmers in the neighborhood using the commons object, thus infringing on the perceived rights of the encloser. He turns to Parliament, successfully, to get proenclosure, anticommunity legislation passed. Between 1760 and 1844, some 2,554 separate enclosure acts were passed by Parliament, the end result of which enclosed an estimated 4,039,023 acres.[2]

The suspicion with which community was held by those who chose to maximize the advantages of a free society meant that community would eventually all but disappear from the list of criteria used in the formation of policy. It also meant that the scales would be tipped in favor of the L-stream in America—for community and the role it played in Montesquieu's political theory clashed in a pronounced way with the vision of the Hobbes-Locke tradition. The America of Hamilton and Madison saw too great a threat in "faction," or, said another way, in aroused communities.

Speaking in general terms, the political theory of England and France differed in significant ways—thus the L-stream and the M-stream—and this meant that when intellectuals of both societies turned their attention to what the triumph of freedom would mean in the economic arena—absent the direction of tradition or the coercion of authority—they came up with different ideas and different economic theory.[3]

But next, risk. The great advantage of life in the preliberal world was its predictability. Barring weather-related exigencies and the frequent specter of war, individuals knew how their lives would unfold, they knew where their next meal was coming from, they knew what comforts they could reasonably expect to acquire and which they could not. In a world defined by freedom, all of this changed. If I leave the farm to seek my fortune, will I find a job? Will it be compensated at a level that provides food and clothing for my children? Or if I leave the estate of my father and invest in the construction of a factory, will I find workers willing to work? Will I find buyers for my product? Will I be able to acquire a loan, if needed? And at what cost?

In many ways it is fair to view the price of political freedom as the assumption of economic risk. And if there is a difference of significance between modern man and his predecessors, it is that modern man has accommodated, culturally and psychologically, to the ever-present stress of risk. Accommodation may be too strong a word, for risk seems to ever-intensify, and here the connection between the consequences of the liberal embrace of freedom—the demise of community and the growth of risk—becomes apparent. As communal solidarity declined, risk increased. Once a source of security and an agent in promoting predictability in life, a diminished sense of community has meant a diminished sense of security—a void that now must be made up by a more feverish pursuit of wealth and whatever security it brings. It is not difficult to see that this trade-off—money for neighbors—is a dubious cultural attribute.

To a very great degree the element or risk continues to rise in the United States and elsewhere—to the point, in fact, that there is considerable scholarly concern for the well-being of the planet, that is, the carrying capacity of the earth itself. And there are grave concerns about the proliferation of psychological maladies: depression, over- and under-eating, and drug dependencies, to name just a few. And there is obviously great concern about terrorist threats, be they nuclear, biochemical, or wanton killing with conventional weapons. The "miracles" of biologically engineered food leave many wondering whether we have just opened the world to new, as yet unforeseen, risks. One could go on and on with concerns in this regard. Risk is all around us, and economic forecasters now tell us that most Americans living today will not reach the real income level of their parents—a circumstance that may well yield yet more risk-taking.

This brings us to another important connection—this one between the ascendancy of liberal political theory and the birth of liberal economic theory. With the risk ushered in by the absence of tradition or authoritative directives came a marked desire to mitigate that risk. Thus the field of economics was born. Most scholars mark that day with the publication of Adam Smith's classic economic text *The Wealth of Nations,* published in 1776, the same year that the American Revolution began. To be sure, the world has always been the site of economic activity, but until Smith's volume was published the world was remarkably devoid of economic theory. In fact, most of what had been written on the subject was better labeled ethics than economics.

Aristotle, like Christian philosophers throughout the Middle Ages,[4] condemned the practice of loaning money at interest. He also praised the farming life, arguing that the virtues of agricultural toil were the sort required for democratic citizenship. Merchants, bankers, and anyone involved in trade was thought to be among the lowly in Greek, Roman, and medieval societies. One of the fascinating aspects of the acceptance of Adam Smith's ideas and the formal study of economics is the near-complete reversal in status that took place in fairly short order. Those involved with manufactures and trade, the "captains of industry," were elevated to a high status while the status of farmers—hillbillies, hicks, bumpkins, and so on; in short, rural dwellers—dropped precipitously. William Cobbett, England's fiery journalist and advocate of parliamentary reform during the first three decades of the nineteenth century, remarked that he had witnessed the transition in the status of rural dwellers during his own lifetime. Said Cobbett, "By degrees beginning about 50 years ago the industrious part of the community, particularly those who create every useful thing by their labour, have been spoken of by everyone possessing the power to oppress them in any degree in just the same manner in which we speak of the animals which compose the stock upon a farm. This is not the manner in which the forefathers of us, the common people, were treated." Identifying the switch from the use of the reference "the commons of England" to such phrases as "the lower orders," frequently used by David Hume and countless other elites, Cobbett blamed this development on "tax-devourers, bankers, brewers, and monopolists of every sort." He noted further that one could hear these sorts of pejorative designations not only from the wealthy in English society but also from "their clerks, from shopkeepers and waiters, and from the fribbles stuck up behind the counter."[5] It is significant to note that this rural-urban status reversal was accepted as fully by Karl Marx as it was by mainstream economists like Smith, Malthus, and Ricardo. Said Marx, "The bourgeoisie has subjected the country to the rule of the towns. It has created enormous cities, has greatly increased the urban population as compared with the rural, and has thus rescued a considerable part of the population from the idiocy of rural life."[6]

The advent of economic theory was very much a part of the ascendancy of urban political and economic power, and in subtle ways it legitimated the increasingly popular view that the rural agrarian world was a thing of the past. The classical and medieval eras lacked even something as simple as price theory, since there were no wages and because interest costs were intermittent given the position of the Church. Consequently they speculated very little about the acquisition of wealth via one avenue or another. Theorizing about appropriate economic behavior was focused on the resulting relations between men—ethics—not about income or wealth generation. Greek, Roman, and post-Roman feudal societies remained tradition-bound in terms of economic activity, and therefore there was no formal role for economic theory. But things change.

The Era of Merchants

The history of economics generally labels the 300-year period between 1450 and 1750 as the merchant or mercantilist era. Improvements in the horse harness as well as in road construction led to increased trade throughout Europe, a development that contributed to the widespread creation of weighted coins and the banks that measured and issued them—in Italy and Holland to start—but later all across the continent. The real catalyst to the stepped-up economic activity of the era, however, was overseas exploration culminating in the introduction of exotic goods from the Orient and, more important, huge infusions of gold, and particularly silver, from the mines of the New World. Christopher Columbus opened the path to what became the Americas in 1492. Vasco de Gama charted the route to India in 1497. With these discoveries the age of the merchant began in earnest.

As the precious metals poured into Spain and Portugal it was immediately coined and diffused throughout Europe such that a general price rise or inflationary period ensued in virtually every European country. Recall that in 1581 Thomas Smith published his *Discourse of the Commonweal of This Realm* as an exploration into the causes of inflation that plagued the nation. Labeling the state a "multitude of free individuals," Smith started a distinctly modern view that held, in part, that individuals were to be economic actors in their own right—and he attributed the nation's inflation dilemma, therefore, to the greed and avarice of those free-acting individuals.

His contemporary and counterpart in France, Jean Bodin, came up with a more sophisticated diagnosis: "I find that the high prices we see today are due to some four or five causes. The principal and almost the only one (which no one has referred to until now) is the abundance of gold and silver, which is today much greater in this kingdom than it was four hundred years ago, to go back no further."[7] Bodin gave voice to what would in time be called the "quantity theory of money," the notion that, trade being held constant, prices will vary with the supply of money.

Of course, the pace of economic activity quickened considerably during this period, and Thomistic strictures regarding usury were routinely ignored. In the 300 years defined by the rise of the merchant, commercial activity, once despised in classical and in early feudal society, became more and more accepted as commonplace, even reputable. Those cities that crafted policies amenable to merchant activity—Antwerp, Amsterdam, Florence, London, and the like—grew by leaps and bounds.

While there was no great economist of the mercantilist era, no scholar who was able to competently describe the economic transition that was taking place, we can see with hindsight that the individual pursuit of wealth was gradually translated into a contribution to the national interest. And the pursuit of national wealth led to an aggressive brand of militarism—as the nations of Europe battled for access to markets and foreign sources of wealth. In fact, the close of the Thirty Years War at Westphalia in 1648 marked the last military conflict in Europe defined chiefly by religious concerns. Henceforth the nations of Europe would do battle in the interest of obtaining a better economic position in the world. And while it is true that no great scholar was able to describe the forces at work during this era, there were a few who were able to describe some of the effects of these forces.

Thomas Mun was one such individual. In 1664 his greatest work, *England's Treasure by Forraign Trade,* was published posthumously. In it he acknowledged that wealth grows when exports outstrip imports. Mun prescribed a variety of options "to encrease our wealth by Forraign Trade, wherein we must observe this rule; to sell more to strangers yearly than wee consume of theirs in value."[8]

Adam Smith would later cite Mun's work as a major contributor to the study of political economy throughout Europe.[9]

Bernard Mandeville, the Dutch-born physician who spent most of his working career in London, is perhaps an even better example. Mandeville published a poem called "The Grumbling Hive" in 1705, describing the interplay of labor and appetites, arguing, between the lines, that satisfying morally questionable urges was in fact good for the larger economy of the nation. Though his success with this poem was limited, he expanded upon it about a decade later, publishing what he called "The Fable of the Bees, Or, Private Vices, Public Benefits." This time the poem created a mild uproar in London and, indeed, throughout England. Mandeville was roundly chastised by individuals representing practically every segment of British society. As a consequence, he was forced to publish a series of remarks explaining various passages of the poem as well as arguing for his vindication from some of the more serious charges leveled against him.

Mandeville's satirical verses were certainly a catalyst for the later more systematic study of the dynamics he identified. Take this passage, as an example:

> ... Whilst Luxury
> Employ'd a Million of the Poor,
> An odious Pride a Million more.
> Envy it Self, and Vanity
> Were Ministers of Industry;
> Their daring Folly, Fickleness
> In Diet, Furniture, and Dress,
> The strange ridic'lous Vice, was made
> The very Wheel, that turn'd the Trade.[10]

In remarks explaining the passage, Mandeville maintained that trade was the principal way "to aggrandize the nation" and that society must not expect to maintain the moral virtue of the populace and economic greatness at the same time.[11]

Mandeville cleverly suggested that the freedom supplied by the political theorists would unleash base human instincts and behaviors previously kept in check by authority and tradition. Importantly, he suggested that this was not something to be lamented, for it would lead to a kind economic boom. Mandeville believed, however, that government nevertheless had to monitor economic activity lest the boom turn into a bust—a position later economists would squabble over at least until the Great Depression and in some measure considerably beyond.

Much happened by way of what we today would call economic policy throughout and especially at the end of the mercantilist era. And to be sure, theory undergirded these policy choices, albeit theory that was largely unarticulated. The era witnessed huge changes, such as the introduction of script—paper money—by various banks and the working out of solutions to the multitude of problems created by the rampant printing of script. The concept of the central bank in England in 1694 and about a century later in the United States partially solved these dilemmas. They smoothed the way, as well, for the governmental use of public debt, that is, the Financial Revolution of Robert Walpole and others, that characterized the first three decades of the eighteenth century in England.

But while the mercantilist era witnessed large increases in trade volume, growing nationalism, and the proliferation of banks and insurance houses, it did not *fundamentally* alter the social structure of England or the United States, nor did it *fundamentally* alter the way most people made their living. That transformation was started, to be sure, but it awaited key technological advances that transformed the concept of what the factory was or what it might be. New technology seemed to be the spark required by Adam Smith to bring his masterpiece, *The Wealth of Nations,* to publication in 1776. From that point on, the formal study of economics would contribute to a subtle cultural shift from a focus on the past and the wisdom it provided for present behavior to a focus on the future and what a particular vision of that future suggested for present behavior. It would gradually become a kind of cultural maxim "to look to the future" and a kind of cultural pejorative to be accused of "living in the past." In fact, it is commonplace today for defenders of the status quo to quickly accuse critics of allowing "nostalgia" to muddle their thinking or to cast criticisms aside by dubbing them "hopelessly romantic." This, of course, constitutes a complete ducking of the issues by wielding the power of cultural shame. Were it not for the now near-complete ideological shift in modern society to a focus on the future, a shift begun by Smith, accusations of living in the past or suffering from nostalgia would appear childish and unsophisticated, little more than name-calling, in fact. But given our cultural fascination with the future, the childishness is not only overlooked, it is remarkably successful.

In my estimation, it is impossible to overemphasize the impact of Adam Smith in shaping these kinds of modern ideological contours. The famous Harvard mathematician and philosopher Alfred North Whitehead once remarked that the entire history of Western political philosophy is but a footnote to Plato. Similarly, I would contend that the entire history of Western economic philosophy is but a footnote to Adam Smith.

Adam Smith and the Advent of Economics

During the mercantilist era, decisions affecting economic policy were based on the hope that they would produce the desired result in the future—generally, the short-term future. The central assumption of the era was that wealth ought to be accumulated and *kept.* The great and lasting impact of Adam Smith, the thing anyone remotely interested in economics should remember if nothing else, is the degree to which he stressed the *circulation* of wealth through markets governed by natural "laws." These laws, according to Smith, operated irrespective of any legislative or entrepreneurial role humans might play. This eighteenth-century insight was quickly translated into a kind of cultural maxim. It is alive and well in the twenty-first century—a tribute to the incredible legacy of Adam Smith. For example, in the wake of huge gasoline price hikes after the damage inflicted by hurricanes Katrina and Rita in the fall of 2005, five oil company executives were paraded before Congress to defend the price gouging and the huge profits it generated. Exxon executive Lee Raymond maintained that "markets work—if you let them." Shell Oil executive John Hofmeister turned the tables and admonished members of Congress, "We respectfully request that Congress do no harm by distorting markets." The implicit argument is that there is such a thing as a market law that operates best if there is no human interference. The fact that markets can't operate without some kind of human action is never brought up. It is the twenty-first century version of believing that the earth is flat (literally, not metaphorically). Markets are made up of (1) producer (supplier) decisions and (2) buyer (consumer) choices, presumably rational decisions based on "comparison shopping." Markets, therefore, are by definition human behavior, and insofar as suppliers compete, they are shot through with interference. But Smith claimed that "natural proclivities" to trade, acquire, and self-enhance would make them function as a better road to overall societal wealth than previous systems (war, hoarding, etc.).

For Smith, the ostensible laws of the market trump all else. This includes, as it has for virtually all pre–twenty-first-century economists, the idea of natural limits on the earth itself, or the fact that the earth's resources might be finite. Such an idea never occurred to Smith. He assumed that economic activity would proceed in a self-correcting fashion in an ever upward mode. This assumption set in motion the idea that still animates virtually all mainstream economic thought in the United States: a healthy economy is a growing economy.

From the vantage point of the twenty-first century these Smithian notions—market laws trump everything, and an economy must grow to be healthy—increasingly are seen as questionable, at least by a growing minority of scholars in the academy. Though it is by no means a sure bet, it is probably possible now for an economist to obtain promotion and tenure at an institution of higher education through the publication of work that suggests that market laws are not laws at all, but general principles that necessarily change with varying circumstance (the 1970s and 1980s stagflation experience is certainly a prime example) and that it is possible, even desirable, to orchestrate an economy on the principle of nongrowth. Not too long ago these were radical ideas. Not radical in a Marxist sense, and this is an important point to keep in mind. Marx would challenge Smith and particularly his successors, David Ricardo and Thomas Malthus, but not on the sanctity of market laws or on the growth principle. Marx was persuaded that Smith was correct as far as these ideas were concerned—a point we will come back to shortly.

For now it is important to recognize the cultural depth and force these ideas acquired, partially because they were shared by virtually everyone in the West—capitalists, socialists, fascists, communists—for almost two centuries. But for all of the sophistication the discipline of economics has acquired over this time, it is increasingly plagued by unpredictable dynamics. Most recently we witnessed unprecedented economic growth during the 1990s, but along with it came growth in the ranks of the poor in the United States and elsewhere, a phenomenon so obvious that even the most staunch advocates of growth economics have had to acknowledge this reality.[12]

Of course, one of the great advantages of participating in the discipline of economics is that the focus is so squarely on the future. It makes it easier to deal with unpleasant present realities: perhaps the growth in the number of poor citizens increased in the 1990s, but the growth benefits of that period will eventually be felt by all. When such economic prognostications prove to be wrong, it scarcely matters, for the prognosticators are already off predicting a new future. Besides, and here is another enduring legacy of Adam Smith, the poor in the United States are much better off than the poor in other places. Smith cast aside the mercantilist assumption that the wealth of nations lay in the accumulation of gold and silver. He almost single-handedly taught the world that the true wealth of nations lies in the production of goods and services. And in these terms, Smith was quick to point out, England (and Scotland, his home) was very wealthy indeed.

> Observe the accommodation of the most common artificer or day-labourer.... All the different parts of his dress and household furniture, the coarse linen shirt he wears next to his skin, the shoes which cover his feet, the bed which he lies on ... the kitchen-grate at which he prepares his victuals ... all the other utensils of his kitchen, all the furniture of his stable, the knives and forks, the earthen or pewter plates ... the glass window which lets in heat and the light, and keeps out the wind and the rain. Compared, indeed, with the most extravagant luxury of the great, his accommodation must no doubt appear extremely simple and easy; and yet it may be true, perhaps, that the accommodation of a European prince does not always so much exceed that of an industrious and frugal peasant, as the accommodation of the latter exceeds that of many an African King.[13]

Smith's enduring contribution with this passage was to augment an already growing tendency, since Locke and Hobbes in the seventeenth century, to view life as purely an economic endeavor. If England's poor have possessions that the poor of Africa do not, then they are better off than the poor of Africa. The same comparison continues to be made about the poor in the United States today: "They may be poor, but at least they have a car to drive, a refrigerator, and a TV. The poor in other parts of the world have none of these things." The extent to which an individual readily acknowledges these claims as obvious and true is also the extent to which that individual has bought into the logic of the L-stream, the

Hobbes-Locke tradition described in the previous chapter. The individual looking at the world through the lens of the M-stream might ask whether the poor in Africa enjoy a more coherent community life, whether they are able to develop skills and competencies in acquiring a subsistence living that garner the admiration and emulation of the young, as well as the respect of friends and neighbors. Or an individual wielding the perspectives of the M-stream might ask whether the poor in Africa are able to exercise a voice in the decisions that affect the way life unfolds around them.[14]

Such questions are not intended to condone or legitimize poverty. They need to be asked, however, because there is a distinction to be made between the poor and the "competently poor," to use an expression taken from Wendell Berry;[15] and between the poor who have some political recourse versus those who have none. The point here is that the business of legitimating huge discrepancies between the wealthy and the poor on the grounds that those in poverty are not as poor as poor elsewhere is imminently simplistic and obviously self-serving. There is a necessary economic dimension to life, to be sure, but it is not the only dimension that can render a life poor—or rich.

Peasants who found themselves dispossessed by the rapid pace of enclosure during the 100 years between 1750 and 1850 soon discovered that the skills they had spent a lifetime acquiring, skills that commanded admiration and respect, were of no use in the burgeoning industrial cities where the "division of labour" was heralded as a kind of market law by Smith, and something to be neglected only at the capitalist's peril. Smith lamented the fact that "agriculture does not admit of so many subdivisions of labour, nor so complete a separation of one business from another, as manufactures." He went on to say that "this impossibility of making so complete and entire a separation of all the different branches of labour employed in agriculture, is perhaps the reason why the improvement of the productive powers of labour in this art, does not always keep pace with their improvement in manufactures."[16]

In fact, it is impossible to read *The Wealth of Nations* without picking up on many such digs aimed at the landed class. Their holdings are so large, Smith maintained, that the possibility of improvement was simply beyond their means. The jabs at the landed aristocracy do not in themselves justify the designation Smith frequently receives as the apologist extraordinaire for the new industrialists, the loom-lords and iron-lords and so on. Smith was hard on these individuals as well, frequently condemning their moral integrity and their "monopolizing spirit."

Smith was content in his misgivings about both loom-lords and land-lords because he believed he had identified an orderly, law-based market system that performed well despite the fact that these individuals might possess serious shortcomings—maybe even because of them. Leave the market system alone and it will self-correct for the excesses of the greedy industrialists or their counterparts on

England's landed estates. The market would ensure that goods would be produced in the quantities demanded at prices that would move down with competition. As wealth accrued in this fashion, improvements in manufacturing technology and in the division of labor would occur. Competition for labor would lead to higher wages, which would in turn encourage workers to have larger families. As the population grew, competition among laborers would drive wages down again, increasing capitalists' profits and encouraging further investment. This was the manner of markets, the order of markets. Government or individuals might tamper with them, but only at great peril. Leave the market alone and things will work out in the long run. Or so Smith argued.

But Smith faced a conceptual dilemma, as have all subsequent economists who assume the inevitability and necessity of economic growth—Marx and his followers included. As noted earlier, there was almost complete predictability related to one's economic role under feudal conditions. The "freedom" awarded peasants as feudalism collapsed meant that dire uncertainties were created. Unemployment became a fact of social existence, and with the exception of hastily amended and ever more punitive poor laws, especially those that led to the proliferation of workhouses, there was not much that separated the dispossessed peasant and his family from starvation.[17] A popular 1830s ballad captured the sentiment of the nation's poor:

> So now my bold companions
> The world seems upside down,
> They scorn the poor man as a thief,
> In country and in town.
>
> They build up large workhouses now to part the man and wife,
> That they may no more children get, 'tis true upon my life.
> They take their children from their arms and send them different ways,
> And fifteen pence allowed to keep a man for seven days.[18]

Do people willingly starve? What's to keep the poor from rising up against their better-off neighbors? For that matter, won't the free pursuit of self-interest lead to societal clashes at all levels? And what about societal projects of common or mutual interest? How will such projects be accomplished if the focus is on *self*-interest?

Smith no doubt puzzled over this. But in the end he decided that his perfect market system took care of this dilemma as well. He was not particularly persuasive on this point, though his argument is often quoted and more often imitated. For Smith decided that if free men merely pursued their self-interest, an "invisible hand" would guide their passions to that "which is most agreeable to the interest of the whole society." In other words, pursue your self-interest and the common good will take care of itself.[19]

Defenders of growth economics to this day are forced into the use of similar language to deal with the same conceptual dilemma that troubled Smith. Elhanan Helpman's recent book titled *The Mystery of Economic Growth* is a good example. Martin Wolf's conservative defense of globalizing growth, *Why Globalization Works,* includes a chapter titled "The 'Magic' of the Market" in which he maintains that "Adam Smith's invisible hand remains as illuminating as ever."[20] An invisible hand is certainly a mysterious concept, and if it indeed exists it is probably fair to call such a thing magical. But for a discipline that prides itself on its allegiance to science and scientific principles, its identification of laws, formulae, theorems, and the like, what are we to make of this resort to the mysterious, the magical, to the unscientific?

We will return to this question, but let it suffice to say for now that the resort to the unscientific suggests that economics is too intimately connected to the intricacies and idiosyncrasies of human behavior to be understood in purely scientific terms. This is true of politics and education as well—though we continue to craft policy on the basis of what science tells us, as if all human dilemmas could be understood in scientific terms. An essay in a recent issue of *Educational Researcher,* a leading journal in professional education, described what the authors saw as prerequisites in "the doctoral preparation of scientifically-based education researchers."[21] A nice example of how deep the fascination for science runs in our culture.

Returning to Smith, however, it is important to point out that his economic analysis, while path-breaking, was too simplistic on many levels. Smith was convinced that labor was the "real measure of the exchangeable value of commodities." Labor became the engine of his economy. When it was in demand, wages would rise. When there was a surplus, wages would fall. With labor representing the real cost of production, rising wages meant rising prices. Conversely, falling wages meant falling prices. Or so it should have worked in Smith's market-driven mechanistic world. Smith was silent on many pertinent questions—such as why the demand for labor should go up and down in the first place—and consequently subsequent economists would have large theoretical gaps to fill.

It is worth noting, too, that Smith was not a fan of bigness. He referred to England as "a nation of shopkeepers" and was deeply suspicious of the growth of large corporate entities. He died in 1790 believing that the market would not countenance their proliferation and that, happily, market laws would alleviate the problems associated with England's unfolding Industrial Revolution. His successors were not nearly so sanguine about England's future. Before turning to the dismal prognostications of Smith's successors—Thomas Malthus and David Ricardo—it is important to at least briefly acknowledge the evolution of a very different kind of economic theory, one that came to fruition in eighteenth-century France.

The Physiocrats

In the forty-year period before the French Revolution, a theoretical perspective related to economics began to take shape in France. Its principal architect was Francois Quesnay, a medical doctor by training who was so successful that he rose through the ranks to become the personal physician of Louis XV. Later in life he turned to the study of economics, and he is probably best known for coining the phrase *laissez faire*, literally, "let do," meaning government ought to play no role in the orchestration of the economy. (More than a century later, in a nonmonarchical world, the phrase would resonate with condoning and promoting industrial interests—a perspective Quesnay and other physiocrats would have been quick to reject had they even been able to conceive of the impact of industrialization.) Adam Smith spent several years in France as the tutor of the young Duke of Buccleuch and during this time became a friend of Quesnay. Smith credits Quesnay with helping to shape his views about the ways of the market—the extent to which it operates in a lawlike fashion to translate the various desires and behaviors of humans into a workable system of distribution.

Quesnay's contribution to Smith in this regard probably stemmed from the tremendous popularity of his *Tableau Economique*, a detailed chart that documented the flow of goods and services, and the wealth they generate, through the various classes of French society. The *tableau* was likely the first sophisticated picture of how an economy works, and it should be no surprise, therefore, that it contributed greatly to the views Smith would make famous via *The Wealth of Nations*.[22]

But for Smith and his English successors, the economic perspectives of Quesnay and the physiocrats (a term meaning the "rule of nature," and therefore very misleading) was marred by one great intellectual handicap. Quesnay and his followers argued that true wealth was generated only through agriculture. Merchants bought and sold, but added nothing. Manufacturers added labor to the products of the soil, but that was all.

On the eve of the Industrial Revolution, such a theoretical perspective was quickly dismissed in England. And, indeed, it had significant detractors in France.[23] But it clearly resonated with the majority of French intellectuals precisely because it resonated, as well, with French culture. To a greater degree than in England, the French took pride in their agricultural accomplishments: cheeses, fruits, and, of course, wines, were produced with extraordinary care and distinctiveness. The physiocrats labeled French agricultural workers—small freeholders, day-laborers, even serfs—the "productive class," a telling contrast to such phrases as the "lower orders" that agricultural workers garnered in England.

Try as they might, the French physiocrats were not able to reform the *ancien regime* quickly enough to forestall the explosive French Revolution in 1789. And in time the views of the physiocrats gave way to economic perspectives that were considerably more amenable to industrial pursuits. But the legacy of the physiocrats has remained in France, and at least partially as a consequence, it has been far more circumspect regarding the application of industrial principles and practices in the agricultural arena. This remains true to this day.

Before dismissing the physiocrats to the dust bin of economic history, as so many have done, their perspectives are worth a closer look. Recall that they were writing at a time before the harnessing and distribution of electricity, steam power, and other energy sources that would shortly thereafter descend upon the global landscape. In such a world, agriculture was the central economic activity. And the fact that food is the only exchangeable commodity that humans absolutely must have legitimates a certain centrality to agriculture. It is the one economic endeavor that we cannot walk away from. We can cease to build ships, shovels, cars, guns, tables, or chairs—but we cannot cease to produce food.

The physiocrats were right about the centrality of agriculture (and perhaps even in the claim that it is the only source of "true" wealth) while it was virtually the only economic activity capable of tapping the energy of *current* sunlight. When the possibility of safely and systematically tapping Paleolithic sunlight (in the form of coal, gas, and oil) became a reality, the physiocratic position was quickly deemed to be useless, or at least hopelessly out of date. But the fact remains that the production of food is the only absolutely necessary economic undertaking, and that the sun, present or past, is the world's only source of energy. Declarations about the uselessness of physiocratic economic theory were directly tied to erroneous assumptions (as we know all too well today) concerning the inexhaustibility of Paleolithic, or alternative, energy sources.

John Locke used the fact that food is the only absolutely necessary economic activity to justify a view of human nature as a purely economic being. In a state of nature, he argued, man would search for food and would stand ready to fight for an economic advantage at a moment's notice. It is no coincidence that the Frenchman Montesquieu, saw the state of nature quite differently; saw it, in fact, as a state of peace rather than a state of war. And it is no coincidence that an economic theory privileging agricultural production would emanate from France.

In nineteenth-century England, as we shall shortly see, the policy arena became a kind of battleground between industrial and agricultural interests, with the industrial interests winning the day. This industrial victory eventually led to a kind of cultural blind spot in the West, even in France. It has been a great failing of the Western mind to unquestionably accept the view of industrialists who maintained that an agrarian state was a relic of the past; outmoded, if not a practical impossibility in the modern world. It is only now in the twenty-first century that such a view is beginning to look like the nonsense that it was. For an agrarian state, as the physiocrats argued, would readily make use of industrial activity—just as the industrial state we have come to know readily makes use of agrarian activity. For now, however, we will leave the French physiocratic vision behind and return to England in the aftermath of Smith's *The Wealth of Nations,* where the Hobbes-Locke predictions of economic man entrenched in a state of war proved to be very prophetic indeed.

An Era Red in Tooth and Claw

Adam Smith died in 1790. Had he lived eight more years he would have had the opportunity to read another economic treatise of lasting impact. It came from the pen of the Reverend Thomas Malthus, who in 1798 published *An Essay on the Principle of Population as It Affects the Future Improvement of Society,* and in the process introduced the study of population "laws" to economic theorizing.

Malthus explained that the passage of time would trigger exponential population growth while the ability of the land, which cannot be reproduced, would lag behind in the production of required food and fiber. In short, according to Malthus, the world was headed for disaster. Whatever one might make of his thesis—and it is one that recurs with some frequency[24]—it cannot be denied that England's population was growing at a rapid clip as the eighteenth century closed. In other words, England was experiencing what would later be called a "Malthusian dilemma," the perception that population growth will soon outstrip society's ability to produce the necessary food, clothing, and shelter.

Though David Ricardo, a contemporary and friend of Malthus, would also contribute to the sentiment, Malthus's *Essay on Population* produced a kind of cultural hardheartedness (this was the term Malthus used to describe accusations against him) that lingers in some circles to this day.[25] Given demographic pressure, or so the Malthusian argument goes, it is simply self-defeating to in any way improve the circumstances of the poor—for this will only stimulate reproduction and add still more poor mouths for the nation to feed. Malthus steadfastly believed this to be the case, and he therefore became a leading voice calling for the abolition of poor relief and low-wage worker housing projects. For these views, of course, he was roundly criticized, but these views nevertheless had a certain appeal—and an obvious utility—for England's industrial entrepreneurs.

That appeal was significantly heightened by the economic theorizing of David Ricardo, clearly the world's leading economist of the first half of the nineteenth century. Ricardo argued that modern society had evolved to the point where it could more or less be divided into three groups: workers, industrialists, and landlords. According to Ricardo, workers survived on wages, industrialists turned profits on capital investment, and landlords generated wealth through rents.

Like Malthus, Ricardo believed that workers would inevitably waste their wages in pursuit of pleasure. Lacking the wherewithal for self-restraint, their numbers would increase, driving wages still lower. Said Ricardo, "When, however, by the encouragement which higher wages give to the increase of population, the number of labourers is increased, wages again fall to their natural price, and indeed from a re-action sometimes fall below it."[26] The combined power of Malthus and Ricardo in shaping modern views about the shortcomings of the poor is difficult to overestimate. The best way to get a glimpse of the effect of their views on the growing business class in England is to think of Ebenezer Scrooge from the Charles Dickens classic, *A Christmas Carol.* Scrooge firmly believed that the poor did not deserve relief and that wages should not exceed that which it takes to keep workers returning the next day. Thanks to Malthus and Ricardo, this was a common ethos in nineteenth-century England. In fact, the corpus of Dickens novels lends a fairly accurate picture of what life was like for wage earners in England's industrial cities: child labor, long hours, dangerous work, no benefits, meager wages, horrific living conditions, and more. Some contemporary accounts claim that an entire class of people was visibly stunted in terms of physical growth over a couple of generations. It is, frankly, difficult to overdramatize the extent of wretched misery suffered by England's poor throughout the middle decades of the nineteenth century. There should be little wonder that Alfred Lord Tennyson described it as an age "red in tooth and claw."[27]

The unfettered profit-seeking behaviors of emerging industrialists that created these conditions and circumstances—legitimated by regnant economic theory—meshed well with the earlier political theory of Hobbes and Locke. Humans are selfish creatures, after all, and in a state of nature they will inevitably fight for economic advantage, thereby "overturning all morality," as Locke put it. The convergence of L-stream political theory and Malthusian/Ricardian economic theory made for inordinately powerful cultural assumptions about the inevitability of vast discrepancies between the wealthy and the poor, between the have and the have-nots. Though much has happened and much has been written that disproves such assumptions, these views nevertheless maintain a curious kind of hold on the modern mind.

A French economist, Jean Baptiste Say, a contemporary and confidant of both Malthus and Ricardo, was a major contributor to this. Say turned his back on the French physiocrat tradition (Quesnay and his followers) and published a treatise on political economy in 1803 in which he explicated the views of Adam Smith for a French audience. But more than this, he put forward what came to be known as "Say's Law," or "Say's Law of Markets," an idea that proved to have amazing staying power. Say argued "that it is production which opens a demand for products." And he explained further:

> When the producer has put the finishing hand to his product, he is most anxious to sell it immediately, lest its value should diminish in his hands. Nor is he less anxious to dispose of the money he may get for it; for the value of money is also perishable. But the only way of getting rid of money is in the purchase of some product or another. Thus, the mere circumstance of the creation of one product immediately opens a vent for other products.[28]

In other words, production creates its own demand. With the identification of this ostensible "law," the science of political economy became much more confidant, much more convinced of its ability to predict future economic activity. There may be temporary imbalances, some brief periods of high unemployment, but these wavelike periods of recession or depression would inevitably right themselves.

Say's Law was challenged by a few scholars, including Malthus and a French economist with the colorful name Jean-Charles Leonard Simonde de Sismondi,[29] but these challenges were overwhelmed by the thunder of approval that dominated nineteenth- and early twentieth-century economics.[30] For almost 130 years, Say's Law was a symbol of respectability among economists. Swear allegiance to it and you were a credible scholar. Question it, and you were relegated to the margins of the profession. Say's Law legitimated the status quo. It promoted production incentives for the "captains of industry." At the same time, it served to squash attempts to prop up demand by coining silver or adding paper money to the economy—policies that would have aided a nation's agrarian interests. Make no mistake about it, Say's Law was a boon to the growth of capitalism—until the capitalist system collapsed in 1929. Since the Great Depression, no one has professed faith in the idea that production creates its own demand. The challenges of Malthus and Sismondi were accurate, though heeded 130 years too late.

The magnitude of the squalor in England's nineteenth-century cities and the vast extent of human misery led to a variety of attempts to ameliorate societal circumstances. Before turning to examine these, however, it is worth noting that David Ricardo played a role in a different kind of drama than the one set in motion for the poor by his "iron law of wages." By depicting the economy as a kind of contested terrain, in particular a place where agrarian interests would inevitably battle with industrial interests for policy amenable to their idiosyncratic pursuits, Ricardo set the stage for a kind of ideological victory for the values of an industrial worldview, and a corresponding defeat for the values of an agrarian worldview. This is a theme we will return to later, as well, but Ricardo's work serves as a nice introduction to this topic. He makes it possible to see the nineteenth-century economic policy arena as the site of a kind of battle to determine which values would prevail and define modern society.

A brief example may help demonstrate this. Malthus had been right about England's population. It was growing and in the process creating an increased demand for food. Heightened demand brought with it higher food prices. This was obviously good for landowners, but bad for factory owners since they had to raise wages sufficiently to allow workers to feed themselves. To get around this, the commercial and industrial interests of England began purchasing cheaper grain from abroad. The landed interests, still dominating Parliament, countered this move by passing what became known as the Corn Laws, restricting the importation of foreign grain.

The Corn Laws incensed Ricardo, who responded with the publication of *An Essay on the Influence of a Low Price of Corn on the Profits of Stock; Shewing the Inexpediency of Restrictions on Importation* in 1815. Documenting the fact that a landlord's "situation is never so prosperous as when food is scarce and dear," he went on to explain that by contrast, "all other persons are greatly benefited by procuring food cheap."[31] This essay was the start of a decades-long contest between the economic interests of agricultural landowners and those of emerging industrialists. Ricardo clearly believed that society needed to move in the direction represented by industrial interests and at least attempt to wrest away the policy hegemony of England's landowners.[32]

The ethos of contest that Ricardo helped to fuel in England had an analogous effect in the United States. Because of the popularity of the M-stream in America, however, and because many believed that America's future could be categorically different from the path taken by England, agrarian ideals would maintain some force for perhaps half a century longer than they did in England. But the contest would eventually come as the nineteenth century closed, bringing a victory for industrial interests and values similar to those that were victorious in England. But this puts us ahead of the story.

Alternatives Arise

The history of nineteenth-century England proves nothing quite so well as the fact that "pure" capitalism is not a viable option for any society. Certain "refinements" are needed, things like publicly supported free schools, worker protections, universally available health care, minimum and possibly maximum wage laws, and social security benefits, to mention a few of the most obvious. While most modern democracies have achieved most of these refinements, the cultural legacy of Malthus and Ricardo—when it comes to legitimating the existence of poverty, placing the blame for it on the poor themselves, as noted earlier—has remained curiously strong. Even the enigmatic John Stuart Mill, heir to Ricardo as the world's preeminent economist, contributed to the commonsense view that "poverty, like most social evils, exists because men follow their brute instincts without due consideration." He added that not much relief was possible until "producing large families is regarded with the same feelings as drunkenness or any other physical excess." Mill explained further:

> A greater number of people cannot, in any given state of civilization, be collectively so well provided for as a smaller. The niggardliness of nature, *not the injustice of society,* is the cause of the penalty attached to overpopulation. An unjust distribution of wealth does not aggravate the evil, but, at most, causes it to be somewhat earlier felt. It is in vain to say that all mouths which the increase in mankind calls

into existence bring with them hands. The new mouths require as much food as the old ones, and the hands do not produce as much.[33]

England's nineteenth-century "captains of industry" found a kind of quiet vindication in Mill's soothing tone. The profound appeal of the idea that increased population drives down wages and creates poverty legitimated the status quo and put the blame for poverty squarely on the shoulders of the poor. It wasn't until near the end of the century, from the pen of Henry George, an American, that this idea was challenged and exposed as vacuous.[34] Still, despite the fact that he often echoed common stereotypes, Mill nevertheless did more than any other individual to eradicate the hardheartedness ostensibly required in emerging industrial societies.

John Stuart Mill was the son of James Mill, a leading English intellectual in his own right. James Mill was a close associate of Jeremy Bentham and one of the founders of "utilitarianism," a political and social theory based on a conception of human nature as essentially pleasure seeking. The central utilitarian idea was that humans by nature seek to acquire happiness and avoid sorrow or pain. Bentham's greatest work, *The Principles of Morals and Legislation,* begins with absolute clarity: "Nature has placed mankind under the governance of two sovereign masters, pain and pleasure. It is for them alone to point out what we ought to do, as well as to determine what we shall do." From this premise Mill and Bentham called for social, political, and economic policy that would derive "the greatest good for the greatest number."[35]

While there was an enviable clarity to utilitarian theory, it was doomed from the start. Critics from all segments of society came forward with example after example of human behavior that could not be characterized as attempts to maximize pleasure or avoid pain. And, worse still, wouldn't the general policy guideline—seek the greatest good for the greatest number—merely exacerbate the potential damage inflicted on minorities via "the tyranny of the majority"? In a half-hearted attempt to defend the theories of Bentham and his father, John Stuart Mill would later attempt an answer to these critics.

But the most significant contribution of James Mill was very likely not the cofounding of utilitarian theory. His greatest contribution may have been serving as the father of John Stuart Mill, for he was a very proactive father. In fact, when individuals first learn about the educational regimen the elder Mill imposed on his son, the phrase "child abuse" often comes quickly to mind. John Stuart was born in 1806. By age three, young John was being instructed by his father in the Greek language. By age seven John Stuart had advanced to the point where he was reading the works of Greek philosophers. At age eight the elder Mill shifted the educational focus to Latin, and shortly thereafter John Stuart was reading the works of Roman intellectuals such as Virgil, Horace, Livy, and Lucretius. He studied algebra, geometry, and calculus as a boy. He wrote several historical works before the age of twelve. As a thirteen-year-old, Mill began the earnest study of everything related to what was then called the field of political economy. It was a boyhood of ceaseless study. He had no age-mate friends whatsoever. He was secluded to the point that he lacked any awareness that other youth led quite different lives.

In what can only seem to contemporary readers as highly predictable, Mill suffered from severe depression during his twenties. He began to rebel against his father, intellectually at least, by reading scholars at the academic fringes—individuals who wrote of matters of the spirit rather than matters of strict reason and rational calculation. In the end, however, it was very likely love that saved him. He met and immediately fell in love with Harriet Taylor, a woman of great energy, deep intellect, and distinctively socialist views. Regrettably, she was married. But this didn't stop them. For twenty years they were together often; they even lived together for a time. When they were apart they wrote volumes to one another. After twenty years, Harriet's husband died. She and John Stuart were quickly thereafter married and inseparable.

That Harriet Taylor had a profound impact on Mill's intellectual development is beyond dispute. He admitted this much in his autobiography.[36] The relationship led directly to Mill's *The Subjection of Women,* published in 1869. Remarkably, considering prevailing views at the time, Mill came out in favor of extending the vote to women (it had not yet been universally extended to males as of 1869). But his greatest contribution was to rescue the distribution of goods and services from the Smithian preserve of law-regulated supply and demand economic behavior. He was satisfied that such laws, perhaps even "iron laws," regulated production, but not so distribution. And here was Mill's contribution to an era grown red in tooth and claw: the distribution of what society produced was up to society.

In other words, wealth could be more evenly distributed. The worst excesses of the age could be curbed through ethical deliberation. In time, Mill believed, the working class would see the Malthusian dilemma and rise above it. In time, income would be increasingly equalized as unearned windfalls and large inheritances would be taxed away. In fact, Mill even prophesied the arrival of a "steady state," which just may have made him one of the most prescient intellectuals of the modern era—for such a concept is only now, under the specter of potentially ruinous environmental circumstances, attracting a following of significance. Mill's conception of a steady state—the idea that an economy need not grow—may yet turn the whole classical tradition in economics on its head.

It is only possible to fully appreciate the extent to which Mill represented an alternative to the dismal views of Malthus and Ricardo by contrasting his gradualist, measured blueprint for improving society against other more immediate, and decidedly more radical, alternatives that came into being during the same era. The world generally only remembers one at this point in history; the acerbic, biting, holistic socialist critique of unfettered capitalism that came from the pen of Karl

Marx. Never has there been an economist who so changed the world. Marxism became the official doctrine of massive revolutions touching well over half the world's population, most notably in Russia and in China. But nearing the midpoint of the nineteenth century, Marx was just one voice among many. France, given its historic cultural embrace of agrarian values, was a prolific source of critiques aimed at the excesses of industrialism. Charles Fourier, Claude Henri Saint-Simon, Louis Blanc, and especially Pierre Proudhon represent a small sampling. There were others in Switzerland, Italy, and Germany, as well as within England itself. One result of their combined efforts was the revolutionary fervor of 1848, a jolt that staggered the old order in Europe—if only temporarily.

But it was Karl Marx—born in Germany, expatriated to France, then to Belgium, then back to Germany, and finally to England—who brought sophisticated social scientific analysis to the socialist critique. It was Marx who lit the communist flame that continues to burn in the twenty-first century. Joseph Schumpeter, Harvard economist and a leading political advisor throughout the 1950s, wrote that "the cold metal of economic theory is in Marx's pages immersed in such a wealth of steaming phrases as to acquire a temperature not naturally its own."[37]

Marx was deeply influenced by the German philosopher G. W. F. Hegel, which is to say he believed the world was in a constant state of "dialectic." Change was omnipresent; new ideas about governance, economics, education—all social phenomena—were inevitable according to Hegel. And the consequences of each new idea of necessity produces an opposite idea. In time these opposing, conflicting ideas merge into a synthesis, and the process continues with the new idea generating its own opposite. Marx applied the Hegelian concept of dialectic—an intellectual history of constant change carrying potential consequences—into an analysis of world history. The landed, feudal order was one synthesis challenged by the merging industrial and financial order. Marx lived through this "dialectical transition" and personally watched it unfold. The next one, inevitably, according to Marx, was to be the workers revolting against the industrial and financial barons (the laboring class against the propertied class).

Clearly, the path of gradual reform and even modest redistribution advanced by John Stuart Mill was preferable to those nations that had already ascended to an era of industrial dominance. England was such a nation; the United States was fast becoming one. Much of northern and western Europe was as well. In time, of course, as Mill had predicted, many socialist reforms became a reality throughout the world. Trade unions, workingmen's associations, cooperative efforts of various kinds all made inroads on the path laid open by Mill: societies can decide how what is produced will be distributed.

Looking at the era red in tooth and claw, it is easy to see the path of slow reform advocated by Mill on the one hand, and the path of dramatic, immediate, even violent reform advocated by Marx on the other. Both paths had their takers. But there was a third option—far less recognized, and of far greater import for today's world than the vision of either Mill or Marx, both of whom accepted, whole cloth, an industrial vision and all that came with it: most significantly, the assumption that the earth's resources were infinite and there to be exploited by those with the wherewithal to do it. But there, too, were assumptions about work, specifically the assumption it could be chopped up and rendered meaningless, devoid of any skillful or artistic dimensions; that leisure—as Thorstein Veblen would later explain[38]—could be converted into a symbol of status replacing work well done. And this is just the start of a dubious list of attributes that spokespersons for the currently regnant industrial worldview have yet to substantively address.

The third option, the alternative to Mill and Marx that emerged in the nineteenth century, was a vision to some degree reminiscent of Winstanley's seventeenth-century depiction of a community-based republic premised on a lifelong commitment to citizen education. It became manifest in the proliferation of community-building experiments in Europe and in the United States—experiments subsequently labeled *utopian,* a word that has come to be defined as synonymous with *naïve,* or with such phrases as "hopelessly romantic" or "overly sentimental." But the word was first used by Thomas More, whose book (published in 1551), *Utopia,* helped clear a path for later critiques of the feudal order. More pointed out that the word *utopia* might refer to the Greek *outopia,* meaning "no place"—a definition that squares well with our current one, but he also maintained that it might refer to *eutopia,* meaning "the good place." Today, any vision of what a society might become that does not look very much like what society currently is, is quickly dubbed "utopian" and therefore impossible to achieve. But whether these communitarian experiments were naïvely "utopian" using our current definition of the word is probably not as significant as the facts that document their incredible proliferation. Whether they were led by famous individuals like Fourier or Owen or by more historically obscure figures, whether they were heavily religious or strikingly secular, built around agriculture or industry, there were profound similarities among them all. In the United States we are most familiar with Hopedale, Northampton, New Harmony, Fruitlands, and Brook Farm, but between 1800 and 1859 there were at least 119 communal societies established; and between 1840 and 1849, the high point of the M-stream in America, there were at least fifty-nine such communities established.[39]

The proliferation of these communities was partially a reaction to the excesses of the emerging industrial era, but it was also partly a reaction to the growing democratic spirit born of an embrace of liberty and freedom. Surely freedom had to mean more than a permission slip to slug it out with others in a competitive economic market? Perhaps Montesquieu was right after all. Maybe human freedom was meant to be applied to the political scene as well, and what better way to infuse a political dimension into the lives of citizens than via community involvement? And just as Montesquieu warned that a democratic republic required a system of schools capable of delivering "the full power of education," the communal societies of the 1840s made educational efforts a central thrust of their experiments, creating one significant similarity among them all.

A second similarity was the degree to which residents of these communitarian projects rejected the so-called scientific "laws" that took economic activity out of the realm of human volition—that there was some force at work that allowed market-driven behaviors to be considered quite apart from the realm of morality. To the contrary, communitarians of the 1840s tried to establish moral economies based on chosen ethical principles; they tried to set moral parameters that would govern the exchange of goods and services within them. The word that generally captured the idea of a moral economy was *cooperation,* and it should be no surprise that political theorizing based on the conception of a state of nature as a state of peace (Montesquieu), rather than a state of war (Locke), would be much more amenable to using cooperation as a guideline for appropriate economic activity.

It turns out that we have to go beyond both Mill and Marx to get a complete picture of the alternative that came into being, albeit piecemeal, during the nineteenth century—for it is within this alternative, I believe, that humankind's greatest hope for a long future lies. Christopher Clark aptly labeled the 1840s as "the communitarian moment," a phrase that suggests certain circumstances came together in such a way as to permit a communitarian vision for what life might be to come to fruition. But "communitarian *moment*" also suggests that other circumstances came together in such a way as to snuff out that momentary vision. To take what instruction we can from the potential of the communitarian moment, we need to examine both its origins and decline.

In 1999 a sizable group of English protestors marched to St. George's Hill in Surrey—now an affluent suburb of London—and symbolically began digging, planting, and building temporary shelter. The effort was designed to commemorate the 350th anniversary of Gerrard Winstanley's digger experiment, and it garnered some limited media attention. The reenactment symbolizes one incontestable fact related to Winstanley and the diggers: what they did was memorable.

At first, of course, it was a memory of events that originally had haunted the landed aristocracy of England; but decades and centuries later it was a memory that served as a source of new possibilities in the world—the establishment of Puritan communities abroad, for instance, or for the establishment of secular communities of the sort that came into being in the nineteenth century. Winstanley and his followers took advantage of that limited window of freedom in the 1640s, that small space of time when the feudal order fell and there was no social institution yet firmly in place to fill the void. In that moment Winstanley and the diggers offered to the world the idea that the earth was a "common treasury" to be protected and used well by all.

There were prehistorical, classical, and medieval antecedents to this idea, to be sure, but the prehistorical conceptions had been irrevocably lost to seventeenth-century Europe, and classical and medieval conceptions lacked the democratic ethos that pervaded England of the 1640s. When the idea of the earth as a common treasury was paired with the idea that an individual ought to have a voice in the decisions that affect her/him, a modern community-oriented agrarian vision was born. For this contribution to humankind, Gerrard Winstanley ought to be listed among the world's great thinkers; his work should be translated into many languages and studied by youth and adults alike the world over. But his agrarian vision was passed over for a vision that fiercely promoted and aggrandized an urban industrial future, and so Winstanley has remained a footnote in history. But while his vision has been kept in the footnotes, kept at the margins of political, economic, and educational theory, it has never disappeared altogether. For that there are others to thank.

An obscure late eighteenth-century professor at King's College in Aberdeen, Scotland, William Ogilivie, is one such individual. Building on the idea of the earth as a common treasury, Ogilivie argued that "the earth having been given to mankind in common occupancy, each individual seems to have by nature a right to possess and cultivate an equal share." If a child is born with the expectation that it will receive mother's milk, "no one can deny that it has the same right to mother-earth."[40] Ogilivie's arguments were laid out anonymously in 1782 in an extended essay sometimes called "Birthright in Land," but the power possessed by England's landed aristocracy was enough to be sure that this idea that every child born on earth was entitled to a part of it would go nowhere. Still, it has proved to be an idea that is difficult to dispute with intellectual argument. If a child deserves food, clothing, and shelter—something no one would attempt to deny—at what point does the child no longer deserve physical possessions necessary for subsistence? Does this occur at age twelve? Sixteen? Eighteen? Twenty-one? And is there some obligation on the part of the members of society to be sure that the means of procuring these things are available to all? Given the vagaries of the market, a society is not in a position to guarantee income for all of those who need it. Then what? Ogilivie's answer was that since each individual has a right "to the use of open air and running water," they also have the right to possess and cultivate a share of the earth.

Of course Ogilivie's contemporaries were quick to point out that such a scheme was not practical, though he did his best to stave off this criticism. "No impractical Utopian scheme can be said to be suggested, in proposing that property in land should be diffused to as great a number of citizens as may desire it: that is only proposing to carry out somewhat farther, and render more extensive, a plan which the experience of many ages has shown to be very practical, and highly beneficial in every public and private respect."[41] This same objection—"It's too impractical"—would be echoed a million times over if someone was able to get the same idea out to a wide audience today—something that has actually happened, as we shall shortly see. For now it is enough to recognize that Ogilivie built on Winstanley's idea of the earth as a common treasury and argued that this conception creates a legitimate entitlement to the possession of the earth for all individuals. Ogilivie pointed out that primitive societies generally operate on the assumption undergirding a birthright in land but added that "whenever conquests have taken place, this right has been commonly subverted and effaced; in the progress of commercial arts and refinements, it is suffered to fall into obscurity and neglect."[42] In other words, as land became an avenue for the acquisition of wealth unencumbered by community obligations, the idea that all individuals have a right to the land has been gradually squeezed out of popular memory.

But the idea didn't die with Ogilivie. It was picked up and refined a few years later by an Englishman turned American citizen, none other than the great pamphleteer of the American colonies, Thomas Paine. In an essay entitled "Agrarian Justice," Paine echoed Ogilivie's arguments and built on the distant memory of Gerrard Winstanley and the diggers.

Paine's career as an agrarian spokesperson developed while he lived in France after the American Revolution. But during the bloody reign of Robespierre, Paine was arrested and charged with being a "foreigner" and was subsequently imprisoned. Gouvenour Morris, America's ambassador to France, refused to acknowledge Paine as a converted and legitimate American citizen, and thus Paine lived for months with the daily threat of the guillotine. When Morris was replaced by James Monroe, the new ambassador quickly lobbied for and achieved Paine's release from prison. Mrs. Monroe nurtured him back to health, and Paine quickly returned to the business of writing pamphlets and essays dedicated to the improvement of mankind. He wrote "Agrarian Justice" during the winter of 1795–1796, though it wasn't published until 1797. It was written as a suggestion for the French republic, though in the author's inscription he noted that "this work is not adapted for any country alone," meaning that its prescriptions might well be used by the United States or even England.

Paine begins the essay by highlighting what Adam Smith went to considerable effort to hide: the fact that the ascendancy of modern "civilization" had created enormous extremes in the quality of life among men.

> Whether that state that is proudly, perhaps erroneously, called civilization, has most promoted or most injured the general happiness of man, is a question that may be strongly contested. On one side, the spectator is dazzled by splendid appearances; on the other, he is shocked by extremes of wretchedness; both of which it has erected. The most affluent and the most miserable of the human race are to be found in the countries that are called civilized.[43]

Recall that Smith legitimized English poverty by pointing to their possessions, the glass in their windows, the silverware on their tables, then compared these possessions to those owned by the poor in Africa, thereafter pronouncing

England's poor to be better off than African kings. Malthus, Ricardo, and even John Stuart Mill berated the poor of England for their moral shortcomings, claiming definitively that they bring on their own circumstances by their inability to contain their "procreative impulses."

Paine would have none of such nonsense. Using the state of nature as a point of departure (as did Hobbes, Locke, Montesquieu, and many others), he noted that neither abject poverty nor incredible affluence existed there. Should a society seek to achieve a natural state, therefore, they must fashion policy that eliminates these extremes. Paine begins with a passage that sounds as if it came directly from Gerrard Winstanley's *The Law of Freedom* or from Ogilivie's *Essay on the Right of Property in Land*:

> It is a position not to be controverted that the earth, in its natural, uncultivated state was, and ever would have continued to be, *the common property of the human race*. In that state every man would have been born to property. He would have been a joint life proprietor with the rest in the property of the soil, and in all of its natural productions, vegetable and animal.[44]

Paine argued that for tens of thousands of years this arrangement was maintained. In time, however, the use of the sword legitimated unlimited acquisition by some and the dispossession of others. Agrarian justice required rectification of this circumstance, and Paine was not satisfied with the objection so many gave to Ogilivie—that his plan was simply not practical. Paine was more than willing to tackle the practicality problem. Like Locke much earlier, Paine acknowledged that improved land is much more productive than unimproved land. But unlike Locke, Paine argued that it was the value of improvements made that constituted individual property—while the land remained necessarily a common treasury. This being the case, every proprietor of cultivated lands owes the community what Paine called a "ground-rent" in exchange for the use of the common treasury.

Paine was aware of the fact that, like the emerging small farms on the Greek peninsula circa 700 BC, the considerable labor involved in cultivation led to property claims where previously there were none. Originally, the land had no owner. The problem with property claims, for Paine, is that the act of establishing what belongs to one is simultaneously the act of denying possession to another. The shortcoming of civilized societies has been their failure to provide an indemnification for those who lack access to the common treasury. Righting this shortcoming was merely a policy question, and Paine went on to demonstrate how such a policy might look:

> I shall now proceed to the plan I have to propose, which is, to create a national fund, out of which there shall be paid to every person, when arrived at the age of twenty-one years, the sum of fifteen pounds sterling, as compensation in part, for the loss of his or her natural inheritance, by the introduction of the system of

landed property: and also, the sum of ten pounds per annum, during life, to every person now living, of the age of fifty years, and to all others as they shall arrive at that age.[45]

He goes on to describe how society might support such a policy—relying most heavily on inheritances taxes, "because it will operate without deranging any present possessors ... and because it will be the least troublesome and the most effectual, and also because the subtraction will be made at a time that best admits it." But as Paine points out, there are many ways to make the resources required by agrarian justice available.

Paine's essay also ought to be required reading for youth and adults everywhere. It is a clearly written, carefully and persuasively constructed argument for a policy intended to minimize the extent to which modern "civilized" society divides people into groups of wealthy and poor. The plan had an impact on those who played a leadership role in establishing America's communitarian moment in the 1840s; it would serve as a catalyst to Henry George's "single tax" plan near the end of the nineteenth century, and it would serve as an indirect inspiration for a contemporary plan, offered by Yale philosophers Bruce Ackerman and Anne Alstott in *The Stakeholder Society* (1993), for the federal government to award a check for $80,000 to each high school or GED graduate. The latter plan was quickly dismissed as impractical.

However, there were other agrarian thinkers who rejected the assumptions and the general philosophy that emanated from the mainstream voices in the field of political economy, that is, Smith, Malthus, Ricardo, Say, and Mill. Ogilivie was one, Paine was another, but there were many more, some of whom were outside of the English-speaking tradition, a fact that has contributed to some degree to their relative obscurity in the annals of economic theorizing. But as with the thought of Winstanley, Ogilivie, and Paine, the ideas are there at the margins waiting for a rediscovery on the part of modern civilized society.

This clearly describes the fate of the ideas offered by the French (though he lived most of his life in Switzerland) economist Sismondi, mentioned earlier as a critic of Say's Law, an economist who began his career as an apologist for the views of Adam Smith. Much like Jean Baptiste Say, Sismondi was enamored with Smith's ability to create a science out of the study of political economy. But he didn't immediately build his career as an economist. His interests were broad. In 1818, for example, he published the last of an eighteen-volume history of the constitutional republics of Italy. He also published extensive works dealing with the literature of southern Europe, noting that its quality seemed to be related to the highs and lows of a nation's economic prosperity.

In time Sismondi had a chance to visit England and, in fact, he lived there for about a year. The visit crushed his admiration for Adam Smith. As M. Mignet put it in 1845,

What had he seen there?—all the grandeur, but also all of the abuse, of unlimited production, every progress of industry causing a revolution in the means of living; every closed market reducing whole populations to die of hunger; the irregularities of competition; the state naturally produced by contending interests, often more destructive than the ravages of war; he had seen man reduced to the spring of a machine more intelligent than himself, human beings heaped together in unhealthy places, where life does not attain half its length; where family ties are broken, where moral ideas are lost; he had seen the weakest infancy condemned to labours which brutalize its mind, and prematurely waste its strength; he had seen the country, as well as the towns, transformed into manufactories; small properties and trades disappearing before great factories; the peasant and the artisan become day-labourers, the day-labourers falling into the lowest and most indigent class, and thus becoming paupers; in a word, he had seen extreme wretchedness and frightful degradation mournfully counterbalance and secretly threaten the prosperity and the splendour of a great nation.[46]

In short, he had witnessed a system legitimated, ostensibly, by the science of political economy, one that clearly sacrificed the happiness of humankind to the production of wealth. It was a system he could not countenance. In 1819 he published his greatest work, *New Principles of Political Economy,* a volume that was not translated into English until 1991. As a consequence, it remained an obscure piece of work, a circumstance with onerous consequences, as history regrettably demonstrated.

Recall that Say's Law maintained that recessionary business cycles would right themselves because production created its own consumption. More than this, it stated that these cycles *had to* right themselves, as if it were a law of nature similar to the law of thermodynamics. Sismondi's response? "It is a grave mistake … to represent consumption as a force without limits always ready to absorb an infinite production."[47] Grave, indeed. As the United States and much of the world slipped deeper and deeper into depression after 1929, American advisors to President Hoover clung ever tighter to Say's Law, waiting for it to exert its mysterious force. It never did.

Sismondi dismissed an economic analysis premised on the idea that human behaviors could be observed and later predicted with lawlike certainty in much the same way that the physicist identifies a law of nature. In so doing, he alienated himself from the classical tradition of Ricardo and Mill, but also from the radical tradition of Marx. Despite this, as we shall see, the world has profited from Sismondi's ideas, and much suffering might have been alleviated by an earlier embrace of those ideas.

Sismondi was unabashedly an agrarian thinker—another reason why his work has been so readily dismissed. There are obvious physiocratic overtones in his work, though he brought much more sophistication to his analysis than

Quesnay and Mirabeau were able to muster at the midpoint of the eighteenth century. Said Sismondi,

> The riches proceeding from land should be the first to engage the attention of the economist or a legislator. They are the most necessary of all, because it is from the ground that our subsistence is derived; because they furnish the materials for every other kind of labor; and lastly, because, in preparation, they constantly employ the half, often much more than half, of all the nation. The class of people who cultivate the ground are particularly valuable for bodily qualities fitted to make excellent soldiers, and for mental qualities fitted to make good citizens.[48]

Sismondi covers much the same ground as Paine in identifying the circumstances leading to property claims. Like Paine, he sees this development as advantageous to society but notes that it also places a burden on society.

> He who, after having enclosed a field, uttered the first *This is mine,* has summoned him who possesses no field, and who could not live if the fields of the first would not bring forth a surplus product. This is a fortunate usurpation, and society, for the benefit of all, does well to guarantee it. However, it is a gift of society and in no way a natural right which preexisted.[49]

In other words, the earth is a common treasury. In order for society to tap the benefits that come with land ownership by the few, limits need to be put in place, lest the landowner lose the ability to adequately care for it. Such limits have the added advantage of maximizing the number of landowners.

This sounds, of course, a bit like Thomas Jefferson, America's leading agrarian spokesperson, and the similarity is indeed obvious. But this similarity also brought charges of being a hopeless romantic from the likes of both Mill and Marx—though both acknowledged the incredible insights Sismondi relayed in the *New Principles,* and both quoted him extensively.[50]

But here is the flaw of Mill and Marx as it relates to Sismondi. They both believed he was a romantic because he foolishly rejected the lawlike inevitability of the Industrial Revolution. They both believed he was an advocate of widely dispersed property ownership and small-scale farming operations as a vain attempt to thwart the inevitable. But this is far too simplistic, whether it is a description of the intentions of Jefferson or Sismondi. And this is the greatest shortcoming in extant scholarship related to each of these individuals. Because the world did not come to look like what they hoped for, they have been charged with romanticism, with living in the past, with every cultural epithet we can think of that says that they were wrong.

An extensive reading of these individuals suggests otherwise, however. Sismondi's agrarianism had nothing to do with a rejection of the Industrial Revolution. It had to do with utilizing economic analysis with the end in mind of improving the human condition—rejecting the leap of faith in the classical tradition that suggests that maximizing a nation's gross national product is synonymous with improving the human condition. Probably the most famous quip of Sismondi's has to do with the position of classical economists who contend that it does not matter if capital employs 100 workers or 1,000, as long as the investment generates a high rate of return. To this kind of thinking—which clearly dominates current "global" economic theory—Sismondi responded that nothing more was needed than for the king of England to turn a crank to produce all the nation's output.

What Sismondi rejected was the inevitable bias for efficiency that was a natural by-product of the industrial mode of production, a bias that would recommend technological innovation (and worker displacement). He rejected, as well, the counterargument of the classical economists that lower costs would offset the downward push on wages created by greater numbers among the unemployed. The system had the effect of dividing classes of people, Sismondi argued, creating a proletariat completely cut off from the surplus value created by their own labor, generating ever-increasing levels of antipathy between classes. Marx may have rejected Sismondi as a romantic, but he borrowed heavily from his analysis.

Sismondi did not seek to hide from the Industrial Revolution. He advocated extensive governmental intervention to deal with it, to check the tendencies it created for ever-greater property and capital accumulation. For example, he argued that day-laborers in the fields or in the factories had a right to compensation for the depreciation of their own work capacities so that they would have the resources to support themselves in old age when they could no longer work. They had a right to governmental protection from the industrial tendency to step up the speed of machines or to increase the length of the work day. Far earlier than anyone else, Sismondi warned of the dangers of massive depressions, arguing persuasively for governmental surveillance over technological innovation; he demonstrated the necessity of a minimum wage whether employed or not, a ceiling on the hours of work, a floor and ceiling on the age of work, and the establishment of profit-sharing plans for workers. Nearly 200 years before the practice became acceptable and demonstrably workable, Sismondi advocated worker-owned industrial operations.

The middle, or agrarian way between Mill, the gradualist advocate of reforming the most objectionable aspects of the new industrial economy, and Marx, the would-be revolutionary industrial reformer, had yet more adherents, though, like Sismondi, they remain at the margins despite the brilliance of their scholarship. We'll examine two more before moving back to the story of the mainstream, the classical tradition that weathered the articulate alternatives generated during the tumultuous nineteenth century. The first is yet another Frenchman, this one with a decidedly mathematical bent.

Leon Walras was born in 1834, the son of French economist Auguste Walras. Early in life Leon demonstrated a passion for literature, and as a young man he took employment as a journalist. He wrote a couple of unremarkable novels before age thirty, which may have helped to persuade him to take his father's advice and devote his life to the study of economics. Once having done so, Walras became a part of a small group of late-nineteenth-century scholars who sought to bring the rigor of mathematics to the business of producing economic theory. Noting that it was one thing to propose a theory "and quite another to prove it," Walras looked forward to the day when "mathematical economics will rank with the mathematical sciences of astronomy and mechanics; and on that day justice will be done to our work."[51]

Despite his marginal status, again, at least partially due to the fact that his work was only intermittently translated into English (*Elements of Pure Economics* was not completely available in English until 1954), Walras made first-rate contributions to the study of economics. He added a more sophisticated conception of scarcity to price theory—now an economic mainstay. He became the most significant contributor (though even here Sismondi was ahead of him, though Walras does not cite him) to the notion of price equilibrium—using curve charts as demonstration. And he wrote extensively about the role of "entrepreneurs" in creating economic activity—all well-regarded contributions to mainstream economics. So why has Walras been relegated to the margins? If John Stuart Mill taught the world that the question of distribution could be left up to society,[52] he did it at a whisper. In contrast, Walras said the same thing at the level of a shout.

Walras labeled questions related to distribution "social economics," likely an unfortunate phrase given the ease with which it can be mistaken for *socialism*. But clearly Walras did go farther than Mill in acknowledging the moral dimensions within economic activity: "Moreover, the appropriation of things by persons or the distribution of social wealth among men in society is a moral and not an industrial phenomenon. It is a relationship among persons."[53]

Walras uses the parable of the deer to explain (note that even Walras, near the end of the nineteenth century, uses a state-of-nature argument to make his point):

> I imagine a tribe of savages and a deer in a forest. The deer is a useful thing limited in quantity and hence subject to appropriation. This point once granted, nothing more needs to be said about it. To be sure, before the deer can actually be appropriated it has to be hunted and killed. Again, this side of the question need not detain us, nor need we stop to consider such correlated problems as arise in connection with the need to dress the deer and prepare it in the kitchen. Quite apart from all of these aspects of a man's relation to a deer, yet another question claims our attention; for whether the deer is still running about in the forest or has been killed, the question is: who shall have it? "The deer belongs to the one who has killed it!" cries a young and active member of the tribe, adding, "If you are too lazy or if your aim is not good enough, so much the worse for you!" An older, weaker member replies: "No! The deer belongs to all of us to be shared equally. If there is only one deer in

the forest and you happen to be the one who catches sight of it, that is no reason why the rest of us should go without food." Obviously we are here confronted with a phenomenon which is fundamentally social and which gives rise to questions of justice or of the mutual co-ordination of human destinies.[54]

John Locke was quite sure that the young man had it right; the deer belongs to the one who killed it. Does the state of nature prompt men to acquire all the deer, apples, and acorns they can acquire? Or does it prompt them to come together to set up norms of behavior related to these acquisitions? This was the splitting point between Locke and Montesquieu, between the L-stream and the M-stream. As political philosophers, they were concerned with what the state of nature meant for the establishment of governmental structures.

But it should be obvious by now that this same state of nature, this same splitting point, was of major import for economists, too, for property claims were clearly made in the act of acquisition. Goods were acquired and inevitably exchanged. What economists added to this splitting point was the idea that economic behavior was determined by natural law. Those who saw the development of industrial production as a part of law-defined life in the modern world—Ricardo and Marx, for instance—tended to take the future out of the realm of human volition. You could count on human self-interest to produce acquisitive behaviors, to seek the maximization of pleasure, and so on, meaning that mathematical calculation and statistical probability were assumed to be powerful tools for economic prediction. Certainly Walras felt that way. He might have made room for himself in the world's economics hall of fame if he hadn't—like so many of the French tradition—insisted that the young man in the forest was wrong.

Was that young man right? Or was he wrong? If you believe he was right, you create a governmental system that does not burden citizens beyond the duty to vote once every few years, freeing them for unfettered economic pursuits. If you believe he was wrong, you create a governmental system that employs citizens in all manner of local political associations so that they have the opportunity to work through the establishment of norms within which economic activity will take place. Turning from political to economic implications, Walras believed that you embrace an "industrial theory" if you believe the young man was right. Such a theory "defines those relations between man and things which aim at the increase and transformation of social wealth, and determine the conditions of *an abundant production* of social wealth within a community." If you believe the young man was wrong, you employ a theory of property, or what might be better labeled as an agrarian theory, which "defines the mutual relations established between man and man with respect to the appropriation of social wealth, and determines the conditions *of the equitable distribution* of social wealth within a community."[55]

For Walras, the relations between man and man need to be worked out; the circumstances that will define life in a community need to be decided. For industrial advocates like Ricardo and Marx, laws immune to human volition will take care of this. For Ricardo, there was nothing that could stop the advance of industrialism; for Marx, that same advance of industrialism would, lawlike, bring about the ascendancy of the worker. Mill opened the door a crack to the idea that through human volition the worst tendencies of industrialism could be ameliorated; Walras tried to throw that door open.

He was not alone. A near-contemporary—this time in England, the hotbed of nineteenth-century industrialism—John Ruskin wrote perhaps the world's most devastating critique of the classical economic tradition as well as the radical socialist tradition represented by Marx. His small book is composed of four extended essays and is entitled *Unto This Last*. It severely chastised the field of political economy, and as a result it was conscientiously ignored; besides, nineteenth-century political economists had no answers for Ruskin's penetrating questions. There wasn't much else they could do except ignore it. In this way, it too fell to the margins of the field, rarely ever read by economists trained during the twentieth century.

John Ruskin was born in London in 1819, the son of a prosperous wine merchant. He demonstrated remarkable intellectual curiosity as a child and as a relatively young man garnered a reputation as an art and architecture scholar, publishing volumes of work that were so popular that he rapidly achieved the status of one of Europe's leading intellectuals. Because of this, the general public was caught off guard when he published four essays on political economy in four successive issues of *Cornhill Magazine*, August through November 1860. Two years later the essays were published together as *Unto This Last*.

Ruskin's essays were an assault on the classical tradition and therefore scorned by many leading intellectuals who ardently believed that the wretched circumstances created by an embrace of industrialism were inevitable, and that rampant poverty was brought on by the poor themselves. Even though Ruskin explicitly rejected socialist doctrine in the essays, much to the chagrin of Marx, he was nevertheless accused of being a socialist in an attempt to discredit him and to minimize his readership. It worked. The book sold very poorly. If it had not been for his impeccable reputation as a scholar in the fields of art and architecture, it probably would have fared even worse. But it is nevertheless there, waiting in the margins for the world to rediscover.

Few today refer to Ruskin as an agrarian thinker, yet he is probably a better fit for such a label than many who possess it. Ruskin argued in a manner reminiscent of the physiocrats,

All *essential* [his emphasis] production is for the Mouth ... hence, consumption is the crown of production; and the wealth of a nation is only to be estimated by what it consumes. The want of any clear sight of this fact is the capital error ... among political economists. Their minds are constantly set on money-gain, not mouth gain; and they fall into every sort of net and snare, dazzled by the coin-glitter as birds by the fowler's glass; or rather (for there is not much else like birds in them) they are like children trying to jump on the heads of their own shadows; the money-gain the shadow of the true gain, which is humanity.[56]

Ruskin's pen was sharp. He was disgusted with the social conditions of England during the middle decades of the nineteenth century. He lambasted the likes of Mill and Ricardo for failing to acknowledge the relationship between the amassing of great wealth and the proliferation of poverty, thus perpetuating a fiction that continues to find believers to this day—that it is possible for everyone to be rich. The motive power of men resides in a soul, argued Ruskin, and "the force of this very peculiar agent, as an unknown quantity, enters into all the political economist's equations, without his knowledge, and falsifies every one of their results."[57] Or consider this barb, "The real science of political economy, which has yet to be distinguished from the bastard science, as medicine from witchcraft, and astronomy from astrology, is that which teaches nations to desire and labour for things that lead to life."[58] And last,

Unhappily for the progress of the science of Political Economy, the plus quantities … make a very positive and venerable appearance in the world, so that everyone is eager to learn the science which produces results so magnificent; whereas the minuses have, on the other hand, a tendency to retire into back streets, or other places of shade—or even to get themselves wholly and finally put out of sight in graves: which renders the algebra of this science peculiar, and differently legible; a large number of its negative signs being written by the account-keeper in a kind of red ink, which starvation thins, and makes strangely pale, or even quite invisible ink, for the present.[59]

Ruskin revealed the true nature of the relationship between wealth and poverty in a manner that has yet to be adequately answered by the classical economics tradition. Said he,

Men nearly always speak and write as if riches were absolute, and it were possible, by following certain scientific precepts, for everybody to be rich. Whereas riches are a power like that of electricity, acting only through inequalities or negations of itself. The force of the guinea you have in your pocket depends wholly on the default of a guinea in your neighbour's pocket. If he did not want it, it would be of no use to you; the degree of power it possesses depends accurately upon the need or desire he has for it—and the art of making yourself rich is therefore equally and necessarily the art of keeping your neighbour poor.[60]

Ruskin's analysis demonstrates the quandary faced by a modern society that chooses to define human nature as essentially economic and then designates freedom as the supreme human value. If life is essentially about economics, then freedom means little more than the freedom to get rich. The problem with this, as Ruskin so ably demonstrates, is that the freedom of the rich is acquired only through the denial of freedom among the poor. The nature of wealth prohibits it from happening in any other way.

The answer to this dilemma is of course the same answer offered in different ways by the likes of Ogilivie, Jefferson, Paine, Sismondi, Walras, and many others: carefully crafted policy that prevents the creation of extreme discrepancies between wealth and poverty. For these representatives of an agrarian worldview, freedom is essentially about having a voice in the decisions that affect oneself, not about the absence of restraints in the economic arena. That is to say, freedom is a political value that, once popularly exercised, will result in morally crafted policy that avoids the discord and divisiveness that necessarily accompanies unlimited accumulation.

There is much more that might be said about Ruskin's *Unto This Last,* like how as early as 1860 he recognized the slogan "free trade" as synonymous with the absence of competition rather than its enlargement—an early commentary on GATT, NAFTA, and other ostensibly "free" trade agreements.[61] But perhaps Ruskin's most prescient insight—the one that speaks most directly to the twenty-first century—had to do with recognizing the power of consumption and the relationship between consumption and a nation's social well-being. "The vital question," wrote Ruskin, "for individual and for nation, is, never 'how much do they make?' but 'to what purpose do they spend?'" Noting that "wise consumption is a far more difficult art than wise production,"[62] Ruskin believed that an unjust economy will be built on indiscriminant spending; a just economy is built around well-considered spending:

> In all buying, consider, first, what condition of existence you cause in the producers of what you buy; secondly, whether the sum you have paid is just to the producer, and in due proportion, lodged in his hands; thirdly, to how much clear use, for food, knowledge, or joy, this that you have bought can be put; and fourthly, to whom and in what way it can be most speedily and serviceably distributed.[63]

There is much more that might be said of *Unto This Last,* but for now it is enough to note that there were plenty of nonsocialist alternatives to the inequities and inequalities that accompanied the rise of capitalism red in tooth and claw. None of the individuals representing alternatives to the classical economics tradition—Ogilivie, Paine, Sismondi, Walras, Ruskin—followed Karl Marx, but neither were they willing to follow Smith, Ricardo, or Mill. In going their own way, they created a third alternative. They gave modern society a glimpse of what it might become, never knowing that humankind would reach the point where environmental exigencies, rather than a humanitarian embrace of justice, would lead us back to their work. That is a main premise of the later chapters of this book.

The Reascendancy of the L-Stream

In a recent exhaustive history of the first half of the nineteenth century, Princeton historian Sean Wilentz reminded his readers that while "elements of democracy existed in the infant American republic of the 1780s," the republic was not democratic. "Nor, in the minds of those who governed it, was it supposed to be."[64] An elite would govern American society and extend to citizens the freedom to pursue their own economic self-interest. But it didn't quite work out that way. Wilentz described America's entrance into the nineteenth century this way: "A momentous rupture occurred between Thomas Jefferson's time and Abraham Lincoln's that created the lineaments of modern democratic politics. The rise of American democracy is the story of that rupture and its immediate consequences."[65] Another way of putting it is to say that the hegemony of the L-stream was severely shaken by tremendous growth of the M-stream—the idea that freedom really ought to be a political value as well as an economic one, that government ought to be, as Lincoln so aptly put it, of, for, and by the people.

Wilentz argues that the Civil War was in no small measure a battle to determine which version of democracy would prevail in the United States, northern or southern, and this certainly seems plausible. Antislavery sentiment was a part of the democratic ethos of the antebellum period, and abolitionist societies were a part of the vast array of local associations that gave citizens a political role to play with their lives. But there were huge economic questions to be answered by the outcome of the Civil War that convolute the interpretation of the war as a battle to establish a certain version of democracy. And, in any event, the Civil War was massively destructive, dividing the nation for decades and in the process severely hindering whatever democratic growth may have emanated from the Thirteenth and Fourteenth Amendments—changes that invested a great deal more democratic possibility in the Constitution than the original version possessed.

In the aftermath of the bloodiest war the nation has ever known, America was ill-poised to build on the democratic trends that emerged from the ruptured Lockean worldview of the antebellum era. In fact, I believe it is accurate to define the post–Civil War era as the period of Locke's reascendancy in the United States. Lingering elements of the M-stream were stymied, thus diminishing the American democracy that had been on the rise for half a century.

To fully understand the genesis of this Lockean reascendancy we have to leave the world of political and economic theory altogether, for shortly after the Civil War the world would begin to sort through the implications of a profound scientific idea, the impact of which seems to rival the impact of the establishment of the world's major religions. I'm speaking here, of course, of the ideas of Charles Darwin. *The Origin of Species,* a distinctly biological treatise, was published in 1859. Had the evolutionary theory therein been restricted to the discipline of biology, the world might have been saved much pain and anguish. That was not to be, however. For elements of the emerging discipline called sociology—especially in England and the United States—quickly took up the theory of evolution and applied it to humanity itself, suggesting that one individual might have more evolutionary wherewithal than another, or that one race might possess more than another race.

An English sociologist by the name of Herbert Spencer was elevated to the status of the world's foremost authority on social Darwinism after publishing *The Study of Sociology* in 1882. In it, Spencer declared that "I am simply carrying out the views of Mr. Darwin in their applications to the human race."[66] Spencer almost single-handedly reestablished a kind of ideological hegemony in the United States and much of Europe related to Locke's interpretation of life as an economic endeavor. Because some species evolve and adapt to changing circumstances and some do not, Spencer looked at human life as a kind of competition. In fact, we have Spencer to thank, not Darwin, for the unfortunate phrase "survival of the fittest."

The L-stream conception of man as fundamentally an economic being, the classical economic tradition of faith in incontrovertible "laws" that play themselves out regardless of human will—human conceptions of justice or morality—this entire ideological package that had been eroding steadily during the antebellum rise of democracy in America all of a sudden received new life in abundance. Now science was at the service of those disciples of Madison and Hamilton who felt that political decisionmaking should be left to the elite, and that citizens should concern themselves with their own economic self-interest. Even the views of Malthus related to the poor—that charity was harmful in the long term—received fresh legitimation from social Darwinist theory. By helping the poor, one only prolongs their inevitable demise. The dime from your pocket will not raise the poor man's evolutionary wherewithal. You are both better off if it stays in your pocket.

America's leading social Darwinist, William Graham Sumner, explained how it worked for those at the top of the evolutionary ladder: "The millionaires are a product of natural selection . . . the naturally selected agents of society for certain work. They get high wages and live in luxury, but the bargain is a good one for society."[67] Obviously, social Darwinism added more fuel to a central theme in classical economics. A healthy economy requires ever-increasing investment in new enterprises, something the wealthy are uniquely prepared to contribute. Though this idea would be challenged from time to time, especially during periods of depression, the idea that a society needs a class of ultrawealthy became nearly sacrosanct with the added legitimation that came from social Darwinism.

The phrase "certain work" in Sumner's comments above is probably as significant as any in the new social Darwinist worldview. Some men are more evolved than others and to them, of course, should fall the very important work, like managing a business enterprise or practicing the art of political statecraft. Those less evolved were *naturally* relegated to less important work: cleaning the streets, farming, or factory work. In time, social Darwinists would stumble onto the idea that by using scientific instruments, such as the IQ test developed in the early twentieth century, teachers could tailor school curriculum to match the evolution-determined occupational destiny of students. Over 100 years later, the public school enterprise in the United States continues to function as though its purpose is outfitting youth for that moment in time when they join the adult "world of work." Such an idea was barely perceptible, a minor theme at best, during the antebellum democratic era when free public school systems were first created. During the postbellum period of L-stream reascendancy, such a marked turn in the purpose of schooling seems imminently predictable.

The new scientific legitimation for a cultural focus on economic activity—on generating wealth—led directly to the era of the "robber barons," the inordinately rich, like J. P. Morgan, Andrew Carnegie, and others. The rise of the M-stream during the first half of the nineteenth century, the idea that citizens ought to play a political role with their lives, gradually gave way to the reascendancy of the L-stream fueled by social Darwinist conceptions, and the idea that citizens need only show up to vote once every so often before going back to their private lives.

Depressions and New Possibilities

Because the economic depression of the 1930s was so catastrophic, people have generally forgotten that the depression of the 1890s was the worst the country had ever endured to that point in time. These two time periods, the 1890s and the 1930s, not surprisingly, became moments where the L-stream reascendancy weakened, moments where citizens demanded a political voice and used that voice to create policy intended to curb the unfettered excesses of the world's industrial moguls, the harsh industrial working conditions, and the growing extremes between the wealthy and the poor.

Much of the force for the democratic movement of the 1890s came from an organization known as the Farmers Alliance, a huge nationwide association of farmers and small-town merchants who objected to the growing power of railroad- and agriculture-related manufacturing and processing industries. The political wing of the alliance became known as the People's, or Populist, Party, which enjoyed considerable success during the decade of the 1890s. Populist candidates created a long list of reforms—everything from guaranteeing free textbooks for public school children, to creating cooperative grain storage, milling, produce, even credit-extending operations, to advocating the implementation of an income tax of 2 percent on all incomes over $4,000 annually—a figure that would have limited the tax to the nation's wealthiest 5 percent. Through some clever maneuvering, a combination of Populist and Democrat congressmen moved this income tax plan into law in 1894.[68]

The robber barons responded quickly to the threat this law represented. In less than a year—remarkably quick—it was challenged in the Supreme Court and struck down on a 5–4 vote. But more than this, the law seems to have generated a kind of collusive strategy among the nation's wealthiest men. In the midst of a severe depression, the Populists and Democrats decided to throw their fates together in the presidential candidacy of William Jennings Bryan; if elected, Bryan stood ready to work for policies, like coining silver, that would ameliorate the tough circumstances faced by the nation's debtors. In the minds of America's ultra-rich, Bryan needed to be stopped. Standard Oil donated $250,000 to the Republican candidate, William McKinley. J. P. Morgan matched that amount. In all, the McKinley campaign spent an unheard of $5–7 million, while the Bryan candidacy spent a mere $600,000. McKinley won an extraordinarily close election.

The Populist threat effectively ended with Bryan's defeat. It was the last time in the nation's history that a farmer revolt would come close to cracking the hegemonic power of industrial interests in the United States. There would be further agrarian agitation during the next depression era, but there was never any question about whether the farmers might obtain the upper hand in policy circles and thereafter create what the Populists called a "cooperative commonwealth." In other words, the vision of the 1840s communitarians, the vision of Jefferson, the vision of Paine; in fact, the vision of Winstanley and Ogilivie, despite the temporary popularity of Henry George's "single tax," gradually eroded to the point that such visions now require rediscovery.

The Populists were defeated, but the memory of the threat they posed remained for some time, as historian Grant McConnell explained: "Although the Populist threat had disappeared, the memory of it was still vivid in the eyes of grain exchanges, heads of farm equipment trusts, and directors of banks."[69] Democrats were able to use that memory to win some political concessions in the years after the Populist revolt. Surprisingly, the idea of the income tax struck a cord with the American public. The demand for such a law seemed to grow with each year of the new century—so much so that Republicans created a strategy to appear as income tax advocates before Democrats could put a bill together. Republican President William Taft proposed a constitutional amendment that would allow Congress to pass income tax bills. This was clearly a political maneuver. Congress had passed income tax laws twice before—and although one was declared unconstitutional by a split court, no one seriously questioned the right of Congress to implement an income tax. By proposing a constitutional amendment, however, Republicans were able to appear as if they were concerned about the common man, while the proposed amendment, they believed, would die a slow death as states failed to ratify it. But it didn't work out that way. To the amazement of Taft and other Republicans, states began to ratify the amendment, making the possibility of an income tax for the rich appear imminent. In 1913, the Sixteenth Amendment was passed. With a Democrat, Woodrow Wilson, in the White House, an income tax bill became a sure bet.

The bill that passed after the Sixteenth Amendment was ratified was actually rather weak. It affected only the nation's top 2 percent of income earners—and not at a particularly high level. A 1 percent tax was applied to incomes between $4,000 and $20,000—and the rate went up gradually to 7 percent on incomes over $500,000. When the United States entered the Great War in 1917, the demand for war revenue led immediately to proposals for higher income taxes and a permanent inheritance tax. The American Committee on War Finance actually proposed a 98 percent surtax on incomes over $100,000. While Congress was not willing to go that far, it did pass a war revenue bill that placed a 50 percent surtax on incomes over $1 million. It increased estate tax rates as well and passed the nation's first excess profits tax on corporations. A year later Congress raised the highest income taxation rate to 70 percent.

From a present-day perspective, these rates seem extraordinarily high. And indeed, when the war ended and newly elected Republican President Warren Harding appointed multimillionaire Andrew Mellon as Secretary of the Treasury, tax cut laws became the order of the day. The highest rate of 77 percent at war's end fell to 25 percent by 1926. The flurry of economic activity during the decade called the Roaring Twenties is now legendary. America's ultrawealthy speculated wildly with the income spikes created with each new round of Mellon's tax cuts. The gap in income distribution between the rich and poor in 1929 was the largest the country had ever known—and it would remain so until the Roaring Nineties at the end of the century.

But the 1930s was a decade like no other—profoundly worse than the 1890s. As noted earlier, Republican President Herbert Hoover was consistently advised to wait for Say's Law to do its magic. After all, an extended depression would be physically impossible. Production creates its own consumption, or so a couple of generations of economic wisdom maintained. But Say never counted on market speculation at incredible levels with borrowed sums. The first hints of bad news created hysteria of the worst sort. Almost everyone with stock market investments tried desperately to sell their shares before the price dwindled to nothing. Over the course of a mere two months, $40 billion worth of share values disappeared. The reverberations of this kind of shock were dramatic and almost immediate, as Robert Heilbroner explained:

> In Muncie, Indiana ... every fourth factory worker lost his job by 1930. In Chicago the majority of working girls were earning less than 25 cents an hour and a quarter of them made less than ten cents. In New York's Bowery alone, two thousand jobless crowded into bread lines every day. In the nation as a whole, residential construction fell by ninety-five percent. Nine million savings accounts were lost. Eighty-five thousand businesses failed. By 1933, the nation was virtually prostrate.[70]

Make no mistake about it: The classical economics tradition was confounded by the Great Depression. By all known economic reckoning, it shouldn't have happened. As one might expect, the egregious social conditions, the veritable armies of unemployed, reawakened socialist doctrine in America and elsewhere. If such ideas were to be held at bay, the classical economics tradition needed a savior—fast. It found one in the English economist John Maynard Keynes.

Keynes was born in 1883, the son of a noteworthy economist in his own right, John Neville Keynes. Up to the onset of the Depression, Keynes was squarely in the classical economics camp. Unlike most others, however, he quickly allowed deteriorating circumstances to convince him that Say was wrong. He attributed this insight to Malthus, who wrote about the possibility of prolonged production "gluts" in his *Principles of Political Economy,* published in 1820. There is some evidence to suggest that Malthus's musings about this possibility were taken directly from Sismondi's *New Principles of Political Economy,* published a year earlier. Regardless, the solution to such dilemmas in the minds of both men was to enlist government spending to stimulate the economy.

In other words, there were "Keynesians" before Keynes—in the United States and in Europe. Hitler himself started massive government spending programs as early as 1933, but the Swedish response to the Depression was probably the most thoroughgoing and successful. Franklin Delano Roosevelt was also a kind of pre-Keynes Keynesian. After ascending to the presidency in 1933, he quickly put government spending schemes into motion in an attempt to stop massive starvation. At this time Keynes was merely discussing his theories. They weren't published until 1936 in his most famous work, *The General Theory of Employment, Interest and Money.* By that time his ideas were merely used to validate the policy Roosevelt felt forced to implement years earlier. Despite the huge range of New Deal reforms, progress was sporadic, and circumstances took a turn for the worse in 1937. To fully shake off the effects of the Great Depression, in fact, took massive wartime expenditures and the full employment that came with America's entrance into World War II.

It is probably impossible to overemphasize the critical worldwide conditions created by the Great Depression. And despite the fact that its steadfast adherence to the notion of unchangeable "laws" contributed greatly to the depth and severity of the Depression, many classical economists were nevertheless elevated to advisory roles at the highest levels during this period, as leaders everywhere scrambled to find a strategy that would alleviate mass suffering.[71] The discipline of economics continues to hold this exulted advisory status today. But the Depression revealed a huge crack in the armor of the classical tradition. The exigent circumstances opened the door to dissenting economists, those whose distinctly nonclassical ideas put them at the margins of the profession. These individuals (Rex Tugwell, who in retirement drafted a new constitution that he felt reflected the realities of the new era; Adolf Berle; and George Warren are a few examples, though there were many others) helped to create the National Recovery Act (NRA), which, though unsuccessful, started a tradition wherein government would act as a catalyst to fair dealing between industry and labor—a tradition that has been profoundly abandoned with extraordinarily negative consequences for labor in this country. It was economists at the margins, "farm economists" as they were derogatorily referred to, like Warren, who completely moved the practice of agriculture out of the classical economics tradition through the auspices of the Agricultural Adjustment Administration—creating a tradition of setting minimum prices and implementing policies required to achieve those prices (making grain storage options available, payments for soil taken out of production, etc.). And it was economics professors at the margins who introduced the concept that came to be known as welfare.

In typical ethnocentric fashion, Americans like to believe that welfare legislation was a uniquely American creation—which, of course, is totally false. The Germany of Otto von Bismarck probably deserves the award for being first in this regard, implementing a state-sponsored accident, sickness, old-age, and disability insurance program in the early 1880s. England itself, under the leadership of David Lloyd George, was able to generate support for unemployment insurance as early as 1911. In the United States, it was the state of Wisconsin—with guidance from University of Wisconsin economics professors, like John R. Commons, who were distinctly outside the classical tradition—that first generated a state system of unemployment compensation. The Wisconsin plan would become a model for the federal system created some three years later.

The exigent conditions created by the Depression generated heavy pressure on politicians to roll back the tax cuts of the 1920s and reinstitute a high tax on the nation's wealthy. "It is a crime to have millions of people starving and hungry while a few others ... are living in luxury," said the Republican senator from Nebraska, George Norris.[72] Louisiana Senator Huey P. Long introduced a resolution in 1932 that would rework America's tax laws so that "no man should be allowed to have an income of more than one million dollars a year." Nor, according to Long, should "one person inherit in a lifetime more than five million without working for it."[73]

Long continually revised what became known as the "share-the-wealth" plan—and in the process generated a huge grass-roots following. Share-the-wealth clubs were created nationwide, 27,000 of them claiming over 7 million members in all.[74] By 1935 the popularity of the Long plan made him a viable democratic challenger to FDR. It also caused Roosevelt to jump on the bandwagon—as he was desperate for revenue to finance a myriad of New Deal programs. The result was the Wealth Tax Act of 1935, which created a top tax rate of 75 percent on incomes over $500,000.

Huey Long's assassination later in 1935 significantly quieted political share-the-wealth rhetoric for the remaining years of the Depression. But with America's entrance into World War II, the pendulum quickly swung back. Said Roosevelt in 1942: "In this time of grave national danger, when all excess income should go to win the war, no American citizen ought to have a net income, after he has paid his taxes, of more than $25,000 a year."[75] As the war progressed, Roosevelt became more adamant about a 100 percent tax rate over a $25,000 income ceiling (roughly $320,000 in 2008 dollars). While the wealthy were outraged, popular support for a "victory tax" of this sort grew tremendously. Congress was forced to respond, though it backed away considerably from what Roosevelt had asked for. Still, it set the highest rate at 82 percent and then added additional surtaxes, effectively making the highest rate 93 percent on all incomes over $200,000.

At war's end, of course, the demand for tax cuts was strong, with the wealthy pushing for across-the-board rate cuts in order to realize the greatest advantage possible. With war with Korea hard on the heels of World War II, however, Congress was able to reinstate high rates on the wealthy—reaching heights of 91 percent for the maximum rate before settling at approximately 88 percent for many years.

Throughout the Vietnam War and the Great Society campaigns against poverty, the graduated income tax remained fairly constant. All of that changed, however, with the election of Ronald Reagan in 1980. The Economic Recovery Act of 1981 reduced income tax rates by 23 percent across the board—thereby reducing the top rate to 50 percent. As if this were not enough, the Tax Act of 1986 reduced the highest rate all the way down to 28 percent. In 1990 Congress raised it back to 31 percent, where it has remained relatively unchanged to this day.

The Big Picture

Johns Hopkins economist Mark Blyth in a wonderful little book called *Great Transformations* (a takeoff on Karl Polyani's earlier book of the same title) argues that the twentieth century is really the story of two great economic transformations. The first was the gradual undoing of unfettered capitalism and the arrival of a kind of "middle way," and the second was the undoing of the middle way and the reascendancy of unfettered capitalism.[76]

In this chapter we have heard from several voices over centuries who have pleaded for policy intended to improve the human condition in manifestly just ways, rather than policy intended to augment the ostensible benefits of passion and greed. It may be that the middle, or agrarian, way is best described by Maurice Childs in an obscure, little-noticed book published in 1936 titled *Sweden: The Middle Way.* It is worth a short digression to describe the arguments laid out within it. Childs tells the story of an impressive group of Swedish economists, including Erik Lindahl, Erik Lundberg, Dag Hammarskjold, and Gunnar Myrdal. These men and others defied the classical economics tradition and led Sweden down an agrarian trajectory implementing, among other things, the kind of social security system recommended by Sismondi back in 1819. As well, they created agricultural price supports and encouraged the creation of a comprehensive system of farmer and consumer cooperatives of the sort sought by the defeated American populists. Much as the United States from the late 1930s through the 1950s, they fashioned policy to flatten the extremes of wealth and poverty.

The New Deal helped the United States move toward the Swedish version of a middle way. By the mid-1950s, for example, there were no longer any billionaires in American society, and the number of millionaires had been reduced substantially from their Depression-era numbers. On top of this, almost a third of all federal revenue (compared to roughly 4 percent today) was generated through excess profits, or corporate income tax.[77] But all of this progress came to a screeching halt as America's wealthy launched a counterattack on the New Deal. They orchestrated a popular reembrace of the classical economics tradition—only this time replacing the word *national* with the word *global*. Every classical argument that legitimated the existence of the poor is back in service in the twenty-first century. Every classical defense of huge fortunes for the few has also been put back to work. The views of Ebeneezer Scrooge have once again become the views of the sophisticate, the individual who lives and works in places designed for the affluent—those individuals who never journey into Ruskin's backstreets, the homes and workplaces of America's 40 million poor. Like Scrooge, today's sophisticate has reembraced the ostensibly lawlike machinations of economic activity. If overseas labor is driving down American wages, so be it. If company pension plans are inhibiting stock price growth, declare bankruptcy and renege on the pension plans. It's a dog-eat-dog world. Hobbes lives again.

The logic of global capitalism is the same that drove the era "red in tooth and claw." The difference is that now the legitimation of passion and greed has resulted in economic activity of the sort that threatens all life on the planet. We simply cannot wait for humanity to marshal the commitment to justice that would trigger another "great transformation" and move us back onto a middle, or agrarian, way. We have to make that move before we exceed the earth's ability to support seven billion people. This book is intended as a kind of primer for human survival in the twenty-first century. Despite the centrality of the political and economic spheres, the largest piece of the puzzle with respect to saving the planet lies in the educational arena. We turn next to a look at the nation's educational efforts.

CHAPTER 3

Education and the Elevation of Private Purpose

The subject of this chapter is educational theory writ large, which is to say that it has to do with how Americans acquire their ideas about how the world works and about their own place within it. As such, it is only partially about formal curriculum and instruction in the nation's K–12 or K–16 schools. For besides learning to read, write, perform mathematical operations, understand rudimentary American history and physical science, and so on, Americans also learn about abortion, about the collapse of savings and loan operations, about global warming, and about whether a foreign power has weapons of mass destruction. In the first instance Americans are exposed to "school curriculum," and in the second they are exposed to what now can only accurately be called "corporate curriculum." In the past several decades American media underwent a profound transformation such that well over 90 percent of all print and broadcast media is controlled by just a handful of large multinational corporations.[1] They give us the "news" in the modern era the same way that clergy during the feudal era delivered news in church on Sunday. So this chapter will consist of two parts—the first dealing with school per se, the second, with corporate impact on learning.

Schools and the Full Power of Education

The concept of a free, mass educational system squares well with certain conceptions regarding how society should function, and not so well with others. For instance, during the feudal era, when power resided in a monarch and economic decisions were based on age-old tradition or coercive authority, the idea of free schools for the nation's youth made little sense. But in Greek society at about 400 BC, with the emergence of small owner-operated farms, the emphasis on human freedom this inspired, and the way this emphasis translated into the spread of democracy—giving people a voice in the decisions that affect them—it all added up to a climate that recommended the creation of schools so that citizens would be well prepared to wield the power that comes with democratic political arrangements.

Even if one rejected "pure" democracy, like Plato, and sought a republican governmental arrangement where representatives of the people would rule, a strong educational system seemed like a great investment since it was never possible to tell who would ascend, as adults, to the representative leadership positions. Eighty percent of Plato's *Republic,* long considered a classic text of *political* theory, has to do with *educating* the city-state's future leaders. Rome during the republic and even later, during the empire, created a loose educational system designed to outfit talented youth with political wherewithal. In both societies, the idea of schooling for a particular vocation, for a particular economic role, was thought to be tainted or crass. To be worthy of the name, an education needed to result in personal traits among citizens conducive to the high-quality governmental arrangements.

Like so many other classical notions, this definition of an education was buried in the rubble that was Rome by AD 450. Throughout the medieval period, learning was sporadic and the chances of the peasant child attending school was nearly nil for better than 1,000 years. As circumstances unfolded in the sixteenth and seventeenth centuries, however, aided at least partially by the invention of the printing press, new political visions became possible. In England of the 1640s, when ecclesiastical censorship was temporarily absent, Gerrard Winstanley and Thomas Hobbes offered nonfeudal options to England's first nonmonarchical leader, Oliver Cromwell.

Winstanley dreamed of an agrarian republic where all citizens might play a political role at the county or ward level. A lifelong educational system was consequently an integral part of his vision. All children were to receive a formal education in arts and sciences, languages, and morals, and in useful trades. So that none would grow up with proficiency in "book-learning" alone, Winstanley believed every student needed to acquire skills that could be used later to generate a living. The curriculum was to be derived from five areas of inquiry—rather than being built around five school "subjects." The first was husbandry, knowing about growing and utilizing the products of the soil; a second area had to do with knowing and understanding minerals and their chemical possibilities; a third area related to knowledge of domestic animals and the uses that could be made of them; the fourth area concerned the utilization of the forest; and finally, the fifth area was knowledge of the stars and their uses for navigation, travel, and so on. In addition to this, adult education was to proceed once a week in gatherings oriented around discussions related to policy matters and what might be done about them. Key individuals would shoulder responsibility for orchestrating the weekly meetings and for arranging public lectures on a range of topics.[2]

In contrast, Hobbes viewed humanity as fundamentally self-interested and overwhelmingly concerned about economic gratification—a natural fit for the commercialist/industrial world he envisioned. The role of education was therefore a conundrum for Hobbes—and he consequently rarely spoke or wrote about it. If freedom was to be the primary social value in his world, then people ought to be free to choose a school for their children, or choose no school. Of course it was Locke's more moderate vision of what the nonfeudal world might look like that was eventually more influential. And unlike Hobbes, John Locke did write now and then about education. But it is important to have a look at what he said about the subject in order to see that despite the fact that the topic fell under his purview from time to time, his thoughts about education stand in stark contrast to those of Winstanley and others who dreamed of a future governed by values quite different from those prized by Locke and Hobbes.

First, Locke's famous *An Essay Concerning Human Understanding*, published in 1690, was an epistemological, not an educational, treatise. It contains no argument related to what the emerging nonfeudal world meant for the education of youth. It was, rather, a prolonged argument about the nature of knowledge versus the nature of belief and an inquiry into which facets of human life could be governed by knowledge and which must remain governed by belief. Locke reinforced and popularized Pierre Gassendi's notion of the mind as a *tabula rasa,* or blank slate, contending that "the senses at first let in particular ideas, and furnish the yet empty cabinet." Or, as he expressed it a little later in the book, the mind was initially "white paper, devoid of all characters, without any ideas."[3]

While there were educational ramifications to the notion of the mind as an empty cabinet, clearly Locke's *An Essay Concerning Human Understanding* was not written with the purpose of illuminating what they might be. In fact, the purpose of the book is still an open question, though it can be read as an argument to dispute the idea that the divine right of kings was anchored in the minds of men as a kind of innate principle. And the book was clearly a kind of epistemological chess match with the French philosopher Rene Descartes. But it is in no way a contribution to emerging arguments about nonfeudal society and the role that formal education might play therein.

The same cannot be said about Locke's 1693 publication, *Some Thoughts Concerning Education,* however. This little book is praised for its even-handed, humanitarian conceptions of what constitutes effective pedagogy. The Pulitzer Prize–winning historian Lawrence Cremin remarked that "balance, moderation, and practicality—these are the qualities that mark *Some Thoughts Concerning Education.*"[4] Largely forgotten is the fact that those thoughts concerning education were not written with the intention of creating a book. They were, rather, a response to a friend who had asked Locke for his opinion on how best to educate their child. Only after some pleading by those with whom Locke's letters had been shared did he reassemble them in an attempt to constitute a book. As a consequence, *Some Thoughts Concerning Education* is strangely reminiscent of Rousseau's *Emile,* in that it is a discussion—a less coherent one—about how to educate one child, and a future gentlemen at that. Locke warns his readers about allowing the child too much discourse with servants as an example, apparently, of the practicality of his educational prescriptions. But he also warns his readers against too much instruction in subject matter rules and encourages active learning strategies, as did Rousseau. The book is not without evident pedagogical insights, to be sure. But it is not a commentary on the role education might play to sustain a nonfeudal governmental structure, or, for that matter, a free market economy. There is no indication, for example, that all citizens should have the opportunity to experience his educational prescriptions. In fact, reading a bit more widely in the large corpus of Locke's work, one finds that Locke had different educational plans for the children of the poor.

As England's commissioner for trade and plantations, Locke drafted a proposal in 1697 intended to amend extant poor laws. He discussed several ideas, such as closing down taverns or yoking the poor to hard labor. But the problem of what to do with the children of the poor was particularly perplexing. He settled on the concept of "work schools" to complement the idea of "work houses" for the poor. There "children of all such as demand the relief of the parish, above three and under fourteen years of age, whilst they live at home with their parents ... shall be obliged to come." These schools would maintain strict discipline. In fact, "any boy or girl, under fourteen years of age found begging out of the parish where they dwell ... shall be sent to the next working school, there to be soundly whipped and kept at work till evening, so that they may be dismissed time enough to get to their place of abode that night."[5]

For Locke, apparently, hunger was a crime. The "balance, moderation, and practicality" that ostensibly dominated his educational vision seems to have disappeared when he turned his attention to the education of the poor. And Locke, of course, made a good part of his large fortune through judicious investments in the African slave trade. There is a kind of symmetry between Locke's behaviors and his steadfast philosophical beliefs about economic man, about man in the state of nature, about man's ostensible propensity to "overturn all morality." Locke merely lived what he believed, and to the degree that we have used Locke's beliefs and assumptions as the criteria for building our political and economic arrangements, there ought to be little wonder why America's cultural development has been so openly tolerant of poverty and racism.

His views were certainly a vivid contrast to those of Winstanley, but they were a vivid contrast to a much more mainstream figure as well, Charles Secondat de Montesquieu of France. Starting, as we have seen in earlier chapters, from a far different premise than Locke, that man was fundamentally political rather than economic, Montesquieu believed that a school system was required for all citizens of a republic. He felt that no republican experiment could possibly be successful without a system that could deliver "the full power of education." It should be fairly obvious that an embrace of Montesquieu's ideas (the M-stream) would have set us on a course of cultural development far different from that of Locke (the L-stream). In fact, this is precisely what was started during the first half of the nineteenth century in the United States, before Darwin's ideas brought its development to a halt by reestablishing the hegemony of the L-stream. It was America's "communitarian moment" when democratic reforms were frequent and state school systems were established left and right.

One can only speculate at this point, but it seems likely that absent the Darwinian legitimation of economic man—man who must compete to survive—we may well have developed the habit and practice of thinking about human freedom in political before economic terms; our school systems would have worked to outfit all citizens, not just a group of gentlemen or those most fit in social Darwinist terms, to play a political role with their lives; we would have been far less tolerant of persistent poverty alongside phenomenal wealth, less tolerant of racism and other forms of discrimination. Fortunately, there are specific things that can be done to move our cultural development toward the M-stream, and that is, in fact, the purpose of the later chapters of this book. For now, though, it is important to see the rather stark contrast that close inspection of various educational prescriptions presents.

This is best accomplished by looking at the educational views of the L-stream authors of the Constitution, Alexander Hamilton and James Madison, and contrasting them with America's greatest M-stream spokesperson, Thomas Jefferson. Again, it's a stark contrast. Hamilton and Madison were virtually silent on the question of how to educate the nation's youth, and as a consequence, the Constitution says nothing about it. This should be contrasted with federal action taken by our pre-Constitution government, the Articles of Confederation and Perpetual Union. Its two most highly lauded pieces of legislation, the Northwest Ordinances of 1785 and 1787, both included federal policies designed to ensure that "schools and the means of education shall forever be encouraged."

Thomas Jefferson, as opposed to Hamilton and Madison, was a perennial advocate of schools. Three times he tried to get his native Virginia to pass laws that would create free schools for all (white) children, even providing full-tuition college scholarships for the most academically talented students who would otherwise be unable to attend. And, of course, as a retirement project, he founded the University of Virginia.

It turns out that the question of how to educate the nation's youth (i.e., educational theory)—a question that, in fact, cannot go unanswered—rests every bit as much on assumptions regarding what human life is, *essentially,* as questions concerning how we will govern ourselves (political theory) and how we will meet our needs (economic theory). Is life just one prolonged economic struggle? Or is it a prolonged association with others? For Hobbes, Locke, Hamilton, Madison, and countless others, life is a prolonged economic struggle. For Winstanley, Montesquieu, Jefferson, and countless others, it is a prolonged period of association with others. To be sure, all of these individuals would say that life is defined by elements of both, but they would also quickly add that the scales tip profoundly in one direction or the other. That is, life is *essentially* one or the other.

Take your pick: life is *essentially* economic or *essentially* social. Now add to the equation the supreme postfeudal value, human freedom. If you add freedom to the life of economic man, he becomes free to make money. If you add freedom to the life of social (or political) man, he becomes free to use his voice in the decisions that affect him, his family, and his neighbors.[6] And, of course, it is possible to add education to the equation. Schooling for economic man will prepare him for his economic struggles—that is, prepare him to make money—whereas schooling for social man will prepare him for shared decision-making—that is, prepare him to play a political role with his life.

While the United States was certainly not devoid of schools during its first fifty years, it had no organized system of schooling, no way to guarantee that all children would receive even a minimal level of literacy. There were charity schools, especially in the large seaboard urban centers, but whether a poor family could avail itself of such an opportunity was clearly a hit or miss proposition. Many called for the establishment of free school systems, just as they called for universal male suffrage, for the establishment of city parks and playgrounds, for prison reforms, and in many locales, for the abolition of slavery. This was Tocqueville's America, the site of the proliferation of Montesquieu's *corps intermediaries*, "intermediate bodies" that gave all citizens a venue for a political dimension in their life. This was America's "communitarian moment" when the idea of democracy—something the Constitution authors sought to hold back—spread like wildfire.

Massachusetts was the first state to take the plunge. In 1836 the state legislature established a system of free schools and appointed Horace Mann, a young lawyer, to be its first commissioner. Other northern states followed suit shortly thereafter so that by the outbreak of Civil War in 1861, most had established state systems to orchestrate the delivery of free instruction in common schools.

The history of America's common school movement has been hotly debated over the years, and it is worth noting a few of the arguments regarding forces that worked for and against the establishment of free common school systems. First, despite fifty years of rejecting the call for school systems that came from individuals of note such as Jefferson in Virginia, Robert Coram in Delaware, Benjamin Rush in Pennsylvania, and Daniel Webster in Massachusetts, the M-stream idea that a republic required a system of schools capable of delivering "the full power of education" never went away. In fact, an argument can be made that pro–common school sentiment grew each time such a plan was rejected.

And what was behind the rejection? As noted earlier, the heavy emphasis on individual freedom in the L-stream made the question of publicly supported free schools a difficult pill to swallow. Would this mean I must pay taxes to support the education of another man's child? What if I preferred not to send my child to school? Certainly I have that freedom, do I not? On top of this, the view of life as essentially economic seemed to suggest that schooling for each family ought to remain a matter of cost/benefit calculation, rather than a matter of right or entitlement.

A second reason for rejecting free common school systems had to do with the very significant extent to which schooling was a quasi-religious endeavor. While touring the United States during the early 1830s, before the establishment of state systems, Tocqueville noted that nearly everywhere he went schools were overwhelmingly "entrusted to clergy."[7] Twenty-first century readers will have a hard time imagining school experiences tightly connected to religion, but daily Bible-reading was a predictable feature of American schools for most of the nineteenth century.

As one might expect, this created some serious problems. There were actually several violent clashes between Protestants and Catholics on this issue, "Bible riots" as they came to be known.[8] But there was significant interdenominational conflict over the idea of free schools within Protestantism itself. For instance, the Calvinist hierarchy on the East Coast (Congregationalists and Presbyterians) had grave reservations about the dramatic growth in the ranks of Methodists and Baptists in the interior states. Consequently, many Calvinist clerics came West specifically to become involved in the direction of state school systems, where they believed they might offset the cultural damage emanating from the dramatic growth in the "popular denominations." In fact, this westward migration of Calvinist clerics who eventually ascended to leadership positions in state departments of education, individuals like John Pierce of Michigan, Edward Beecher of Illinois, Caleb Mills of Indiana, Calvin Stowe of Ohio, and Edward Neill of Minnesota, actually resulted in significant popular opposition to the establishment of free school systems. Caleb Mills, Indiana's second state superintendent of public instruction, wrote concerning his successor, "Let him be elected by popular vote, or appointed by Executive authority, or chosen by a joint ballot of the Legislature, the question would be immediately asked by thousands, not is he qualified, but is he *Presbyterian*?"[9] Methodist and Baptist farmers across the Midwest were not enamored by the thought of state systems of education controlled by Calvinist clergy.

And then there was massive immigration into the United States, by the tens of thousands, especially from Ireland. The nation had never witnessed anything like it. As thousands of immigrants annually spread into the Eastern Seaboard cities, appalling conditions appeared almost overnight. How were the children of these immigrants to become capable, contributing democratic citizens? Perhaps a school system could keep Irish youth out of gangs and off the streets? And what about the utilization of child labor in the ever-growing number of industrial centers? Could schools alleviate this social ill?

All of this is to suggest that there were many different reasons to either support or oppose the establishment of free school systems. That the scales were tipped in favor of support for such systems in the late 1830s and 1840s, during an age historian Sean Wilentz contends was defined by "the rise of democracy"—during the era in which Tocqueville toured the United States and made note of its distinctively democratic ethos—indicates that the M-stream emphasis on an educational system to support the view that all humans require a political role to play with their lives was a huge part of the establishment of free common school systems.

Significantly, Americans came to describe their public schools as *common schools*. Not common as a reference to the "lower orders" or commoners of feudal society, but schools providing free instruction in a curriculum common to citizens of a democracy. The common schools were to deliver sophisticated literacy and numeracy skills to all citizens—or at least to as many as desired to receive them. And in time this was changed as state after state began to pass compulsory attendance laws so that no citizen of the republic would lack the intellectual wherewithal to decide for him- or herself what policy options secures or endangers freedom.[10]

But it is perhaps more important to note what was not a part of the common school project as it was initially developed in this country. For this system was not created as a vehicle for enhancing economic wherewithal among the nation's youth. In fact, any economic benefit extending from a common school education was deemed to be merely a fortunate residual. The education provided in nineteenth-century common schools was an education congruent with the M-stream conception of life as essentially social—as essentially a prolonged association with others. This suggested an education that would enable citizens to play a political role with their lives and to ably shoulder the burden of democracy on behalf of oneself, one's family, and one's neighbors. Farther still from the vision of the common school founders was the idea that the nation's schools must outperform the schools of other nations in order to ensure a kind of global economic dominion or outright military superiority. These were twentieth-century conceptions, and it doesn't take a great deal of insight to see the degree to which such ideas cheapened the definition of an education.

What caused such a profound shift in the mission of the nation's schools? How did they go from being "pillars of the republic," the title of Carl Kaestle's award-winning history of the common school era, to becoming an element in economic and/or military analysis?[11] To fully understand the answer to this question, one needs to recognize that these school systems were created at the height of the M-stream in America, at a point in history when the excesses of free market capitalism had created a kind of worldwide revulsion manifest in what many have derogatorily, and erroneously, called a romantic period.[12]

During this period school systems designed to support the republic were established, democratic political reforms were abundant, and a myriad of alternative
economic theories were created: Mill's gradualism, Marx's radicalism, and the
middle or agrarian way promoted by the likes of Ogilivie, Sismondi, Walras, and
Ruskin. And what was it that pushed the L-stream back to the fore? What was it
that helped bury the great variety of alternatives to capitalism red in tooth and
claw? What was it that shifted the focus of the nation's schools from the provision
of democratic arts designed to enhance the political lives of citizens to a great
"sorting machine," as historian Joel Spring has aptly named America's twentieth-
century schools? The answer is the same in each instance and was introduced in
the previous chapter.

Nothing proves the power of ideas quite so well as Darwin's theory of evolution.
To be sure, there was racism in the world prior to the misguided translation of
Darwinian biology into Spencerian sociology. But racism never before possessed
the credibility that came with the official sanction of science. Much mischief
and much suffering can be traced back to the power of the idea of evolution.
Darwin argued and tried to demonstrate that all species must adapt to changes
in their environment, and to the world's first generation of social Darwinists
this clearly applied to the "races" of humankind. As early as the second decade
of the twentieth century, for instance, scientists from America's top universities
were claiming that blacks were at least 200,000 years behind whites in evolution.[13]
"Scientists of the mind," as historian Clarence Karier has called them,[14] worked
assiduously at creating tests that would prove which human groups were more
or less "evolved"[15]

This all led inevitably to organizations devoted to eugenics, race-purity clubs,
and the massive expansion of the Ku Klux Klan, as well as above-boards legal
efforts to provide for the sterilization of "feeble-minded" women, immigration
legislation, and stiffer penalties for violating racial segregation—to say nothing of
what it meant elsewhere for the victims of Adolph Hitler and his cronies. It is extraordinarily lamentable history—some of humankind's worst—and it tainted the
development of virtually all twentieth-century institutions in the United States,
perhaps none more profoundly than the American system of public education.

Before describing the impact of social Darwinist science on American schools,
however, it is probably a good idea to reiterate the ideological symmetry between
the social Darwinist view of life as a kind of economic struggle with the environment, one that only the most fit individuals survive, and Locke's view of the state
of nature as a kind of prolonged economic struggle. In many ways, social Darwinism simply confirmed Locke's view about what life is, *essentially.* What citizens
needed, therefore, was to select a government of the most fit to make decisions
for them and thereafter return to the pursuit of their own economic self-interest.
Given the gradations of evolution among humans, the *last* thing a progressive
society would want to do is give all citizens a voice in political decisionmaking.

This would be one and the same as giving power to the *least* evolved in American society, those *least* capable of making important decisions.

The nineteenth-century school system that grew out of the M-stream cultural milieu, schools as almost literal pillars of the republic, required a major overhaul as a result of the Darwinian-inspired reascendancy of the L-stream. With economics once again firmly established as the essence of the human condition, didn't it make sense, social Darwinists argued, that an education ought to match a child's economic destiny? Those with very little evolutionary wherewithal, for instance, will end up in low-skill jobs, whereas those who were among the highly evolved would ascend to positions of power and influence. One group *deserves* our best educational efforts, and on the other group such efforts would be a waste.

By the first decade of the twentieth century, this transition in America's schools was well under way. And, curiously, it received even more momentum from a famous black educational spokesperson, Booker T. Washington. Starting with very little, Washington built the Tuskegee Normal School into a large (and profitable) educational center for blacks in the South. Having received accolades for a speech given at the Atlanta Exposition in 1895 in which he claimed that blacks and whites were as one hand in all things economic, but as separate as the fingers in all things social, he gradually began to garner thousands of dollars from northern white philanthropists. With the influx of these dollars Tuskegee grew, and Washington became a national spokesperson for a vocationally oriented educational philosophy—one that suggested that an education was about acquiring whatever skills or knowledge was necessary for the world of work.

It was an unfortunate philosophy. As early as 1902 William Torrey Harris, then the U. S. Commissioner of Education, declared that the Booker T. Washington solution "applies to the downtrodden of all races without reference to color."[16] By 1917 Congress had stepped squarely into the world of educational policy by passing the Smith-Hughes Act, a law that generated funds for the creation of "shops" and "home economics" classrooms in high schools all across the country. According to longtime Harvard president Charles Eliot, such classrooms were needed if schools were to identify the "evident and probable destinies" of children and give them each an education appropriate to that destiny.[17]

The idea that schools should provide a common curricular experience, or one common to the citizens of a republic, was rejected as out of date. In fact, what was needed was not common schools, but "comprehensive" schools capable of delivering instruction in differentiated curricular tracks that were in step with the evolutionary gradations of humankind. It was a given, for instance, that minorities, be they black, Hispanic, or Native, would require a strictly vocational curriculum. This led to the construction of "tech high schools" in the larger cities of the nation—schools that still exist, though the worst excesses of a strictly vocational curriculum generally have been eliminated. But in today's tech high schools, like all schools, the shift in focus to "preparation for a job" has not changed at all. If anything, it has intensified as schools came to be blamed for America's poor economic performance during the 1980s.[18] This was a crime so onerous, apparently, that the next couple of decades witnessed a veritable testing fetish among policymakers. Even educators who knew better acquiesced in the face of tremendous pressure to define an education as a series of test scores. It was analysis similar to the kind that we might expect from a child, and yet it remains state-of-the-art thinking among most educational policymakers in this country, regardless of their political persuasion.

A Closer Look

Even among those with a keen interest in U.S. history there is inadequate appreciation for the cataclysmic nature of the decade of the 1890s. It was an era, according to historian Nell Painter, when America was "standing at Armageddon."[19] As noted in Chapter 2, the severe economic depression during the middle years of the decade became overshadowed by the depth and severity of the 1930s depression. But the circumstances of the 1890s were a catalyst to changes of great significance, changes that need to be understood in order to make sense of twentieth-century developments in any arena, be it politics, economics, or education.

The most profound change was one that took place among the nation's intellectuals and profoundly colored their interpretation of virtually all developments throughout that tumultuous decade and for a few decades thereafter. Prior to the advent of social Darwinism, scholars thought about the world in mechanistic terms, as if the universe were a giant machine that trudged on regardless of what humans might choose to do with their lives. This view was at least partially a by-product of Newtonian physics and so dates back to the seventeenth century. As such, it was a view of the world that grew alongside the movement from feudalism to industrial democracies justified by the idea that liberty ought to be the value that guides all political and economic behavior. Oddly enough, a close connection exists between believing in human freedom and conceiving of human societies as machinelike entities that would trudge on in accord with the laws of nature. In fact, it was this mechanistic conception of society that gave rise to the liberal notion of progress. Human choices can be seen as another set of complex cogs in the machine of society. Thus men like Locke argue that although a revolution might occur, bringing anguish and suffering, the world would continue to trudge on, to make progress toward the ever-increasing improvement of humankind. Jefferson's faith in progress was so strong, he thought there should be a revolution every fifty years or so. In short, because the world functioned as a kind of perpetual machine, progress was considered inevitable.

Social Darwinism changed all that. By the 1890s scholars began to conceive of human societies not as machines but as organisms with life cycles that included birth, growth, decline, and death. Looking around during the depression of the 1890s, the nation's intellectuals did not like what they saw. There were threats to the status quo everywhere one looked. The surprise showing of Populist presidential candidate James Weaver in the 1892 election, for instance, was a shock to many. The agrarian crusade against the growing power of corporate America, if state and even national election results were any indication, was not something to be taken lightly. And the decade witnessed significant growth in the ranks of the American Socialist Party, too. On top of this, labor unions were springing up across the country and the number of worker strikes spiked dramatically during the depression—sometimes setting off pitched street battles between workers and the Pinkerton "detectives" hired by corporate management. Rail companies that had severely overextended themselves collapsed; in fact, one out of every six American corporations folded during the 1890s depression. Unemployment reached an unheard of 25 percent—a mark that was only slightly eclipsed by circumstances during the 1930s depression.

And university professors shared more bad news. Frederick Jackson Turner, a University of Wisconsin historian, declared the frontier closed as of 1893. In a famous paper delivered before the American Historical Association, he argued that there was no longer room for the disaffected or disillusioned of American society in the nation's western states. The frontier, Turner argued further, had been the key to America's vitality—what would become of American democracy without the frontier? Sociologists like John Lee Coulter at the University of Minnesota raised even greater alarm by identifying a population trend of potentially devastating consequences. The nation's rural youth—fine, upstanding, white, Anglo-Saxon, and Protestant—were leaving the countryside and migrating to the city at rapid rates. There they would doubtless intermingle with immigrants from less-evolved races. To capture what they believed to be the ominous ramifications of this development, sociologists coined phrases like "folk depletion" and "race-suicide."

If society is a kind of organism, almost everything about the 1890s suggested that America was in deep trouble. If we were going to get out of the tailspin that defined the decade, we couldn't merely wait for a thing called progress, we had to create it. American society, like individuals within it, had to adapt to changing circumstances or face extinction. In other words, progress was something that couldn't be taken for granted, it was something that needed to be skillfully engineered.

What has come to be known as America's "Progressive Era," roughly 1900–1917, was a response to the anxiety produced by the 1890s—anxiety born of a powerful, though vacuous, idea: that the life of a society is closely, even strictly, analogous to a human life. Such biological terminology is at best heuristic and metaphorical, and is palpably dangerous when taken literally. Yet the simplistic and false biological analogies became common in educational literature of the Progressive Era, with experts arguing that society was indeed an organism, and that individuals were merely the cells within it. And, since each cell in an organism has a specific function to perform in order for the organism to be healthy, each individual in society had a specific function to perform as well. Failure to do so, or failure to perform the right function, meant an unhealthy society. Schools, therefore, had a tremendous burden to shoulder. They had to accurately identify the role each individual should play in society, and make sure each received an education conducive to that role. That schools became first and foremost a sorting procedure was no accident or by-product; it was explicitly planned and implemented.

How were schools to shoulder this burden? How could they be certain that they wouldn't make a mistake? Fortunately, the same scientific minds that gave us the society-as-an-organism metaphor were ready to give teachers the tools they needed to do their job. In 1912 Joseph Mayer Rice summarized those tools in a book called *Scientific Management in Education.* In it he called for clearly defined, fixed standards that students must meet, a scientific system of pedagogical management, and the use of scientifically based measurement tools that could tell teachers whether standards were efficiently met.[20] Readers today who are familiar with the educational philosophy undergirding the 2002 No Child Left Behind Act will recognize that it is exactly the same philosophy that Rice was spearheading almost 100 years ago. It is a kind of inside joke among professional educators that any grant proposal headed for a federal office these days must modify every noun with the phrase "scientifically based."

It should be clear that thanks to the backdrop provided by the tumultuous 1890s, the business of profoundly shifting the nation's educational agenda from one designed to deliver political wherewithal and only secondarily economic utility, to one designed to deliver economic utility near-exclusively was serious, if not a matter of societal life and death. With the same enthusiasm that the nation invested in building national guard armories all across the country so that strikes could be quickly put down, we set about the business of building high schools designed to provide a curricular track matching the "evident and probable destiny" of each student.

The idea that schools should be a kind of direct conduit to a particular economic role gradually became conventional wisdom, though not without generating dissent. By 2009, however, those who question whether it is appropriate for schools to serve what the late Neil Postman called "the god of economic utility" are few. The average legislator or congressperson, for instance, has virtually no idea that schools might serve a different purpose from what they do now, or that they ever did. This is one among a few critical societal shortcomings that this book is intended to address.

Not everyone was convinced that Darwinian-inspired organism metaphors aptly described societal circumstances or, for that matter, legitimated the profound shift that took place in the perceived purpose of public education. For there was a nagging difficulty that came with this shift, and it continues to haunt the public educational system in the twenty-first century. Though very few are aware of it, our public schools still function on the basis of social Darwinist theory. In fact, the only way to find comfort in light of this nagging difficulty is to prove beyond the shadow of a doubt that some of the races of humankind are intellectually inferior to others—less evolved, to use Progressive Era terminology. Once this has been accomplished, we can have a clear conscience about the fact that some American youth receive a better education than others. We no longer need to suffer any angst over the fact that various minority groups disproportionately populate the "special" education classrooms of the nation, or that they are disproportionately represented among those who "drop out" of school. All will be as it should.

The problem is that proof of the intellectual inferiority of certain racial groups has been elusive—remarkably so, considering that scientists have been hot on its trail since the second decade of the twentieth century. But as each twentieth-century decade passed, the scientific community was forced to grudgingly admit that new understandings took them even farther from the proof they so adamantly sought. Genetic study, for example, eventually brought us to the point where we could see that the entire concept of race itself was flawed, making the task of proving the intellectual inferiority of various racial groups nearly insurmountable. In fact, before the twentieth century closed, scholars—even fast-track scholars, those who conduct research intended to legitimate the status quo in exchange for public accolades, high visibility, and financial reward—had ceased in the attempt to scientifically legitimate racism.[21]

So the nagging difficulty remains. As long as the purpose of education is the provision of economic wherewithal, the system builds in toleration for its own poor performance. Some jobs require very little intellectual acumen. Someone, as we all know, must sweep the streets. That will be the students who can't seem to learn to read. If such students are disproportionately minority group members, it must be a grand coincidence.

Since the scientific community failed to generate the kind of proof that would legitimate disparate educational results, the professional education community gradually came up with a kind of coping mechanism—that is, they created a concept that would help them feel better about the nagging difficulty hounding American public education ever since the social Darwinist shift occurred. That concept came to be known as "equal educational opportunity," a palatable expression that masks the essence of the concept, which is blaming the child—or her parents—for the lack of academic achievement. All children have the opportunity to acquire an education via America's public schools. If some choose not to avail themselves of this opportunity, it's their own fault.

It shouldn't be surprising that throughout the twentieth century there were those who rejected the idea that school performance was a mirror reflecting racial intellectual wherewithal, or the idea that school performance was an accurate account of those who chose and those who chose not to avail themselves of equal educational opportunity. In fact, what should be surprising is that those who rejected these views were so few in number.

The Dissenters

The most thoroughgoing and far-reaching among those who rejected social Darwinism was not an educator at all, though one would be hard-pressed to find a more persuasive advocate of education and the contribution education might make to the improvement of humankind. Lester Frank Ward was in fact many things, but most prominently, he was America's first distinguished sociologist. Within ten years of his death in 1913, however, he had been profoundly forgotten. In fact, he is today as much a footnote in America's intellectual history as Winstanley is in England's, for like Winstanley, Ward's views did not prevail. If Winstanley's vision was rejected in favor of that of Hobbes and Locke, Ward's interpretation of modern life at the close of the nineteenth century was rejected in the face of the immense appeal (and obvious utility) of Herbert Spencer's social Darwinism.

Ward didn't fail through lack of effort. He took on the intellectual underpinnings of Spencerian sociology, and he exposed them as seriously lacking. But Spencer had already acquired the status of something like a modern-day rock star—someone so popular that he could withstand even well-constructed arguments that proved him wrong. The life of Spencer's most successful American disciple, William Graham Sumner, represents a telling contrast to Ward, for they were very nearly the same age and they tackled the same set of social problems. But that's where the similarity ends. Ward was the youngest of ten children, the son of a tenant farmer and sometimes day-laboring mechanic who died when Lester was sixteen. From that point on, he was on his own. He drifted from job to job, all the while demonstrating an earnest desire to educate himself, studying everything he could get his hands on. In 1862 he enlisted in the Union Army and served for a little more than two years. He was seriously wounded at Chancellorsville and then again a year later. He was discharged late in 1864.

Hanging around Washington, he eventually found work in the growing number of civil service offices. At the age of twenty-six he began working for the Bureau of Statistics, learning all that he could both on the job and in night school. By 1870 he received a B.A. from Columbia University in Washington, D.C.—and a master's degree two years later. Not satisfied, Ward picked up additional degrees in law and medicine from Johns Hopkins University. In 1883 he became the chief paleontologist of the U.S. Geological Survey. That was also the year he published his two-volume masterpiece, *Dynamic Sociology*.

In contrast, William Graham Sumner purchased a substitute to take his place in the Union Army so that he could continue his studies at Yale—and later several European universities. Sumner was a life-long academic, while Ward moved from one government post to another, completing his scholarly publications at night and on weekends. He did not join a university faculty until an invitation came from Brown University in 1907. Sumner was a devout social Darwinist, arguing that "if we do not like survival of the fittest we have only one possible alternative, and that is survival of the unfittest. The former is the law of civilization, the latter is the law of anti-civilization."[22] Nature had a kind of supreme decisionmaking power, according to Sumner, when it came to the evolutionary process. Nothing could be done about evolutionary law. To the emerging American postwar elite, the robber barons, as they came to be called, the doctrine of survival of the fittest and, in particular, the ostensible inevitability of this doctrine, was immensely self-satisfying. Their success, however ruthlessly ill-gotten, was proof of their high evolutionary status—proof that they were a cut above those who could not boast of similar success. That this is a classical example of circular reasoning did not occur to them, given its emotional appeal and power as legitimation.

The unconditional embrace of social Darwinism among the nation's wealthiest and most powerful citizens, as well as among most intellectuals in colleges and universities across the country, meant that Ward's effort to expose social Darwinism as intellectually vacuous was a tall order. But he started by asking precisely what was meant by the phrase "survival of the fittest." What does it mean to be demonstrably more fit to survive? Is that a circumstance or condition that will necessarily create more happiness or more good in the world?

Ward exposed the doctrine as no more than a kind of insidious self-congratulation, calling it "the great stubborn error, so universal and ingrained as to constitute a world view." He claimed that "every form of sophistry" is used to support the idea "that the difference between the upper and lower classes of society is due to a difference in their intellectual capacity, something existing in the nature of things, something preordained and inherently inevitable."[23] And he argued further, "No matter what class of society you may select from—taking a corresponding number from each—the individuals from all classes will be equal in their native capacity for knowledge."[24] Intellectual inequality existed, to be sure, but it existed among all classes alike.

The primary difference between the upper and lower classes of American society, according to Ward, was not a difference in intellect but a difference in the possession of knowledge. Thus, for Ward, education was all important. In this respect he was a civic republican of the M-stream mold. All citizens required the full power of education, according to Ward, in order to create a people's government. And those citizens selected to be a part of such a government would require even more education in the form of legislator training academies of the sort he envisioned.

Ward steadfastly refused to buy into the social Darwinist notion that natural evolution would chart its own course. He believed that human history demonstrated the reverse of this position—that humankind, through the application of intelligence, could guide the course of societal evolution. Ward concluded in 1895 that "nothing is more obvious today than the signal inability of capital and private enterprise to take care of themselves unaided by the state," noting their propensity for "besieging legislatures for relief from their own incompetency ... through a trained body of lawyers and lobbyists," all the while shouting "laissez faire."[25]

Government intervention was surely needed—Ward agreed—but the nature of that intervention had to be in the interest of generating happiness among citizens, not saving corporations that had overextended themselves. In *Psychic Factors of Civilization,* published in 1893, Ward argued that to get the kind of government planning and action that would ensure productive social evolution, concerted and widespread educational effort was necessary. Not an education designed to outfit one for his or her ostensible evolutionary status, but one fitted to participation in the political system regardless of race or class origin. The book was reviewed by a young philosopher at the University of Michigan who concurred with Ward's arguments. His name was John Dewey.

Born and raised in rural Vermont, Dewey held a lifelong appreciation for the centrality of community to the human condition—an appreciation that was evident in his educational experiments and in his educational philosophy. He attended the University of Vermont as a young man and after graduating, taught high school for two years in Oil City, Pennsylvania. That was followed by a short stint as a teacher in a village school in Charlotte, Vermont, but Dewey eventually made his way to graduate study in philosophy at Johns Hopkins University in Baltimore, where he found his niche. He was an excellent graduate student, publishing first-rate peer-reviewed work even before receiving his doctorate. His first academic position came in 1886 in the Department of Philosophy and Psychology at the University of Michigan. In 1888 he accepted a chair in philosophy at the University of Minnesota, but stayed only one year before returning to Ann Arbor. Dewey was a prolific writer and had built such a solid reputation in so short a time that William Rainey Harper, president of the University of Chicago, included Dewey as one of several accomplished scholars that he felt he must recruit to the new university; this group included such luminaries as Albion Small, Thorstein Veblen, and George Herbert Mead.

It is clear that almost upon his arrival at Chicago in 1894, Dewey had begun making plans to create an experimental school near the university campus. It was an idea that excited President Harper, for unlike most private college presidents, he sought to make the University of Chicago tightly connected to the city's public schools and its teachers. The Dewey school opened in 1896, and Dewey remained intimately involved with it for eight years. But just a year into the experiment,

Dewey, like Ward, rejected the growing sentiment that schooling ought to be tailored to individual, racially determined, occupational destinies.

> We cannot, whether we approve the fact or regret it, educate the child for special membership on the basis of habit, routine, or tradition. The society for which the child, to-day, is to be educated, is too complex, makes too many demands upon personality to be capable of being based upon custom and routine without the utmost disaster. We must educate by giving him the widest powers and most complete tools of civilization. Only a study, only the knowledge, of what those powers are and how to master them, and what would instrumentally aid or hinder in their development, and how, is in any way adequate to this task.[26]

He explained more fully a few years later: "What the best and wisest parent wants for his own child, that must the community want for all its children. Any other ideal for our schools is narrow and unlovely; acted upon, it destroys our democracy."[27] There has scarcely ever been a more penetrating insight written in the English language. Dewey argued persuasively that to educate youth for particular roles was contrary to the idea of government of, for, and by the people. He sharply criticized the idea that individuals were merely cells in a societal organism, each with a preordained function to perform. In *Democracy and Education,* published in 1916, he noted that "the notion of 'organism' is thus used to give a philosophic sanction to class distinctions in social organization," a kind of academic fad that Dewey could not countenance.[28]

While Dewey was at Columbia, the university's colorful longtime president, Nicholas Murray Butler, stated that

> For a generation or more past[,] the center of human interest has been moving from the point which it occupied for some four hundred years to a new point which it bids fair to occupy for a time equally long. The shift in the position of the center of gravity in human interest has been from politics to economics; from considerations that had to do with forms of government, with the establishment and protection of individual liberty, to considerations that have to do with production, distribution, and consumption of wealth.[29]

The social efficiency school reformers of the Progressive Era were evidence of this shift in the "center of gravity of human interest." But it was not only the undemocratic nature of the grand shift in the purpose of schools that bothered Dewey. It was also the fact that the shift necessarily entailed schooling as preparation for something that may (or may not) occur later—and this, he believed, was tantamount to impeding learning in its own right. "Children are not regarded as social members in full and regular standing"; they are, rather, "placed on the waiting list."[30] Subject matter, under such circumstances, has little or no immediate relevance. But if the goal of education was shifted to the practice of social membership, productive life in association with others, shouldering community responsibilities, and the like, teachers could focus on "the interaction of subject matter with pupils' present needs," thereby reducing "the artificial gap between life in school and out." Dewey condemned curriculum based upon "other men's knowledge" and instructional approaches he called "frontal attacks," something he deemed to be "even more wasteful in learning than in war."[31]

Dewey's philosophy gradually came to be associated with a loose movement called "Progressive education," which in turn came to be captured by many phrases, including "child-centered," "learning by doing," "active learning," and the "project method." People gradually began to invoke Dewey for most any kind of reform, and partially as a result of this, the Progressive movement never posed a serious threat to the dominant Darwinian view of education as preparation for later economic life (with the possible exception of a few of the darkest years during the 1930s depression).

Dewey and Harper had a serious falling out in 1904, which led to Dewey taking a position in the Philosophy Department at Columbia University in New York City. His scholarship gradually drifted away from educational questions, though he revisited education questions now and then and remained keenly interested in schools until his death in 1952. In 1927, while at Columbia, Dewey was joined by a young education professor who had received his doctorate at the University of Chicago, a place still profoundly influenced by the educational philosophy Dewey generated there during his eight-year affiliation with the lab school. His name was George Counts.

Born in 1889 in rural Kansas, Counts graduated from Baker University in 1911. Five years later he received his doctorate from the University of Chicago. He worked at several colleges after that, including Yale, before joining the faculty at Teachers College Columbia University in 1927. Counts established himself as an early critic of the modern, occupationally focused schools. His book, *The Selective Character of American Secondary Education*, published in 1922, documented the fact that America's high schools were disproportionately serving the upper classes in American society and that the practice of what came to be called "tracking," dividing students into different curricular groups ostensibly on the basis of ability, was in fact further exacerbating the social class distinctions found in America's schools. A few years later he conducted a study of school board membership across the country. In *The Social Composition of Boards of Education*, published in 1927, Counts argued that whether the school boards were urban or rural they tended to be dominated by local elites—which had the effect of encouraging schools to preserve the status quo.

While his work in the 1920s garnered a small following, it was nothing compared to the way his popularity grew during the darkest days of the 1930s depression. In 1932 he published three speeches as a kind of pamphlet or small book.

Though the speeches had separate titles, the book was called *Dare the School Build a New Social Order?* Said Counts:

> Consider the present condition of the nation. Who among us, if he had not been reared among our institutions, could believe his eyes as he surveys the economic situation, or his ears as he listens to the solemn disquisitions by our financial and political leaders on the cause and cure of the depression! Here is a society that manifests the most extraordinary contradictions: mastery over the forces of nature, surpassing the wildest dreams of antiquity, is accompanied by extreme material insecurity; dire poverty walks hand in hand with the most extravagant living that the world has ever known; an abundance of goods of all kinds is coupled with privation, misery, and even starvation; an excess of production is seriously offered as the underlying cause of severe physical suffering; breakfastless children march to school past bankrupt shops laden with rich foods gathered from the ends of the earth; strong men by the millions walk the streets in a futile search for employment and with the exhaustion of hope enter the ranks of the damned. One can only imagine what Jeremiah would say if he could step out of the pages of the Old Testament and cast his eyes over this vast spectacle so full of tragedy and of menace.[32]

For Counts, the loose reform movement known as Progressive education, inspired by John Dewey, lacked a specific and well-articulated direction. In order for the movement to be successful, in order for the schools to generate necessary cultural changes, "changes in our ideals," they needed to "face squarely and courageously every single social issue, come to grips with life in all its stark reality, establish an organic relation with the community, develop a realistic and comprehensive theory of welfare, [and] fashion a compelling and challenging vision of human destiny." If teachers were unfettered from curricular restraints, if they were allowed to see themselves as educational statesmen, they could produce educational experiences designed to bring a political role out of each and every citizen. Keeping the focus squarely on preserving human dignity and enriching the life "of the common man," schools could foster substantive ideals that would move in the direction of a just and equitable society instead of the shallow materialist ideals so poignantly identified by Veblen a few decades earlier.[33]

While Counts was certainly no Marxist, he didn't back away from proclaiming the need for certain socialist reforms. He cast aside criticisms that such reforms would be an infringement on freedom. There would certainly be restraints. The individual, he maintained, "would not be permitted to carve out a fortune out of the natural resources of the nation, to organize a business purely for the purpose of making money, to build a new factory or railroad whenever and wherever he pleased, to throw the economic system out of gear for the protection of his own private interests, or to amass or attempt to amass great riches by the corruption of the political life." Rather than an infringement, Counts argued that a new poverty-free era would be marked by freedom's dramatic extension, since "freedom without a secure economic base is only a word: in our society it may be freedom to beg, steal, or starve."[34]

Counts believed schools could change all that. Joined by Harold Rugg and other colleagues at Teachers College, Counts spearheaded the creation of a journal, *Social Frontier,* that served as a vehicle for social reconstructionist educational theory. Rugg went on to create a series of social studies textbooks with a serious social reconstructionist flavor. Teachers attended the lectures presented by these men, they read the *Social Frontier,* and many tried to live up to the injunction to politicize their pedagogical imaginations.

Although Counts and other Progressive educators gained a considerable following during the depths of the depression, they were still dissenters, still a long way from representing mainstream opinion on educational questions. Social Darwinist educators such as David Snedden and Franklin Bobbitt sneered at the idea that schools might reconstruct American society. And as World War II replaced the Great Depression as the country's primary concern, anything perceived to be a criticism of American society was increasingly labeled "un-American." By 1940 the National Association of Manufacturers openly condemned Rugg's social reconstructionist textbooks, joining forces with the American Legion.[35] Even the Education Policies Commission of the National Education Association had by that year moved away from the production of annual reports emphasizing the pivotal connection between free schools and democracy—a frequent focus during the depression years—back to an economic focus, *Education and Economic Well-Being,* with a new visual featuring an industrial gear emanating out of an open book like the sun rising on the horizon. This report featured chapters highlighting the connection between "education and productivity" and the "kind of occupational education [required] for economic well-being."[36] Social Darwinist schooling had survived the threat posed by the Depression.

American Schools and the "God of Economic Utility"

Though the focus of America's schools as the nation emerged from the Great Depression returned to serve what the late Neil Postman called "the god of economic utility," the consequences of the depression years in the economic realm were many. The New Deal effectively buried most intellectual allegiance to the doctrine of laissez faire (though it has made a comeback recently). Over the next couple of decades, through income and estate taxes, billionaires were eliminated and the number of millionaires was dramatically reduced. Social security protected the lives of millions from starvation and misery. Welfare programs protected children whose parents could not or would not work. But in all of this, the school's role was minimal.

Educational reforms came and went. Students experienced the "life adjust-ment curriculum" and "new math," but the focus remained squarely on outfit-ting youth for an eventual occupational destiny. The second half of the twentieth century saw its share of dissenters, too, including such luminaries as Jonathan Kozol, John Goodlad, and Theodore Sizer. But these individuals were never able to shake the educational system loose from the social Darwinist assumptions that drove it. And these dissenters were rendered even less effective by something unprecedented in American educational history: an attack on the educational system by the government itself.

Ronald Reagan campaigned for the presidency in 1980 on a platform that called for the abolition of the federal Department of Education, something he was not able to accomplish. But he also introduced a variety of "reform" initiatives into discussions related to schooling—things like tuition tax credits, vouchers, and school prayer. Successful in his bid for the presidency, Reagan consented to Secretary of Education Terrence Bell's appointment of a commission of noneducators to study the educational problem in the United States. The commission prepared a report and submitted it to the president in April of 1983. It was titled *A Nation at Risk*, and it claimed that school performance in the United States was evidence of "a rising tide of mediocrity." In fact, the commissioners claimed that "if an unfriendly foreign power had attempted to impose on America the mediocre educational performance that exists today, we might well have viewed it as an act of war."[37]

The crisis rhetoric in the report signaled the beginning of a new era in terms of the relationship between the federal government and the nation's schools—an era marked by consistent and persistent allegations of poor performance and goal-oriented policies ostensibly designed to improve that performance. But it is interesting to examine the evidence upon which this trend-setting report was based. Or rather, the lack of evidence, as Gerald Bracey and many others have demonstrated. Said Bracey regarding the report's claim that "there was a steady decline in 17-year-olds as measured by the national assessment of science in 1969, 1973, and 1977":

> Maybe, maybe not. The National Assessment of Educational Progress (NAEP) was not originally designed to produce trends, and the scores for 1969 and 1973 are backward extrapolations from the 1977 assessment. In any case, the declines were smaller for 9 and 13-year-olds and had already been wiped out by gains on the 1982 assessment. Scores for reading and math for all three ages assessed by NAEP were stable or inching upward. The commissioners thus had nine trendlines (three ages times three subjects), only one of which could be used to support crisis rhetoric. That was the only one they reported.[38]

Many other claims were made for which scholars could find no evidence, and for which none could be supplied by commissioners who were asked after the document's publication.[39] It is likely that no president-sponsored commission report has been as fabricated, as devoid of an evidential base, as *A Nation at Risk*. But beyond a skeptic or two in the media ranks, it was nevertheless overwhelmingly embraced and heralded by print and broadcast media. In fact, in the wake of the release of this report, the American public was taught that its schools were failing.

But it taught the American public something even more pernicious, and even more false. It taught Americans to believe that there is a direct connection between the performance of American schools and the performance of the American economy. "If only to keep and improve on the slim edge we still retain in the world markets," wrote the commissioners, "we must dedicate ourselves to the reform of our educational system."[40] The Pulitzer Prize–winning educational historian Lawrence Cremin commented on the strength of the connection to a nation's school performance and the fate of a nation's economy:

> American economic competitiveness with Japan and other nations is to a considerable degree a function of monetary, trade, and industrial policy, and of decisions made by the President and Congress, the Federal Reserve Board, and the Federal Departments of the Treasury, Commerce, and Labor. Therefore, to conclude that problems of international competitiveness can be solved by educational reform, *especially educational reform defined solely as school reform,* is not merely utopian and millennialist, it is at best foolish and at worst a crass effort to direct attention away from those truly responsible for doing something about competitiveness and to lay the burden instead on the schools.[41]

Two abundantly obvious circumstances shatter any semblance of confidence one might wish to put in the good schools–good economy thesis. The first has to do with America's economy of the 1990s, the most prosperous anywhere at any time, and yet our schools continued to fail, at least according to leading multinational CEOs like Louis Gerstner, who's "op-ed" essay in the *New York Times* in May 1994 declared, "Our Schools Are Failing: Do We Care?"[42] The second is a similar example in reverse. While Japan's economy has stumbled and consequently garnered headlines such as "The Sinking Sun" for the past decade, Japanese schools have nevertheless continued to shine, producing ostensibly world-class test scores, and in so doing destroying the argument for a causal link between school performance and economic growth.[43]

As Cremin so aptly described it, the good schools–good economy thesis is such an exaggeration as to make it largely propaganda—there is no evidence to support it, and much that renders it false. But it has been effective propaganda, becoming a mainstay in the corporate curriculum taught to Americans via media networks. Cremin left open the possibility that educational reform *could* make a direct contribution to economic well-being, but not if educational reform is limited to school reform. This is a point of departure for the second part of this chapter, for Americans are educated in many ways, and we have yet to explore nonschool contributions to what Americans come to know and understand. First, though, we should bring the school story into the twenty-first century.

The two presidencies that followed Ronald Reagan—George Bush and Bill Clinton—both followed the trend set in motion by *A Nation at Risk*. Each created a similar educational agenda to solve the "crisis" gripping American education. Goals 2000 (Clinton) and America 2000 (Bush) called for reform of the nation's school system such that eight goals would be met "by the year 2000." Had we met these goals, which of course we did not, America would have been "first in the world" in mathematics and science achievement. And, true to form, every American would have possessed "the knowledge and skills necessary to compete in a global economy."[44] Speaking before the American Academy of Arts and Sciences in 1995, Ernest Boyer noted the irony in the Goals 2000 agenda:

> In his inaugural address, President George Bush declared as the nation's first educational goal, that by the year 2000 all children in this country will come to school "ready to learn," Yet we have more children in poverty today than we did five years ago. Today a shocking percentage of the nation's nineteen million preschoolers are malnourished and educationally impoverished. One wonders how this nation can live comfortably with the fact that so many of our children are so shockingly impoverished.[45]

The Y-2K dilemma seemingly drew the attention of America's media away from the fact the Bush and Clinton programs were failures, and they of course have consistently refused to expose the poverty epidemic in this country. We did not meet the goals set for the year 2000, so a new piece of educational legislation soon grabbed the headlines early in the George W. Bush administration. It was called No Child Left Behind (NCLB), and its basic premise was that all schools would raise every child to grade-level achievement within a twelve-year window. Further, all schools had to demonstrate annual progress toward that goal or suffer from a spate of possible punishments.

The bill was some 1,200 pages long and included over 500 separate measures for schools to meet. Clearly the second Bush administration was undaunted by the fact that prior administrations were unable to meet a mere eight goals. And, indeed, the Bush Education Department has continually had to make exceptions and allowances for unexpected developments. Because education is by constitutional default a state-administered burden, some freedom had to be given to the states to determine what might constitute acceptable annual progress toward the ultimate goal. This in turn meant that some states looked very good in the first years of the program while other states looked very bad. It created a kind of public relations nightmare and an incredible statistical mess for state departments of education. The general consensus of the educational research community is that

No Child Left Behind is bad policy at best, and potentially damaging at worst. Gerald Bracey described it this way:

> It has been 20 years . . . since *A Nation at Risk* appeared. It is clear that it was false then and is false now. Today, the laments are old and tired—and still false. "Test Scores Lag as School Spending Soars" trumpeted the headline of a 2002 press release from the American Legislative Exchange Council. Ho hum. The various special interest groups in education need another treatise to rally around. And now they have one. It's called No Child Left Behind. It's a weapon of mass destruction, and the target is the public school system. Today, our public schools are truly at risk.[46]

There are really so many problems with No Child Left Behind it is difficult to know where to begin to delineate them, but perhaps the most significant one is the manner and emphasis with which it conflates the definition of an education with a test score. Anyone interested will look in vain throughout the corpus of the best literature the West has to offer for any definition of what constitutes an education—or an educated person—that includes a single reference to performance on a test. And yet we have come to the point in this country where we wholly define education in those meager terms. It is a sad commentary on American culture, to be sure, but it is also pernicious, for the simple truth is that if those students who score in the bottom half nationally move to the top, we would be forced to come up with new tests to give us a new bottom half. Tests may illuminate curricular and instructional issues of concern to educators, but they are not a vehicle on which we can ride en route to a better school system.

Critics, of course, quickly rush in here and sling accusations about not wanting "to be held accountable." This, of course, is ludicrous. The whole point is that test-driven assessment systems don't tell us enough to make any kind of accurate judgment of how "accountable" we've been. We can do much better in the realm of accountability than we are doing now, though that is a topic for the next chapter. Before going there, we need to have a look at the other primary educational venue in the United States.

America's Corporate Curriculum

There is a persuasive argument often made that suggests that NCLB was not intended to be a catalyst to educational reform at all, but rather a kind of death sentence that could easily be followed by privatizing schools once the sentence was fully carried out. The argument stems from the fact that a kind of gospel of "privatization" is clearly evident among conservatives going back to the Reagan administration. H. Christopher Whittle is one such conservative. During the 1980s he created Channel One, a company that provides televisions free to schools who agree to force children to watch specially packaged news programs interspersed with commercials targeting preteens and teenagers. According to contract terms, this must occur during the school day, in 90 percent of all school days, and in 80 percent of the school's classrooms. In this way firms like Pepsi and Reebok reach eight million viewers for a price tag that hovers around $200,000 for a thirty-second slot.[47] Channel One takes home all of the profit; schools receive only televisions for supplying the advertising targets.

The upside of this arrangement, in my view, is that schools routinely ignore the contract specifications since there is no real enforcement, and the worst that could happen is that Channel One would take back the televisions—which it is extremely hesitant to do for this would mean that students would need to be subtracted from the list of those "reached," thus driving down the price Channel One can ask for advertising minutes. It is not hard to find people adamantly opposed to the inherent exploitation of children via Channel One contracts. What is more difficult to find is people who oppose Channel One for the exploitive advertising *and* for the content of the specially packaged news shows. For these shows are merely scaled-down versions of adult news shows aired by the major networks. The range of issues exposed via Channel One and ABC, for example, is about the same. It consists of relatively "safe" topics that have the effect of teaching students and adults that American "free market" policies are always on the side of justice and, regardless, that the majority of Americans support those policies. The "free market" is elevated as a kind of social and economic panacea, without the slightest indication that there may be a connection between free-market policy and dramatic social and economic inequality. Channel One, then, serves as a kind of obvious example of the "corporate curriculum."

Christopher Whittle moved from his successes with Channel One to a bold project predicated on his firm belief, and the firm belief of many conservatives, that a private company could easily and vastly outperform heavily bureaucratized public school districts in the business of providing an education—which is to say, in the current context, the business of producing test scores. He called his initiative the Edison Project, and solicited contracts from public school districts that wished to turn over the management of one or more of their schools to Whittle. The Edison Project received extensive media fanfare, and Whittle boldly predicted that by 2020, he would be running one out of every ten public schools in the United States. When the project went public after accumulating 183 schools to manage, share prices soared to $38. It was at the very height of Whittle's success, in 2001, that No Child Left Behind was conceived, drafted, and passed into law—a circumstance that lends additional credence to those who argue that NCLB was created to make public schools appear to be failures, thus smoothing the way for privatized takeovers.

But since NCLB was passed, the Edison stock price has collapsed. The company was investigated by the Securities and Exchange Commission for misrepresenting revenues, and as a consequence, it is now the subject of multiple class-action lawsuits—one coming from the firm that is handling a major class-action suit against Enron. On top of this, many school districts have become disillusioned with Edison and what they claim are "hidden costs" charged by the company. Rumors continue to haunt the Edison Project, especially those charging that administrators routinely attempt to "counsel out" students who they believe will not perform well on tests. Although all signs indicate Edison is headed for financial collapse, revenue from huge firms has poured into the project before and may do so again—a move that may be deemed necessary if the vision of a privatized education system is to be kept alive.

Privatizing education is just one more example of a kind of free market ideology that praises any and every attempt to open up social interchange to the possibility of realizing profit. George W. Bush steadfastly tried to privatize Social Security only to discover that the American public saw the blatant self-interest on the part of American corporations in such a plan, and they rejected it. But the ideology survives, and for every defeat there has been a victory, such as drastic reductions in the estate tax, rhetorically dubbed the "death tax." The ideology that has gripped the nation since the Reagan administration has consistently promoted the re-embrace of laissez-faire economics, weakening antitrust action to the point that it can scarcely be recognized, consistently promoting privatization as a kind of cure-all for the nation's problems, and consistently insisting on an interpretation of the free speech and freedom of the press clauses of the First Amendment to the Constitution that invests the right defended by the amendment not in the viewing or listening public but in the multinational corporations delivering the speech.

The freedom of speech extended to all persons was legally extended to corporations in the 1886 Supreme Court case *Santa Clara County v. Southern Pacific Railroad.* As the media in this country have been increasingly centralized into the hands of fewer and fewer corporations, the power of these entities to control what constitutes "news" has become nearly absolute. Pulitzer Prize–winning scholar Ben Bagdikian first alerted the nation to the growing power of media corporations in his book *The Media Monopoly,* published in 1983. At that time Bagdikian demonstrated that the vast majority of print and broadcast news was controlled by a mere fifty corporations.[48] This was a fairly shocking revelation for the very limited segment of the population with access to the book. After publishing several subsequent editions over the years, Bagdikian published *The New Media Monopoly* in 2004. During the twenty-one year interval between the first edition of *The Media Monopoly* and *The New Media Monopoly,* the number of multinational corporations dominating print and broadcast media in this country was reduced from fifty to five: Time-Warner, Disney, News Corporation, Viacom, and Bertelsmann.

Through a process called conglomeration, these corporations have expanded into all media areas, buying up movie studios, theater chains, newspapers, professional sports teams, magazines, music studios and record labels, television networks, telephone companies, cable stations, and of course, news programs. The list of companies owned by the "Big Five" is extraordinarily long. Time-Warner, for example, owns the WB network, but also CNN, Headline News, CNN International, TNT, Turner Classic Movies, HBO, TBS, Primestar, New Line Film Studios, Hanna-Barbera studios, several movie-theater companies, and more. Disney owns ABC, ESPN, ESPN2, Lifetime, A&E, the History Channel, the Disney Channel, the ABC radio network, Miramax and other film studio companies, magazine and book publishing companies, hundreds of Disney retail stores, and, of course, several world-famous theme parks—to provide a very partial listing. But there is no need to delineate all of the holdings of the Big Five to recognize the power that resides in their ability to program what constitutes the news Americans will hear and what they will not hear, for that power translates directly into what Americans will debate and discuss at work, at school, at home, in the grocery store, or at the local pub. In short, it is a veritable public educational program—teaching Americans what constitutes the issues of the day, and what to think about those issues.

If it is not quite clear why this oligopolistic control of the media is a serious problem, consider this. Most would agree that if an American company were utilizing foreign sweatshop labor to maximize its profits, and in the process proliferating Third World poverty and misery, we might reasonably expect an investigative reporter, or a team of them, to expose this practice on a network nightly news program. Disney utilizes sweatshop labor in Haiti and elsewhere, but since it owns ABC, we won't find such investigative reports on the ABC nightly news.[49]

Given all of the talk about the wonderful benefits of competition in a free market, one might also reasonably expect that NBC would expose Disney's dubious production practices in an effort to draw viewers away from ABC. If this were done, however, then ABC would have to try to control the damage done by producing an equally revealing exposé on the production practices of General Electric, the multinational corporation that owns NBC. But this only highlights another danger of oligopolistic control within an industry. Such a move would start a kind of internecine war that would ultimately damage everyone. So such reports are strictly off-limits—not only for the multinational corporations that control a particular industry but for all multinational corporations. For example, when a couple of reporters working for Rupert Murdoch's News Corporation, the owner of Fox News, produced a devastating documentary condemning the corporate practices of Monsanto, a multinational agribusiness firm, the reporters were immediately fired. When a Fox executive was publicly questioned about this action, he responded that News Corporation "paid $3 billion for these TV stations. We will decide what the news is. The news is what we tell you it is."[50]

Controlling what people hear and don't hear, what they then discuss and don't discuss, has long been a highly desirable goal among those with power. As Bagdikian put it, "Leaders of democracies no less than medicine men, shamans, kings, and dictators are jealous of their power over ideas, as eager to control information as they are to control armies."[51] The topic of Sunday sermons during the feudal era could be commanded by the king. Ecclesiastical censorship of information dominated the era. The Enlightenment cry for separating church and state was every bit as much an attempt to carve out room for intellectual freedom as it was to realize religious freedom. Now, as a consequence of our embrace of free-market ideology and our near-complete inability to recognize the assumptions undergirding this ideology as the very same assumptions that undergirded the era of capitalism "red in tooth and claw," we stand in dire need of the same kind of separation, only this time we must demand the separation of corporation and state.

The public doesn't hear much, for obvious reasons, about the growing demand for media reform. But citizen concern is growing nevertheless. On those rare occasions when media corporation spokespersons are forced to defend themselves, they fall back on their First Amendment right to "free speech," a right they accrued after the dubious 1886 Supreme Court decision that gave corporations the right of "personhood." A 1976 Supreme Court decision, *Buckley v. Valeo,* extended the free "speech" of corporations to include the donation of money to political campaigns—a decision that has transformed political deliberation in the United States into a kind of spending battle, a fact that privileges candidates who themselves possess enormous wealth or can curry favor with others who have it. Both decisions were enormous blows to the vitality of democracy in America, and both must ultimately be overturned if the United States is ever to reembrace the democratic values that we ostensibly wish for others around the world.

The existence of media domination by the Big Five rests on a particular interpretation of the First Amendment, which means it might be useful to briefly revisit the circumstances surrounding the addition of this amendment, and the entire "bill of rights," to the proposed Constitution. Thomas Jefferson and a large number of anti-Federalists—generally individuals with an agrarian, civic republican, M-stream orientation to the idea of postfeudal government—roundly rejected the Constitution, in part because of its failure to delineate the rights of citizens. In order to improve the odds that the Constitution would be ratified, Hamilton and Madison reluctantly agreed to the inclusion of what was popularly called the "bill of rights." Thus the first ten amendments came into being.

The absolute insistence of the farmers and artisans who demanded the right of "free speech" clearly had nothing to do with any sort of vision on their part that multinational corporations might one day need this right to protect their ability to control what constitutes news or their ability to spend a candidate into political office. The very idea is ludicrous. These farmers and artisans wanted to be sure that they would not be denied the information they needed to ably exercise their right to a voice in the decisions that affected them. This is why the First Amendment also stipulates that Congress will make no law abridging the freedom of the press. They knew that a diverse and free press was crucial for access to information and therefore to democratic functioning. The First Amendment did not include the freedom of harness-makers to establish shops, or the freedom of blacksmiths, hatters, carpenters, or any other commercial endeavor. The free press clause, like free speech, was about protecting the nation's ability to remain democratic. The rights pertaining to commercial endeavors were included in the Fifth Amendment with the freedom to enter into contracts. The rights delineated in the First Amendment were there to ensure that the majority would not be abused by a powerful minority, a possibility that seemed ever so likely given the popular Federalist quip, "those who own the country ought to govern it."[52]

One shouldn't be too surprised that judges in the American judicial system have utilized a dubious interpretation of the First Amendment to protect multinational corporations. One need only recall that learned men seated on the nation's highest courts at one time actively defended the rights of individuals to own human slaves, and, after the Civil War, new judges actively defended the rights of some individuals to discriminate against and segregate others. It should not be surprising that most federal judges steadfastly defend corporations, especially since they are unelected and accountable only to those who put them in office, and so, indirectly, to the monied interests that put those in office who put them in office.

It is interesting to look at the initial judicial reaction to the slow development of media corporations in this country. In the 1940s, the courts clearly separated the commercial interests of newly arrived media corporations from the First Amendment. It was not until the 1970s that the this position was reversed, and in the previous two decades the courts have become a kind of impenetrable shield defending the "rights" of multinational corporations. But glaring weaknesses remain. Consider Robert McChesney's position on this question: "If the rights to be protected by the First Amendment can only be effectively employed by a fraction of the citizenry, and their exercise of these rights gives them undue political power and undermines the ability of the balance of the citizenry to exercise the same rights and/or other constitutional rights, then it is not necessarily legitimately protected by the First Amendment."[53]

Free speech is not an absolute right, as Americans well know. If its use will put people in danger, that right evaporates. The example every American has heard is that no one has the right to shout "fire" in a crowded theater. The same principle applies in the case of oligopolistic control of print and broadcast media. If Americans are endangered by this circumstance—an easy proposition to demonstrate—then the right of the Big Five to exclusive control of what Americans hear and see evaporates. How might this endangerment be demonstrated?

One could point to the number of Americans who die needlessly each year due to the fact that they have no health insurance—a statistic that is not permitted on the airwaves or in the newspapers because if it were generally known, Americans might demand changes to the health care system. And then, of course, there are the wars in which young Americans have died by the thousands. Recently Americans were taught by the media the false propositions that (1) Iraq held "weapons of mass destruction," and (2) that a connection existed between Iraq and those responsible for the terrorist attacks of September 11, 2001. In this way the Big Five helped to create the conditions that have led to the death of thousands of young Americans. At the time of this writing, Americans are still dying in Iraq, even though no citizen has a clear understanding of why we are there, since the initial rationale has been proved false. Exporting democracy is constantly touted as the new goal for the war, but such a goal makes Americans uneasy because other than vague references to Saddam Hussein as a dictator and a murderer, citizens do not know the extent to which the Iraqis lacked democracy before the war. The average American has no idea whether Hussein was popularly elected to office or not. And there is this nagging thought in the consciousness of Americans: why must we spend billions and billions of taxpayer dollars to foist democracy on a country that evidently doesn't want it? With respect to the war and the life of our young sons and daughters, Americans stand in desperate need of information that the Big Five will not provide.

But they will put on a show. Anything that includes violence, trauma, sex, or death will dominate the airwaves. Corruption and scandal, so long as it doesn't expose key members of the power elite (unless they have been targeted for expulsion, à la Bill Clinton), is also a hot "news" topic. In July 1989, the ABC Nightly News ran a segment describing an American diplomat who ostensibly leaked key state secrets to the Russians. To captivate its audience, the program switched to a shrouded scene of a man handing a briefcase to a Russian agent in Vienna. The scene was completely fabricated and staged by ABC news personnel who were not identified as such.[54] While staged film clips are not generally this egregious, snippets of gun battles, explosions, and running refugees are routinely used despite the fact they may depict circumstances completely unrelated to the story being reported.

Longtime newsman Daniel Schorr, who has worked for NBC, CBS, and NPR, publicly revealed the incredible push to report violence on the nightly news. Schorr described his efforts to question Martin Luther King Jr. in February 1968. King held a news conference to discuss the upcoming "Poor People's March," an event scheduled to take place in the nation's capital later that spring. Said Schorr:

> I came to his news conference with a CBS camera crew prepared to do what TV reporters do—get the most interesting sound bite I could in order to ensure a place in the evening news lineup. I succeeded in eliciting from him phrases on the pos-

sibility of "disruptive protest" directed at the Johnson administration and Congress. As I waited for my camera crew to pack up, I noticed that Dr. King remained seated at a table in an almost empty room, looking depressed. Approaching him, I asked him why he seemed so morose. "Because of you," he said, "and because of your colleagues in television. You try to provoke me to threaten violence, and if I don't, then you will put on television those who do. And by putting them on television, you will elect them our leaders. And, if there is violence, will you think of your part in bringing it about?"[55]

Let me share one last example of the danger involved in using the First Amendment to protect commercial speech. It is a more contemporary example, and it involves the incredible campaign to eliminate the estate tax in the United States. It is likely that there were only a few sentiments shared by virtually all of those living in the incipient, post-Revolution United States. But one of those was surely a rejection of the feudal mechanisms that enabled wealth to be passed down within families from one generation to the next. These mechanisms, like primogeniture, solidified class structures and created barriers to social and economic mobility. In the new postfeudal world, with its heavy emphasis on human freedom, Americans were determined to set a new example. In time this meant the establishment of estate taxes that would mitigate the ability of the wealthiest Americans to create a financial aristocracy. While there has always been debate about the level at which the estate tax should kick in, there has been remarkably little disagreement regarding the legitimacy of the estate tax itself.

Not anymore. Michael J. Graetz and Ian Shapiro have chronicled the remarkable story of the 1990s fight over taxing inherited wealth in their book *Death by a Thousand Cuts*.[56] The 1990s were a heady time for conservatives. Wealth was accumulating at fantastic rates in the hottest economy the nation had ever known. Additionally, in 1994, Republicans took control of both houses of Congress. With the incredible rapid accrual of wealth, philanthropic foundations sprang up everywhere, doubling the nation's total in a mere ten years. Think tanks, entities set up to conduct research legitimizing preferred policy, multiplied quickly, with two out of three falling under the classification of "conservative."[57] Coalitions concerned about the estate tax came together to create a public relations campaign aimed at selling the idea of repealing the estate tax to the American public.

Given the facts, one might be hesitant to undertake such a task. The estate tax throughout the 1990s affected only the wealthiest 2 percent of Americans. If you died single, there was no estate tax eligibility unless your estate was worth more than $650,000. For married couples, the exemption limit was a $1.3 million estate. Despite the fact that so few Americans paid the estate tax (roughly 19 percent of the estate value), it generated significant federal income—$24.4 billion in 1999.[58] In short, the estate tax seemed to be doing what it was designed to do: curbing the growth of a financial aristocracy while augmenting federal income.

With the estate tax affecting so few individuals, and with it seemingly working, that is, doing what it was designed to do, advocates of its repeal faced a difficult challenge. Their strategy was essentially twofold. First, they had to make the public believe that the estate tax threatened average Americans; and second, they had to make the tax appear as a kind of injustice, or morally skewed practice. Again, this was a tall order given the fact that the average estate in this country is not expected to top $100,000 until sometime after 2015, a figure that is light-years from the exemption limit, and also given the fact that a rejection of inherited wealth was a founding value of the nation.[59]

Tall order or not, the campaign to repeal the estate tax picked up incredible steam during the 1990s. Horror stories were circulated widely about small businessmen and farmers who were not going to be able to pass their businesses and farms on to their children. Several individuals ostensibly caught in this bind were brought before Congress to testify about the impending burden their families would face upon their death. One individual in particular made a huge impact on Congress: a black Mississippi tree farmer by the name of Chester Thigpen. In February 1995, Thigpen told the members of Congress how he was descended from slaves, how he managed to buy some land in the 1940s, how he plowed with mules, how he built up an 850 acre tree farm, and how he was now in danger of not being able to pass it on to his son.

Thigpen was a huge hit. In fact, some conservatives felt that they should name their proposed estate tax elimination bill the "Chester Thigpen bill."[60] As it turned out, however, Thigpen's estate was not in danger, as its value was actually well below the exemption limit. Thigpen's son, Roy, was asked recently if his father wrote his own congressional testimony, to which Roy laughed and guessed that it was probably written by some professors.[61] Many other small businessmen and farmers were brought before Congress who, one hopes, wrote their own testimony and were actually subject to the tax they lamented. But it was not only Congress that needed to be persuaded to eliminate the estate tax; the American public needed to be convinced as well. For that, conservatives had another strategy.

This example demonstrates the great danger of a school system geared to providing occupational wherewithal and held accountable by mere test scores. With such a system in place one can count on the American public to be uninformed about most matters of direct political concern to them, especially matters related to taxation and finance, a circumstance exacerbated by a commercialized media dedicated to the perpetuation of the status quo. Even so, with an education system predicated on preparing citizens for an active role in a democracy, sophisticated policy surveillance is much more likely—a circumstance that could have stopped the campaign to eliminate the estate tax dead in its tracks. But in a clever ploy for which several claim credit, the estate tax was renamed the "death tax" for the benefit of the American public.

Newt Gingrich, Rush Limbaugh, George W. Bush, and countless others hammered the phrase "death tax" into the consciousness of the American public. When they had used the phrase often enough, they sprinkled in the "death of the American dream" without the least bit of worry that some might envision that dream as something other than joining the ranks of the super-wealthy. Americans everywhere began to wonder if their families, too, might "get a visit from the undertaker and the IRS on the same day." Everyone dies; does everyone pay a death tax? Good question. Some polls indicated that the majority of Americans, as high as 77 percent, didn't really know if they were affected. More than a third believed that their families would definitely pay a death tax. That's better than one out of three when the reality was that only two out of 100 would in fact owe an estate tax.[62] Ninety-eight percent of the population agreed to put $24 billion back into the hands of the top 2 percent of the population, and to cover the federal revenue shortfall on their behalf. No other single circumstance better demonstrates the power of corporate-controlled media or the utility of an educational system designed to shuffle youth into their eventual occupational roles.

The sad truth is that Americans stood in desperate need of information on this issue and that the major networks, recklessly utilizing the phrase "death tax" as if it possessed some explanatory power, refused to provide it. Democracy, as Thomas Jefferson well knew, rests on the availability of information. That's why the freedom of the press was included in the First Amendment. That's why Montesquieu argued that an effective republic required a school system capable of delivering "the full power of education." That's why the establishment of common schools occurred at the height of the M-stream in American society. And that's why it is imperative that now, in the twenty-first century, citizens figure out some way to bring about media reform.

Many like to point to "public broadcasting" as the answer to commercialized media, and indeed, as the power of the airwaves became increasingly apparent in the 1930s, a kind of public versus commercial decision needed to be made in terms of who would dominate the media arena—a decision almost exactly analogous to that which needed to be made in the early 1990s regarding how the Internet would function. In both cases the advocates of commercialism won out, leaving little space for a public broadcasting or public Internet system to function. Essentially, public broadcasting advocates were left with two options: either fill a niche bypassed by commercial media, or give up the enterprise altogether. Gradually, then, public broadcasting stations began to arrange cultural programming with appeal to the nation's highly educated elite. But throughout the 1930s, 1940s, and 1950s, it was hounded by conservative politicians who demanded that public broadcasters not stray from the political issues deemed appropriate by commercial media. The conservative attack against public broadcasting went on into the 1960s, ending in 1967 when Congress passed the Public Broadcasting Act, a piece of legislation that set up the Corporation for Public Broadcasting (CPB), and subsequently, NPR and PBS.

While this should have been a major victory, the financial footing for the CPB was rendered tenuous, necessitating a reliance on large donors who then possessed the ability to limit news coverage to the narrowly acceptable confines established by commercial media. In short, public broadcasting was relegated to the margins and stripped of its ability to provide the kind of information Americans need in order to make informed decisions related to the political arena.

One might think that the American public would get fed up with the fact that their only source for news is limited to what is deemed acceptable by large multinational corporations. And certainly many are. But the system is held together by a fiction that is constantly taught and retaught to Americans: the media are liberal. Everything hinges on the majority of Americans believing this to be true. So the message will come from politicians, from conservative broadcasters, and from conservative think tanks—though these last entities often find themselves in a quandary. If they produce too much propaganda, they might begin to lose their legitimacy. This is why they jump all over studies conducted by university professors that say what they want to hear. This is why we have a "fast track" phenomenon within the academy. Would you like high visibility and notoriety quickly, without having to spend years acquiring the respect of peers through rigorous, time-consuming research and publication? Then produce a study that says one of the following:

- The media are liberal
- There is no such thing as global warming, or if there is, humans didn't cause it
- Multiculturalism is damaging American society
- The feminist movement is destroying the American family
- Minorities have only themselves to blame for their socioeconomic status
- Nationalizing health care would be an egregious mistake

It's your ticket to fifteen minutes of fame. You can become the Chester Thigpen of the academy. The price, of course, is respectability within the profession, but it's a price many academics are all too willing to pay. After all, there's a think tank out there somewhere that will gladly put you on the payroll if you say the right things.

The truth is that virtually nothing liberal makes it to the airwaves.[63] Broadcasters will pepper politicians with questions on insignificant issues to give the appearance of being liberal, and this seems to work to satisfy the public as to the charge that media are indeed liberal, but it is a charade. At times, the media will report a story that reflects badly on conservatives in power, such as when the Bush administration bribed Armstrong Williams, a conservative black TV commentator with his own nationally syndicated talk show, to the tune of $250,000, to say good things about No Child Left Behind.[64] But these incidents hit print or broadcast news one day and are gone the next, never mentioned again. The public has little chance to scrutinize the ramifications of the offense before it disappears. Yet the fact that it made the news, however briefly, serves to perpetuate the myth that the media are liberal.

This shouldn't be considered an argument for the establishment of *liberal* media so much as an argument for recognizing the educational dimension of media and then reforming the system so that it fulfills its educative role in a manner conducive to the effective functioning of a democratic society. Because the commercial aspects of media will always trump the public service aspects, government regulation is going to be required. This is a difficult switch to make because for the first half of our history as a nation, the fear was that government might withhold, or share false, information. Now, in the twenty-first century, to ask government to assume the power required to regulate the flow of free and accurate information seems like a complete reversal of the assumptions that dominated the minds of our founders. Further, given the revolving door between corporate America and political positions of all kinds, it seems like a huge and nearly impossible task to accomplish. I certainly won't argue with that. But as the anthropologist Marvin Harris once ended one of his books, "The rational response to bad odds is to try harder."[65]

Media reform advocates, environmentalists, political reform advocates, economic reform advocates—they all generally try to work for change within their realm of interest. This is a mistake, in my view, and probably attributable to the establishment and hardening of disciplinary boundaries within American higher education. Work needs to occur on all fronts, that much is true. But reformers have generally disregarded the extent to which public education determines public wherewithal for the kind of changes that are necessary, and so school change needs to be a big part of the reform agenda.

The systematic focus on the "god of economic utility" in the nation's schools combined with the policy emphasis on the production of higher test scores serve to undermine the ability of the American public to obtain any intellectual leverage over the insidious nature of the corporate curriculum, the print and broadcast news controlled by a mere handful of multinational corporations. This loudly suggests that it is imperative to balance the goals of public education so that its original purpose—preparation for life in a democracy—reemerges as part of what constitutes a P–12 or P–16 education. Creating this change is no small task, but of the three large realms most closely affecting the human condition in the twenty-first century—politics, economics, and education—it may be the one that citizens have the best chance to change. With success in that arena, the odds are considerably heightened for success in the other two. For this reason, I begin the second part of this book with a chapter that focuses on strategies for citizen action in the educational arena.

Chapter 4

Elevating Education's Public Purpose

Political, economic, and educational theory are deeply connected. This is inevitable since the subject matter of these three classes of theory—that is, power and policy, the distribution of necessities and wealth, and what people learn and believe—interpenetrate so deeply. Still, American citizens are generally unaware of these deep connections as well as the degree to which each arena functions on the basis of certain key assumptions about the human condition. L-stream logic contends that we remain economic men and women in a state of nature that boasts an inexhaustible supply of acorns and apples. Because passionate self-interest is "sewn into our very nature," a smooth-functioning republic needs a governmental structure that limits citizen participation, it needs a free market economy that endorses unlimited accumulation, and it needs a school system that focuses on the eventual economic contribution of youth.

But introduce just one flaw, one mistake, in the L-stream logic and it becomes increasingly clear that we need different political, economic, and educational arrangements. I believe the assumption that passion and greed is a central characteristic of humans everywhere is baseless. Humans certainly have a capacity for these attributes, even worse ones, but it would be a difficult proposition to prove that they are "sewn into our very nature." Perhaps, though, there will be readers who disagree. And what about the assumption that humans are *essentially* economic beings? Once again, I believe the preponderance of the evidence suggests that this is wrong. Humans are profoundly social, so much so that they suffer physically, not to mention psychologically, when social connections are lost. But again, some readers may disagree.

There is one L-stream assumption, however, that is becoming increasingly difficult to support, even for steadfast defenders of the status quo, and that is the assumption that the resources of the world are infinitely abundant. Recall that

John Locke supported the unlimited accumulation of apples so long as others could use money to purchase the apples they didn't possess. What happens when the supply of apples is exhausted, or hoarded, and can't be purchased at any price? The question becomes a serious one when oil is substituted for apples. Do the L-stream assumptions work in a world where energy is not abundant and cheap, but scarce and expensive? Do they work in a world filled with people? I don't believe they do. This suggests to me that profound changes are needed in the way we think about and ultimately do politics, economics, and education.

I invite the reader to look upon the last three chapters of this book as a long list of possible changes that might be made in the interest of creating a better, more just, and more secure future for ourselves and others throughout the world. Some may appeal to you, others may not. It is my hope, though, that one change strategy or another might resonate and become a cause to which the reader will contribute some part of him- or herself. Keep in mind the often-quoted words of Margaret Mead: "Never doubt that a small group of committed people can change the world. Indeed it is the only thing that ever has."

Throughout the 2008 presidential election "season," *change* became the buzz word, the critical slogan for aspiring candidates in both parties. In addition to problems with our health care system and the continuing war in Iraq, our very infrastructure had begun to fail, and it failed in plain sight of the American public.[1] The food supply, as an example, was interrupted in turn by the 2006 "spinach crisis," a green onion scare a few months later, and then the recall of tons of tainted meats from the Midwest early in 2007. According to researchers at the Center for Disease Control and Prevention, food contamination causes more than 325,000 hospitalizations and 5,000 deaths each year—statistics ignored by the nightly news.[2] Even the pet food industry was shaken by a tainted production process that resulted in the death of hundreds of cats and dogs and suffering on the part of thousands more. This was followed by the revelation that tens of thousands of Mattel, Inc., toys were produced with lead paint—a potentially deadly circumstance for American youth. And in July 2007, a massive bridge collapsed without warning during rush hour in Minneapolis, Minnesota.

Beyond our infrastructure difficulties there is a deeper looming concern that haunts many Americans. What if it is true that an ever-growing economy is a biophysical impossibility? Will we, one day, if that day has not already passed, discover that further efforts at growth will only render the vast majority of the earth's inhabitants poorer, not richer? Will more growth efforts—more buildings, more factories, more irrigation, more appliances, more roads—speed up the depletion of the earth's finite resources and render the health of local ecosystems increasingly more tenuous? The classical economics tradition has great faith in the concept of growth—faith built up over a couple of centuries in which the world was sparsely populated by people—but that faith cannot change the fact that the earth is now filled with people (approaching seven billion), nor can it change the fact that the biosphere is finite. Commenting on the difficulty involved in changing human behavior in recognition of these circumstances, former World Bank economist Herman Daly wrote:

> Because establishing and maintaining a sustainable economy entails an enormous change of mind and heart by economists, politicians, and voters, one might well be tempted to declare that such a project would be impossible. But the alternative to a sustainable economy, an ever growing economy, is biophysically impossible. In choosing between tackling a political impossibility and a biophysical impossibility, I would judge the latter to be more impossible and take my chances with the former.[3]

Change "in the mind(s) and heart(s)" of economists, politicians, and voters is another way of saying "change in the way we *do* economics, politics, and education." We discussed in Chapter 3 two of the largest educational institutions in American society: the public school, and the print and broadcast news that makes up the corporate "school." The latter is not subject to much of anything in the way of democratic control. Citizens who are aware of this share the burden of trying to create media reform, but we should also recognize that the most direct path to that end may be through the other large educational institution: the public school. By comparison, for instance, a local school is much more amenable, or at least potentially much more amenable, to grass-roots change efforts.

Our schools were originally created to enable citizens to shoulder the burden of democracy; that is, they initially had a distinctly public purpose. As we saw in the previous chapter, by 1918 that public purpose had been effectively buried in favor of elevating private purpose and in the process leaving matters of statecraft to the nation's elite. Said another way, the goal of schooling was converted almost exclusively to outfitting the nation's youth for jobs in the economic arena. In recent decades, that goal has become cemented by educational policy that has greatly increased the amount of standardized testing in schools on the dubious assumption that higher test scores would mean students are learning more of something with presumed value—or perhaps on the even more dubious assumption that higher test scores would increase our lead as the world's dominant economic and military power.

The truth of the matter is that performing well on exams is not a skill that lends itself particularly well even to the world of work, much less to more substantive goals, like the well-being of a democracy. The testing fetish that currently dominates the educational policy landscape will perhaps die a natural death unless conspiracy theorists are accurate, meaning this fetish is actually a part of a concerted effort to delegitimize schools so that they may be turned over to for-profit investors and managers. But numbers tell us so little of consequence, and besides, even if we arrived at a point where the exams resulted in steadily increasing scores, they cannot go up forever. There are certainly admirable uses to be made of standardized exams, diagnosing learning difficulties, identifying curricular gaps, and so on, but to convert them into the end goal of an educational system is to expose a kind of intellectual poverty—a general lack of real insight into the nature of the human condition—the natural result of allowing our educational system 100 years worth of institutional momentum moving away from any sophisticated definition of a true education.

Although like political and economic reform, educational change is a monumental task, there are a couple of key differences that may mean that it is in fact the arena most susceptible to citizen action. For one, the system is composed of local schools. For another, citizens are rightfully accorded a voice in the affairs of the local school since it so profoundly touches the deepest concern of parents— their children. What can citizens do to move schools in the direction of something approaching the ability to deliver "the full power of education"? For one, they can reconsider some of what I take to be very worthy reform proposals of the past. Second, there is a growing list of current proposals with great promise as well.

Past Change Strategies to Reconsider

A significant educational experiment took place at the height of America's worst economic depression. At what came to be called "coal camps" in West Virginia, particularly one called Scott's Run, poverty, sickness, and the most dreadful of living conditions pressed in on laid-off miners and their families. Conditions were so bad that Scott's Run became a focal point for New Deal reformers, many of whom had fashioned a community-oriented vision related to desirable political, economic, and educational arrangements. Guided by the efforts of Eleanor Roosevelt and funded by the financier Barnard Baruch, reformers decided to purchase a farm belonging to a man named Arthur a short distance from Scott's Run. There they created a model community called Arthurdale with an economy based on part-time employment and subsistence agriculture. An elaborate application procedure was created, and applications were distributed to the idle miner families in Scott's Run. Those selected to become a part of the experiment moved into newly built houses with small plots of land during 1933 and 1934.

The architects of Arthurdale took great pains to center the new model community around the school. They chose a progressive educator with a distinguished reputation, Elsie Clapp (a former student of John Dewey's), to be the director of School and Community Activities. Clapp and other reformers involved in the project believed that the poverty and degradation of the coal camps had destroyed the communal bonds that existed among the miners prior to the arrival of the coal companies. The school at Arthurdale would design its curriculum so that these communal bonds could be restored.

The new community residents worked with reformers to design and build the school buildings. They were constructed separately and detached from one another and were designed to mirror the architecture of the new houses in the community. The school buildings were to be shared by community residents for use as a club meeting place, a place of worship, a place of study (in the library), and for work (in the shops or the home economics room). In fact, clubs of all sorts were started in Arthurdale in concert with adult education efforts, including cooking and canning classes, woodworking classes, and well-baby health care classes.

School officially began in Arthurdale in the fall of 1934. Young children came to the nursery school, and older children and youth took their seats in K–12 classrooms. They didn't stay seated long, however, for the community-based curriculum of the Arthurdale schools was based on an active pedagogy. First-graders studied farm life. They were frequently out watching and taking rudimentary notes on the work being conducted in the small fields and plots of Arthurdale. Those working the fields became de facto teachers as they were asked to explain why and how they were doing their work. Class gardens were planted, butter was churned, and replicas of all the economic activity of Arthurdale were created with blocks produced in the school shops. Second-graders focused on the continuing construction of the entire village of Arthurdale. They learned about carpentry and stone masonry through the use of hand tools, but more important, they were introduced to mathematical concepts through their study of community construction. Third-graders studied Native American life by constructing teepees, meat-drying racks, looms, fireplaces, and the like. Fourth-graders restored an old log cabin and studied pioneer life. The log cabin, it turned out, was part of the property owned by the area's first white settler, Colonel Fairfax, a friend and contemporary of George Washington.

Efforts were made to enculturate the community's older children into a sustainable local economy by providing skills centered on food production, furniture making, and glass production through cooperative efforts. High school teachers believed that character and integrity were developed through substantive contributions to community life, and they tried to orchestrate their lessons in literature, history, science, and mathematics with this larger goal in mind. As the school director, Clapp worked hard to be sure that teachers allowed traditional school subjects to grow out of the study of community life—not the other way around—a significant distinction. In fact, this emphasis, and the steadfast dedication to it on the part of Arthurdale teachers, is one reason why this eighty-year-old experiment in progressive education remains, even today, perhaps the best example of communitarian theory applied to schooling.

But there were problems on the horizon. The National Association for the Advancement of Colored People (NAACP) railed at the fact that while a quarter of the applicants for Arthurdale were black, none were chosen to join the community. In fact, a deliberate decision was made to keep Arthurdale white. Further, because Arthurdale applicants had to produce a recommendation from a former employer, those Scott's Run residents who had been most involved with union activity were not accepted. This contributed to animosity between the residents of Scott's Run and their near neighbors in Arthurdale. Other West Virginia residents saw the community as a radical venture, and the small stream of local funding began to dry up as a result. Even some of Arthurdale's own residents began to question whether the community-based emphasis of the schools might be inhibiting the social mobility of their children.

Clapp and other Arthurdale reformers clung to the idea that reinserting the self-sufficient culture of West Virginia was the secret to allowing Arthurdale residents to lead fulfilled lives. They consciously avoided any curricular entanglement with larger political and economic issues, such as the behavior of coal companies or the suffering of their former neighbors still living in Scott's Run. Although the ancient log cabin they restored had been a slave dwelling, they refused to engage the history of slavery in the region.

As the initial momentum of the Arthurdale experiment began to subside, it became clear to Clapp and to others that the community needed some connection to the nation's larger political economy. Arthurdale's defenders lobbied Congress for the funds needed to establish a factory in the community that would supply post office furniture to the federal government. For a host of reasons, not the least of which was the diminished federal budget during the depression years, Congress denied the request. This decision symbolized the end of the experiment for most of the reformers working at Arthurdale. Clapp and many other teachers left for other positions. Before the decade was over, Arthurdale schools were operating, for all intents and purposes, like every other West Virginia school.

The accounts of former students indicate that the pedagogy of Arthurdale schools during the height of the Great Depression was highly successful. Students understood that there was little delineation between the subjects they were taught and the life of the community. Arthurdale's failing, however, lay in its monocultural approach to curriculum, its acceptance of racial segregation, its failure to allow a cross section of even the local white population to become involved, and its uncritical embrace of preindustrial West Virginia culture at the expense of engaging contemporary dynamics caused by the intrusion of industrial forces in their own backyard. Insert these into school systems operating with the same steadfast dedication to community-based curriculum, and it is possible to envision a dramatically new way to do schooling in this country.

Something called "the project method" was introduced to American teachers during the Progressive Era. John Dewey and others wrote in particular about the ways that science instruction could benefit by engaging students in various projects. Dewey argued that rather than storing up information, students might experiment and generate scientific understanding through the process of doing science. The still-prevalent "science fair" is an outgrowth of this early movement related to what came to be called the project method. It was another Columbia professor, however, William Heard Kilpatrick, who published an article titled simply "The Project Method" in *Teachers College Record* in 1918, who is credited with popularizing this approach across all grade levels and all school subjects. The article was enormously popular. In fact, it took 60,000 reprints of that issue of *Teachers College Record* to satisfy the enormous demand.[4]

At a time when Internet-based research opportunities have greatly expanded possibilities for the project method, its deployment has diminished in the wake of standards-based instruction and testing, though many educators are actively working to repopularize it. The ascendancy of constructivist learning theory, in fact, seems to beg for use of the project method. If learning is indeed a constructive process, students working through projects of various kinds would seem to naturally facilitate the gradual construction of student understanding.

In 1983, shortly after President Reagan's commission of noneducators released *A Nation at Risk*, John Goodlad published the results of a massive study of schooling in America in a book titled *A Place Called School.* He concluded with some fairly radical recommendations for public education—all of which, of course, were ignored. Had we moved quickly as a nation to implement the structural reforms he described, we wouldn't labor today with a 40 percent high school dropout rate in our large cities, and the teaching profession wouldn't be paralyzed by straightjacket policies like NCLB. In fact, improvement in the quality of American culture, let alone American schooling, would be well under way. As a consequence, it is worth a short digression to describe Goodlad's recommendations.

The essential thrust of his plan was to move the educational experience up by a couple of years in order to begin at age four and finish something analogous to the current K–12 curriculum by age sixteen. Under his plan, the school experiences of America's youth would unfold, roughly, in three four-year blocks. The primary block would begin on each child's fourth birthday, their first day in school. In this way each child begins with a birthday party and the warmest of welcomes into the culture of the school. According to Goodlad,

> The timing and rate of departure would approximate the timing and rate of entry—departure from the first phase at or near the eighth birthday, from the second near the twelfth, and from the third near the sixteenth. Children beginning a primary school would enter, more or less randomly, one of up to three or, at the most, four nongraded, four-year units of not more than 100 children each. For each unit this means the entry and departure every year of 25 children—two or three out and two or three in each month. The tumultuous business of socializing 25 or so beginners each September is completely eliminated. Schooling immediately takes on a highly individualized character.... Given the maxima of four units and 100 children per unit, the maximum enrollment of a primary school is 400.[5]

The interested reader can find much more detail related to this plan by picking up a copy of *A Place Called School.* For now it's merely important to get a glimpse of the many advantages Goodlad's proposal represents. Indeed, given all of the advantages, one can't help but wonder why the United States never attempted a change of this kind. The few criticisms that were voiced regarding the plan had to do with what kids ages sixteen through eighteen would do—and, predictably, how this might affect high school athletics.

But imagine what might be done with a civil service dimension to the educational endeavor in this country. Imagine community colleges everywhere orchestrating work experiences for those who avail themselves of civil service options in health clinics, in community neighborhood restoration projects, in pre-age-four childcare, in after-school youth clubs, on newly created cooperative urban farms—the list could go on and on. Military service and college, too, would be among the options for sixteen-year-olds. The opportunities are really quite endless, and the potential benefit for improving the quality and feel of America's public places is almost beyond calculation.

John Goodlad's proposal is merely one example of a plan for structural change that might have moved American society into a far healthier position as a nation— positively affecting lives the educational system cannot currently reach—and at the very same time infusing youthful energy into the restoration of public places and into the care of America's most helpless citizens. The first U.S. president to put a distinguished educational statesman, someone like John Goodlad or Linda Darling-Hammond, in charge of the federal Department of Education stands at least a fighting chance of getting structural reforms of this magnitude under way. A parade of ex-governors or cronies of one sort or another into that cabinet position, with virtually no insight into the huge array of issues that come to bear on educational questions, will leave us mired in our current circumstances.

It should be obvious that a theme of this book is that community is a fundamental dimension of healthy human life. Community provides the place where democracy can become real, community can provide a kind of check on needless economic production and consumption, and, it turns out, community is central to optimizing the educational opportunities afforded youth. Scholars have come to these conclusions in the past, Winstanley, Montesquieu, and Jefferson most notably, perhaps, but the list is much longer and includes such contemporary and near-contemporary figures as Mohandas Gandhi, Martin Luther King Jr., Wendell Berry, Aldo Leopold, David Orr, and E. F. Schumacher.

The Arthurdale experiment demonstrates that an attempt to create community in the absence of democracy or by ignoring injustice will inevitably fail. Writ large, that lesson looks like this: when one portion of society's population receives the best medical care available and another portion goes without it altogether, or any similar significant societal discrepancy occurs, a sense of community diminishes. In such places we should assume that disaffection, apathy, despair, drug use, and crime will become quite prominent. When imbalances grow to a global scale, as they clearly have done, antipathy, hatred, and violence are the imminently predictable result. The threat of terrorism in the twenty-first century is a perfect example of the outgrowth of politics, economics, and education unfettered from the standards created by healthy human communities. When one adds to that the development of impending environmental catastrophes from overheating the earth and overutilizing the earth's store of Paleolithic sunlight (i.e., fossil fuels), the stakes premised on reinserting community as a value into political, economic, and educational reckoning are enormous—indeed, they have never been larger.

The Progressive Era switch in the ends of education, from enculturation into democratic political life to enculturation into the world of work, was a major step backward for democracy in America. This "world of work" approach to education became embedded in American culture by reliance on accountability mechanisms limited, for all intents and purposes, to standardized tests. Because of the huge array of cultural/linguistic issues that confound the results of these tests, we have built an educational system that privileges white students of wealth and discriminates against various minority groups and the poor, collectively.

To make matters worse, during the past twenty years or so, the education policy arena has clamped down on schools with such vigor that the system actually performs poorly even for the most privileged in American society. No Child Left Behind was built on the assumption that the establishment of learning standards was optimal education policy. But there's something embarrassingly childlike about the logic of standards, a logic that goes something like this: "Let's decide what all students should know. That way we can test them to see if they know it." The proponents of standards-based reform were apparently untroubled by questions related to the nature of knowledge, or the relationship of knowledge to the places where it is utilized, or the burden of seeing that knowledge is used well in the world, or any other kinds of questions that might confound the idea that all kids in each state should learn the same things at roughly the same time in their lives. Or worse still, that all kids in *every* state should learn the same things at the same time.

Beyond this shortcoming, there is a large, looming dark side to standards-based reform—though few like to talk about it. Standards undeniably shift the pedagogical focus of schools to right and wrong answers. The result is a kind of pedagogical tragedy as the development and nurturance of problem-solving skills and creativity becomes the first and most obvious casualty in the nation's schools. Yale's well-known creativity expert, Robert Sternberg, described this circumstance. Said Sternberg, "The increasingly massive and far-reaching use of conventional standardized tests is one of the most effective, if unintentional, vehicles this country has ever created for suppressing creativity."[6] At a time when the world has been declared metaphorically flat, creativity seems like a highly desirable characteristic for American youth to possess—but current educational policy might just as well overtly censor its development in the nation's schools.

The second casualty of standards-based reform is a broad curriculum. Because of the design of NCLB, performance on math and reading, and to a slightly lesser degree science, has been the primary focus. Stories of elementary schools that limit the curriculum exclusively to math and reading abound. Social studies, art, music, and even physical education have been jettisoned, the latter despite rapidly rising rates of childhood obesity. On top of this, governors meet frequently to collectively berate state departments of education for not doing enough to focus the high school curriculum on math and science—implicitly maintaining that dubious idea that widespread knowledge of math and science is the key to economic growth and development.[7]

The hubris behind the narrowing of America's school curriculum is nothing short of staggering. In over 2,000 years of Western history we have been exposed to countless sophisticated definitions of what constitutes an education, or an educated person, and none of these call for a curriculum built near-exclusively on math and science. In fact, it is fairly easy to make a good argument as to why such a narrow educational focus would be culturally and in other ways devastating to the United States. While math and science may be the well-spring of technological advances, they yield little intellectual leverage over how new technologies will interact with human society. It takes students who have studied literature or history or philosophy or art to protect society from the unintended consequences of technological advance—from the damage done by chlorofluorocarbons, for instance, or from CO_2 emissions. It takes students who have studied art, music, folklore, and similar subjects to prevent mining companies from removing mountaintops in the search for coal deposits. In short, a healthy society needs citizens who are broadly educated and who only thereafter specialize across the spectrum of academic disciplines.

The third casualty of standards-based reform is innovative, passionate, instruction. The teaching act has two inescapable dimensions: one is curricular, the other instructional. The standards movement has had the effect of removing curricular judgment and curricular decisionmaking from the professional lives of teachers. The result has been that a huge part of what makes the profession fulfilling was taken away—leaving only decisions about how to teach the material. And even this decision is far from sacred as more and more principals demand a certain type of instruction in the foolish hope that *one* instructional approach will raise test scores for *all*. In point of fact, it is not just principals who have begun to demand a kind of instructional uniformity. We have recently witnessed the emergence of a totally new class of school personnel sometimes described as "textbook police." When a large district purchases a curriculum from a large textbook company, it will send "police" out to schools to make sure teachers are teaching the right way, with the right amount of time, and so on. Company profits increasingly depend on improving test scores in large districts, a circumstance that cannot be left to the idiosyncratic instructional practices of teachers. If these companies are going to make huge profits, teachers must be policed to see that they are doing their part toward that end.

The standards-based milieu in schools, flanked by a kind of "big brother" federal educational policy in NCLB, is slowly converting the teaching profession into a technical enterprise—sapping the passion and excitement teachers might otherwise bring to the classroom. It is ironic that this would happen in the face of clear research results that demonstrate that the teacher is the largest single variable affecting student achievement. Given this, you would think there would be a strong push to improve the professional lives of teachers rather than diminish them. And in this regard it would be fruitful to take heed of Antonio Damasio's research. A world-renowned neurobiologist, Damasio argued in his best-selling book *Descartes' Error* that human rational power can only be brought to its highest levels through the deployment of feeling, emotion, and passion.[8]

The federal government, thanks to the Constitution, has no official role to play in education. Many have viewed this circumstance as an indication of judicious wisdom among the Constitution authors. I don't believe this was the case. Education, or citizen improvement, was simply not a part of the project that the Constitution represents—and thus they did not condone or even make mention of the notion of public education. Those issues that went undiscussed in the Constitution by default became the province of the individual states. Again, that is our good fortune, for it legitimates local and state efforts to turn away from federal education policies like NCLB. Regrettably, many states are just as much in the grip of powerful corporate interests as is the federal government. This means there may be little opportunity for those states to declare educational independence from the strictures of federal education policy. If that is the case, however, there is always the local school itself.

New Change Strategies for Consideration

Most teachers will tell you that it is far easier to assess a child's progress via daily contact over the course of a school year than to make that attempt on the basis of one afternoon with a test booklet and a sheet full of bubbles. Most will tell you that if they had the opportunity they could create exciting lessons for students, lessons that pique student interest and generate real enthusiasm for learning. Most will tell you that a classroom does not have to be a deadening, emotionally flat place where mandated "stuff" is covered and recovered, taught and retaught. Most will tell you, however, that in order for these things to happen, the school must have a degree of curricular and instructional independence it does not currently possess.

There are ways this may be changed locally, however, if the will is there to do so. Parents have the right to expect that their child's school will nurture creativity and will expose students to a broad curriculum—and thus multiple approaches to problem-solving. And parents have a right to schools that will staff classrooms with teachers who exhibit passionate teaching. If you would like to see real change in the local school, build a coalition of parents intent on demanding these things. For those teachers and administrators fully committed to their profession, such a coalition of parents would constitute a breath of fresh air. Via school-community forums it may be possible to generate enough commitment to convince the local board of education to act courageously on behalf of the school's children. It might convince the local board of education, in fact, to openly embrace an act of civil disobedience of sorts by rejecting the mandate that they submit AYP (adequate yearly progress on test scores) data.

Almost on cue, as if defenders of the status quo anticipated the possibility of such action, an attack on democratically elected school boards has already begun. Implausible as it might seem, school boards have been declared "weak" and undesirable. If they could somehow be replaced by the kind of board of directors industries possess, perhaps via mayoral appointment, public education might be saved, or so the argument goes. As much as they would like to see control of the nation's schools taken out of the hands of local citizens, they have been forced to admit that "the American people are accustomed to school boards" and that "it is doubtful whether an effort to change the school board structure would be successful."[9]

Any school board, or any school community, intent on rejecting NCLB needs to be equipped with a better plan for assessment, a better plan for demonstrating and documenting the academic achievement of all children who attend the local school. As well, a school declaring curricular and instructional independence must have the support of parents and community members that surround it. Citizens whose first passion might be the health of the environment, or media reform, or term limits, or campaign finance reform, or any other sort of political or economic reform, need to recognize that a crucial first step to achieving those ends may well be a genuine conversation about what goes on in the local school. Allow teachers to mine the curricular and instructional potential of the local community, the local neighborhood, and you have taken a major step toward raising the consciousness of the next generation with respect to the full range of circumstances—political, economic, social—affecting one's home, family, neighbors, and neighborhood.

It is impossible to overemphasize the need for an alternative plan for concerted, systematic assessment of student learning. Periodic standardized testing can certainly be a part of this, but it will not replace genuine oversight on the part of teachers *and* community members. In fact, one structural change that should probably occur at the state level is a demand that each school select a Board of Assessors by lot—that is, a group of adults charged with assessing student learning and monitoring the curricular decisions of teachers. Teachers, in fact, should make periodic curricular reports to such a board, in effect forcing them to think deeply about their curricular choices and how they might affect the subsequent achievement of students across the full range of school subjects, art and music no less than math and science.[10]

Here is what such a reform might look like. Each school could convene a ten-member Board of Assessors chosen by lot for a two-year term from the vicinity surrounding the school. This board would take over the curricular and instructional monitoring duties of the elected school board, leaving them free to deal with personnel, infrastructure, and budget issues. A process could be created that would allow citizens to decline to serve on the Board of Assessors if there are good reasons to do so, but, generally speaking, the selection process should be analogous to the one used to select jurors for legal trials. The responsibility of the board would be to engage in discussions with teachers about their curricular and instructional choices, to decide how well these choices articulate across grades and subjects, and to become intimately involved in the assessment of student learning. Annually, the Board of Assessors should make a report to the State Department of Education relaying their level of satisfaction with the progress made at the school. In this way the matter of accountability is given substance, and a school's community will be allowed to decide how well its school is doing, rather than leaving this to a distant testing agency where the employees have never met the local students on whom they pass statistical judgments.

With curricular and instructional freedom, teachers will be able to craft lessons that capitalize on the relevance of the local context, including how the neighborhood and the school's neighbors have been treated by past and current policy decisions. In other words, the schools can become an invaluable laboratory for policy surveillance, an invaluable agent in the promotion of import substitution and ethical consumption. Through learning in the traditional school subjects, students can do the research required for community members who wish to know the conditions they create among the producers of what they buy.

Educators will recognize the "project method" and elements of what has come to be called "place-based pedagogy" in this reform. Some might be quick to argue that the large majority of the nation's teachers may be unfamiliar with these approaches. But I believe that the act of curricular and instructional liberation itself will move teachers in this direction on their own devices, and I think that that development could be augmented with help from the nation's schools and colleges of education. Higher education, generally, could play a major role, too, especially in terms of assisting local Boards of Assessors to do their jobs well. This would be an invaluable sort of professorial service that could come from professors across a range of disciplines. We have a little experience with this stemming from Chicago's experiment with Local School Councils—the elected members of which were required to participate in eighteen hours of training initially provided by three Chicago-area higher education institutions, but later taken over by the Chicago school district itself.[11] While there are many positive developments stemming from this 1988 reform effort, immersing the councils in personnel decisions, particularly decisions related to hiring and firing principals, has been a huge drawback for the effectiveness of the councils, in my estimation. Further, the fact that council members have been elected rather than being selected by lot has introduced some of the worst elements of American politics—meetings attended by parents and community members who demand that the council take or rescind some action or another.

A nonelected Board of Assessors, whose focus is on curriculum and instruction, might very well orchestrate occasional public hearings, but the vast majority of the issues and concerns that generate antipathy and disruption at school board meetings would be left to the elected board. Part of the training colleges and universities would offer newly selected Assessor Board members would be how to communicate its role to the general public.

Still, as everyone has heard, "democracy is messy." Within this reform measure there is potential for conflict between the nonelected Board of Assessors and the elected School Board, or between the assessors and teachers, or between the assessors and administrators. The American system of education has not prepared citizens well for the kind of give-and-take conversations that the assessors would need to embrace. Colleges can be a huge help by providing assistance toward that end, however.

Still, most of the assistance from institutions of higher education would entail helping the board members build a new vision for schools—helping them see the potential for connecting schoolwork to the vitality of the community that the school serves, helping them understand the pivotal role of context, of relevance, to human learning. I have no intention of prescribing what a local school might do, but it is easy for me to envision a school that chooses to require a well-crafted piece of local legislation from each grade-level class, or a school that requires each grade-level class to adopt a neighborhood building—one that is currently an eyesore—for a complete restoration. Schools might identify a range of areas within which students must wield traditional school subjects in the interest of community betterment—aesthetics, health care, housing, historical preservation, oral history, community music and theater, local poetry, the identification of economic niches working catalytically toward import substitution, state and federal policy analysis, research related to the production of goods and services consumed locally, opinion surveys, cash-flow surveys, and environmental monitoring and testing, to name a few. A school's Board of Assessors would need to elicit from teachers how students will benefit academically from such projects and how what is learned will serve as a foundation for future learning. Additionally, they would need to serve as witnesses to student academic growth.

Teachers who have both the time and the incentive to be creative, to work together, can find an infinite number of ways to embed curriculum into local circumstances and conditions such that the traditional school subjects are taught within a context, the relevance of which would be abundantly evident—dramatically increasing the likelihood that school subjects will be well learned. The great shortcoming of what is now all the rage—standards-based education—is that it decontextualizes curriculum so that its use is unknown, or at best, assumed to exist somewhere far off in every student's future. This is why John Dewey chastised American education, claiming it put children on a waiting list and kept them there until they were released by adulthood. The net effect of what we are currently doing in the name of education all across this country is very much like assigning the study of Spanish without the opportunity to use it. Five years later it is forgotten with ease. Any piece of the curriculum, devoid of an opportunity to wield it, suffers the same fate as unutilized Spanish instruction. The time-tested colloquialism is accurate: use it or lose it.

The best intentions surrounding learning standards fly in the face of what we know about how humans learn. But even if this were not the case, there would still be ample reason to liberate teachers such that they might embed lessons in the context of the immediate community—ample reason if there is general agreement about the ends of education, that economic productivity does not solely define the human condition; that is, that one's occupation is not the only means by which a life may be rendered rich or poor. A republic requires a school system that delivers "the full power of education," to quote Montesquieu once again. Such a system will of necessity utilize the immediate community to balance economic *and political* enculturation. And, to our great good fortune, reinvigorated communities mean a reinvigorated democracy.

Short of statewide legislation mandating Boards of Assessors, however, those schools that garner the commitment of a sufficiently large group of community members, teachers, and administrators enough to orchestrate an official act of curricular and instructional independence may well wish to build a local Board of Assessors into their alternative assessment plans. It would be almost impossible for a state department of education to punish a school for declaring pedagogical independence when the declaration comes with the support of the majority of the school's immediate community.

A school that frees itself from curricular and instructional shackles represented by policies like NCLB is free to take full advantage of what we know about learning and the development of human understanding. While the current policymaking regime seeks to entrench the status quo with an accountability movement that will effectively limit curricular or instructional creativity, research into the nature of learning and the development of understanding suggests that we need to promote an educational agenda that celebrates and expands what the current accountability movement limits and restricts. Human understanding is largely believed to be a constructive process.[12] It requires certain key elements such as new information, old information, and a kind of cognitive negotiation between the two in an attempt to appraise and exercise judgment regarding an evidential base. It is this last element that is widely neglected in America's schools but is a *sine qua non* with regard to the development of understanding.

One reason why so little attention is paid to the cultivation of judgment concerning evidence has to do with the purpose of schooling. If the enterprise is predominantly about occupational preparation, then the verdict, so to speak, is already in. We know what students need to get if they are going to be ready for the job market. Our best students, those clearly headed for the important and interesting jobs in society, are often afforded an education that includes the cultivation of reasoned judgment. They are the exception, however, for most students are merely asked to acquire certain sets of facts and skills. Our stepped-up accountability efforts are designed to be sure that our students get them.

If we step out of the Lockean tradition and into Montesquieu and Jefferson's view of the world, however, it becomes apparent that at least one purpose of schools must be to attend to developing wherewithal for the political role youth will play as they move into adulthood. Given their interpretation of what makes us fully human, all children require the ability to look at problems from multiple perspectives, and all children require the ability to form reasoned judgments regarding evidence. The dignity of a life doesn't reside totally in an individual's ability to affect his or her economic condition; it also resides in his or her capacity as a citizen affecting the lives of others. In other words, there is a social or communal dimension to life that requires educational cultivation.

This suggests that it is not enough for students to acquire history or math facts; they must also acquire the ability to wield them. This will do two things. One, it will provide practice at playing a political role, perhaps through local associations, thus invigorating democracy; second, it will provide a catalyst for cognitive activity, that constructive process that results in the development of understanding. This is the essential thrust of what has become known as place-based education.[13]

Mathematics, history, and virtually all of the traditional school subjects can be taught in such a way that students feel compelled to use them. There is likely no better path to the development of disciplinary understanding and no better preparation for the political role democratic citizens should play. As student skills and abilities increase, the scope of the curriculum can broaden. For example, math students can be asked to use algebra, geometry, and statistics in ways that are beneficial to the policy makers in their community. They can examine a huge range of issues that dominate debate in the policy arena, including demographics, environmental concerns, income distribution, tax structures, the availability and cost of goods and services, safety concerns, housing patterns, employment opportunities, interest rate fluctuations, corporate citizenship, and health care. Virtually every school subject could provide a viewpoint from which to examine these issues. All subjects could contribute to the development of wherewithal regarding the merits of evidence, for all children are political actors every bit as much as they are economic actors.

Moving the educational narrative in this country away from what the late Neil Postman called the "god of economic utility" toward a balanced approach that yields skills and knowledge of the sort necessary for the economic arena and the capacity for reasoned judgment among all students necessary for the political arena, is the great educational task that faces this nation.[14] It should be noted that shifting the educational narrative in this way would constitute at least a partial return to the schooling purposes identified by the founders of the common school in the 1830s and 1840s, a period that marked the high point of the M-stream tradition in American consciousness. I do not mean to suggest that the vision of Henry Barnard, Horace Mann, Caleb Mills, and the rest of the common school founders was not marred by dubious ulterior motives: assimilating immigrants, posturing for denominational hegemony, and so on. But whatever else one might say about them, the idea that schools would exist to provide economic wherewithal for citizens, or to create a well-oiled economy, was a minor theme at the very best. In other words, preparation for democratic life is what public schools were created for in the first place. It is past time to put an end to our century-long amnesia related to what schools are for. Though the current policy context yields little reason to be optimistic that this might happen, the larger scholarly trends under way all point to a renewed interest in the role played by community in what it means to be human, a development that suggests that the insertion of community in public school curriculum may not be as far off as one might think.

The essential message of this chapter has to do with curricular and instructional liberation for teachers and schools. Teachers need to be free to frame lessons in light of neighborhood dynamics, the conditions that affect the real and everyday lives of students. In other words, teachers need to take children off what Dewey called "the waiting list." The end result is that they will thereby educate citizens rather than self-interest pursuers. Students so educated will be far more likely to shoulder the burden of democracy, to interrogate the sham public-relations campaigns sponsored by corporate media, things like "eliminating the death tax."

This process has the additional benefit of resting on a completely new opportunity for civic engagement on the part of citizens: participation on a local Board of Assessors selected by lot. The curricular and instructional liberation of teachers must be monitored by the community so that the public can gradually feel greater and greater comfort with an educational system that minimizes the use of standardized exams. If we are unable to raise the social and political dimensions of life to at least an equal educational status with the economic dimension, none of the political and economic reforms in the remainder of this book have a serious chance of coming to fruition—meaning America will inevitably succumb to what Jane Jacobs has called a Dark Age Ahead.

Create study groups composed of teachers, community members, administrators, and school board members. Read this book or any from a long list of those written to challenge Americans to revitalize communities and thereby invigorate democracy. Make a bold step. Create a Board of Assessors and liberate local teachers. Declare independence from educational policy ill-suited for local circumstances. Do these things as a commitment to a better future across the full range of dimensions to life that make it worth living. Economic reform of the sort created by agrarian economists or political reform of the civic republican political tradition embodied by the likes of Winstanley, Jefferson, and Tocqueville can put us on a far healthier cultural trajectory, but only if they are buttressed by schools that specifically reject social Darwinism in the interest of upholding new ends for education. Create those schools, and allow economic and political reform to unfold in their wake. As Wendell Berry observed many years before NCLB, local schools no longer serve the local community; instead, "they serve the government's economy and the economy's government."[15] In so doing, they destroy the promise of democracy. Find the courage to change the schools, and the doors to economic and political reform are once again open.

CHAPTER 5

Genius and Virtue

What we do with our children will determine what we are, collectively, as a society. Accordingly, Wendell Berry once noted, "There can be no greater blow to the integrity of a community than the loss of its school or loss of control of its school."[1] Our failure to see the connection between schools and healthy communities, and, one step further, the connection between healthy communities and the well-being of democratic processes, was perhaps the most serious intellectual shortcoming of the twentieth century. The great sins of that century—racism, prejudice, sexism, homophobia, discrimination, environmental degradation, ceaseless wars of dubious merit, and a generalized indifference to the sanctity of human life beyond the fetal stage—they can all be connected to our failure to come to grips with the centrality of community to the human condition.

It should be clear by this point that by *community* I am referring to an authentic process of sharing, negotiating, and finding meaning in social experiences, including decisions that emerge and the actions involved in trying to implement decisions. Community is a process for getting things done in a manner fundamentally distinct from bureaucracies (or other hierarchic organizational structures) that often depend on the charisma and vision of leaders. Community is a place where people can will, and work for, a better world through efforts at home. Community is a place where genius and virtue are not constrained by the dictates of line authority—a place where democracy, therefore, can flourish.

As Robert Putnam and his colleagues discovered in Italy, democracy works best in communities with high levels of participation in local associations. This is the very essence of M-stream political thinking, for Montesquieu shared this insight back in the eighteenth century. When citizens come together in a local neighborhood association, or in a quilting club, or in a bowling league, they inevitably get around to discussing the circumstances they share, the circumstances surrounding them. "Can't something be done about that abandoned house across the street from the school?" is the kind of question that gets asked in these settings. The question can lead to a petition brought before local government officials. Action frequently results. But dramatically diminish American participation in these kinds of local associations and you simultaneously diminish the number of conversations that focus on shared circumstances. As local associations and conversations disappear, a sense of community erodes. Engaged and invigorated communities, then, are the key to creating a healthy democracy.

I believe that the first step to rebuilding community in America is to reconnect the local school to it. This requires a kind of curricular and instructional liberation for teachers, but one closely monitored by the parents and community members who surround the school. To those who will quickly ask whether the nation's teachers possess any greater intellectual leverage over the significance of the relationship of the school to the community, or community to the well-being of democracy, than any other occupational group, I will confess quickly that they do not. To those who ask whether teachers are just as much in the dark as doctors, lawyers, police, or brick layers with respect to the corporate control of media, the interlocked interests of corporations and our governmental system, the extent to which industrialized agricultural practices have endangered our food supply, and so on, I would answer that they are.

Still, the nation's teachers are well educated, and they lead lives surrounded by learning. If they are asked to hone their curricular judgment with respect to traditional school subjects, to identify instructional practices that motivate students, to reignite the passion that brought them to the profession in the first place, they will turn of necessity to the circumstances that surround their students. Recognizing that part of the mission of public schools is to prepare citizens to take their place in a democracy, they will move in the direction of socializing students to assess the justice or injustice afforded the local community. It is not hard to imagine the kind of democratic revitalization that will occur in the wake of millions of students intellectually engaged in the life of their communities.

Curricular and instructional liberation, of course, will not automatically result in this kind of school-born democratic revitalization. Teachers will need a glimpse of that vision in order to begin working toward it. There are currently organizations out there trying to spread that vision, like the National Network for Educational Renewal. This is a coalition of school and university partnerships dedicated to pursuing educational efforts as a contribution to democracy. The membership currently stands at approximately fifty institutions of higher education supporting established partnerships with nearly 1,000 schools. While this is evidence that the vision is spreading, it nevertheless represents a small portion of the nation's total. Still, any school can build this vision anywhere through concerted efforts via school-community meetings, book clubs, or even petition drives.

I should add here, as we saw in previous chapters, that the intention of our common school founders was to create local institutions that would operate in the interest of democracy, various ulterior motives notwithstanding. This is not to say, however, that schools should *exclusively* attend to the educational preparation of future citizens in a democracy. Students will eventually need jobs; they will need to play an economic role with their lives. And so we now turn to that dimension of the human condition. To start this discussion, I'll begin with a very brief review of the circumstances laid out in Chapter 2.

When the feudal world succumbed at last to the powerful arguments of political theorists, an era defined by the elevation of human freedom was born. All nonfeudal Western governmental arrangements created after the great English political drama of the 1640s were premised on the concept that men were, by right and by nature, free. For some this meant that a government must be as democratic as possible, and for others it meant that government needed to be as insensitive to democracy as possible. But once feudal ideas were discredited, a society could not espouse human freedom and deny citizens a political voice altogether. Initially there was room to exclude the political voice of women and slaves, of course, and even those free males who held insufficient property, but a sizable expansion of political participation was inevitable.

In the face of this circumstance some argued, like Jefferson, that in combination with a mass educational system, widespread democracy will work just fine. Fearing that, others, like Hamilton and Madison, claimed that the best sort of government will limit that political voice, or control for its effects. This is, of course, precisely the strategy they weaved into our Constitution. The voice of the people was limited to the occasional selection of representatives. On top of this, access to these representatives was deliberately limited further by the decision to allow one congressional representative to represent 30,000 citizens—effectively removing the possibility that the represented might meaningfully participate in decisions made by representatives. As the United States has matured as a nation, instead of amending this circumstance, we have exacerbated it to the point that today's representative represents 650,000 individuals.[2]

But in keeping with Lockean theory, or with the logic of the L-Stream, this is forgivable provided that (1) people have at least some vehicle to select leaders, and (2) they have some vehicle to get rid of them if they fail to do their job. In fact, this is not only forgivable but desirable, because it frees citizens so that they may indulge their ostensible primary passion. That is, it enables people to pursue their own economic self-interest.

In this way, passion and greed were elevated to the status of cultural virtues, "gods," John Maynard Keynes would call them, as the feverish pursuit of money, of acquisition, came to be seen as the fuel that drives a nation's economy. This was an early insight into the conditions created by a free society. Recall the subtitle of Bernard Mandeville's great eighteenth-century poem "The Fable of the Bees," in which he explained that the feverish pursuit of wealth might expose "private vices," but from those we could expect "public benefits." Keynes once described the "essence of capitalism" as "the dependence upon an intense appeal to the money-making and money-loving instincts of individuals as the main motive force of the economic machine."[3]

One can readily see that if men are thought to be *essentially* economic beings, an assumption of great significance, governmental and educational arrangements will come to take a predictable shape. Looking deeper, however, we can see that there are assumptions embedded in the conception of economic man itself that require scrutiny. As it turns out, as Keynes noted above, these more deeply embedded assumptions have to do with the concept of "instinct." For Keynes and indeed most intellectuals of the first half of the twentieth century, the idea that humans contained "instincts" that were presocial or precultural was unquestioned. Today, most social scientists are deeply skeptical of the concept, arguing that humans are always simultaneously the product of biology and society. Without the benefit of this critique of the concept of instinct, Keynes and any number of economists of the classical tradition believed that the economic instincts of significance were those that pushed us to pursue money and love wealth. Given those instincts, we were practically duty-bound to create an economic policy context that maximized the odds that these instincts might be gratified. Thorstein Veblen once described such a context as "legislative safeguarding by the businessmen who have a pecuniary interest in industrial affairs." He noted further that such policies are quietly accepted "in the naïve faith that the material interests of the community at large will coincide with the opportunities for gain so secured to the businessmen."[4]

The fact that communities all across the country, particularly those that we now call "inner city" and countless rural villages in every state, have not shared in the material benefits that have accumulated in the business class has not made a dent in our resolve to maintain an economic context that privileges the right of the captains of industry to do as they please—up to and including paying lobbyists to write legislation and thereafter find congresspeople willing to sponsor it. But here's the thing. What if this assumption about economic man is wrong? What if money-loving is more a matter of societal enculturation than presocial instinct? What if, in fact, the essential economic "instinct" is, as Veblen claimed, workmanship?

The Nature of Work

Twenty-first century citizens may find the word *workmanship* unfamiliar, except perhaps when used while complaining about particular products. It is worth a short digression, therefore, to examine the analysis from which Thorstein Veblen derived his claim that workmanship is as natural—or more so—than greed.

Veblen argued that human life at its earliest was group life out of necessity. Early human societies lived "very near the soil" and were "unremittingly dependent for their daily life on the workmanlike efficiency of all members of the group." Work, then, was not primarily about self-interest but rather was undertaken to enhance the well-being of the group. Veblen explained, "The prime requisite for survival under these conditions would be a propensity *unselfishly* and *impersonally* to make the most of the material means at hand and a penchant for turning all resources of knowledge and material to account to sustain the life of the group."[5]

What one received in exchange for work was not money. It was the means to sustain one's self and one's family, to be sure, but it was additionally gratitude, admiration, and respect. It was additionally those human characteristics that motivated individuals to bring as much quality, as much workmanship, to their labors as they could possibly muster. In doing so, work of *any* kind, done well and done for others, became a source of pride.

For thousands of years, according to Veblen, these conditions defined the world of work. For thousands of years, humans culturally cultivated the "instinct" of workmanship. To change this, to realize a world marked by unlimited accumulation based on the assumption that money-loving was central to the human condition, profound disruptions had to occur. For one, money needed to be a pivotal feature of the economy. Potential employers had to say, in effect, "In exchange for the pride, admiration, and respect you once received, I will give you money." This was an abrupt and serious change. Any historian of eighteenth- or nineteenth-century Europe—or the United States, for that matter—will tell you that workers did not rejoice when they were offered the substitution. That money-loving predilection on which we base our economic policy was nowhere in sight at the transition to wage labor, at least not among what shortly came to be known as the "working class."

Why not, one might reasonably ask. Can't people change? Veblen answered: "In so slow-breeding a species as man, and with changes in the conditions of life going forward at a visibly rapid pace, the chance of an adequate adaptation of hybrid human nature to new conditions seems doubtful at best." He went on to explain our present predicament: "As the matter stands, the [human] race is required to meet changing conditions of life to which its relatively unchanging endowment of instincts is presumably not wholly adapted, and to meet these conditions by the use of technological ways and means widely different from those that were at the disposal of the [human] race from the outset."[6]

In a word, no. You can't take a predilection bred through countless generations and expect it to disappear, or become inconsequential, overnight. On top of this, we are talking about more than the mere substitution of money for qualities like respect and admiration. We are talking about a desire to do work guided by a completely different standard. The social nature of work throughout history, as Veblen demonstrated, tended to advance the pursuit of quality. Work undertaken in the pursuit of money-making moved in the direction of the standard of efficiency. The standard of efficiency can only work against the standard of quality.

It should be noted that Karl Marx, like Veblen, identified the social nature of work, as well as the community cohesion created when people are able to create useful products and exchange them face-to-face in the town square. Industrial managers and owners removed the creative and distributive dimensions of work and thereby contributed to worker alienation and the erosion of a sense of community. Still Marx saw a certain inevitability in the logic of industrial efficiency. His project was not to condemn the ill-effects of efficiency-driven production but to put workers in a position where they would share the surplus value it created.

The movement toward greater efficiency meant breaking up work tasks to the point that very little skill was involved—a circumstance that would, among other things, make workers easier to replace. These developments came with a toll paid in blood and violence, as anyone casually familiar with labor history knows. Almost until the Great Depression of the 1930s, capital seemed willing to enter pitched battles with labor, if need be, to force the cultural transition millions found so distasteful. Until the 1930s, Say's Law was still intact. Optimism about an abundant future was everywhere. After the Crash in October 1929, all of this changed. People gradually made peace with the idea that perhaps the end result of a culture that elevates passion and greed as desirable attributes was not prosperity, but rather depression and devastation. If this was the case, drastic changes were indeed in order. If this was the case, the policies and practices laid out by disregarded agrarian philosophers might prove useful after all.

We won't revisit the New Deal and all of the agrarian-inspired reforms that came with it. Nor will we stop to revisit the dismantling of the New Deal with the post-Reagan conservative ascendancy. I want to begin this argument for creating an economics driven by genius and virtue, replacing the current one driven by passion and greed, by honing in on one by-product of our reembrace of pre-1930s economics: the crisis of meaning in the lives of citizens, the veritable tidal wave of mental ill-health in the United States. As early as the era of the Great Depression itself, insightful scholars caught a glimpse of it. Acknowledging Veblen's analysis, for instance, Keynes argued that "We have been expressly evolved by nature—with all of our impulses and deepest instincts—for the purpose of solving the economic problem. If the economic problem is solved, mankind will be deprived of its traditional purpose." He noted further that he "looked on with dread of the readjustments of the habits and instincts of the ordinary man, bred into him for countless generations, which he may be asked to discard within a few decades. To use the language of today—must we not expect a general 'nervous breakdown'?"[7]

Keynes knew that the end result of (1) forcing workers to substitute money for admiration and respect, (2) forcing them to dutifully attend to deskilled and in many cases mind-numbing tasks, and (3) forcing them to do these things at the lowest possible wage was a prescription for societal ill-health of one sort or another—a general nervous breakdown, perhaps, but violent class struggle was a possibility, too. The exigencies of the Great Depression therefore created fertile ground for new ideas, including the prospect of paying workers middle-class wages in exchange for giving up, in the name of industrial efficiency, meaningfulness in their work.

A bargain of sorts was struck: meaningless work for meaningful pay. In the process, vast discrepancies between the rich and poor were diminished over the ensuing decades of the 1940s, 1950s, even into the 1960s. Billionaires disappeared. The number of millionaires shrunk. Wealth was dispersed broadly at rates that would have compared favorably to present-day Japan or Sweden. But, of course, as we all know, it did not last. The bargain was broke. In the spirit of classical economics of an earlier era, it is now deemed to be acceptable to pay workers at the lowest rate possible. Capitalism is once again defined by its appeal to the money-loving predilection within us. Only this time, corporations have a wide range of media outlets that can pound home the message that this is legitimate, that this is how it should be, that justice requires creating a policy context that allows the wealthiest to maximize their income.

Coincident with the conservative reascendancy of the last quarter of the twentieth century has been a breakdown of social connectedness in the United States, a breakdown of astronomical proportions. Robert Putnam exhaustively documented the "collapse of American community" in his now-famous book titled *Bowling Alone.* In that work he did his best to identify the reasons why Americans are taking a less and less active role in the social and political life of their communities, why they are less likely to know and trust their neighbors, or to donate to charity, or to take part in community projects. He attributed much of this to the advent of television, to increased work demands, to urban sprawl and commuting, but the largest factor in the demise of community in America he called "generational change," a slightly ambiguous reference to changed ideas about how the world works and the role of citizens within it.

My own view is that what Putnam calls "generational change" is in reality the surging ideology of the L-stream—the vision of life as an atomistic journey in which fulfillment is tied to the material acquisition available at the mall. This brand of hyperindividualism, this "culture of narcissism," as the late Christopher Lasch called it, has contributed significantly to the social disconnection Putnam documented so persuasively. Further, it has contributed to the proliferation of loneliness and depression. In fact, "depression imposes the fourth largest total burden of any disease on Americans overall," according to Putnam.[8] Depression, of course, like all human experiences, has physiological dimensions, physiological correlates that these days are commonly labeled as "causes" of depression. This classic misinterpretation of correlation as causation leads to an incomplete understanding of depression as well as other mental health phenomena. A prominent psychologist has argued that depression is tied to our cultural emphasis on individualism—our cultural insistence on carving one's own path in life and our cultural rejection of engaging in collective efforts of mutual benefit.[9] When individuals fail at individual pursuits, there is no built-in support system to cushion the fall. There is only sadness, isolation, and depression.

The physiological dimensions to social disconnectedness have been well documented. People who have few social ties are at significantly greater risk of heart attack and other diseases. Put simply, depression depresses the immune system—or its capabilities; this fact suggests that, revitalizing democratic processes aside, the "revival of American community" is a necessary project solely in terms of the health of American citizens, solely in terms of our ability to cease to be the "Prozac nation."

But let's bring this discussion back to the economic arena. Given the abundance of research related to America's health difficulties, particularly our mental health difficulties, one might ask whether or not we can reorient our culture in the direction of group membership, of community renewal, of doing things for and with others. Granted, such a goal will require significant effort in the educational arena, first and foremost, and political changes are obviously needed, too. But we can make changes in the economic arena in the interest of pursuing this goal as well. It requires only insight into the problem and the will necessary to do something about it.

Economics guided by the efficiency standard thrives on anonymity, something Mattel, Inc., will work desperately to reclaim as it recovers from the 2007 "lead paint scandal." Every attempt is made to limit the knowledge of consumers to recognition of a brand name. Beyond that, the less consumers know about a company the better. It is not in the interest of multinational corporations like Mattell to widely announce how it conducts its business, or how its employees are treated or compensated, the point of origin of raw materials, or the location and oversight levels of manufacturing processes. The name of the game is money-making. It should be obvious that an economy driven by money-making has contributed significantly to our demonstrably unhealthy culture.

Veblen's work helps us see that the opposite of an economy driven by money-making is one driven by workmanship—an appeal to the desire within us to do work well because work is ultimately undertaken in the interest of more than just one's self. It is culturally difficult for us to see this in a world where work has been broken into small pieces in the name of efficiency. But whether I design a manufacturing machine, operate it, or clean it at night when it is idle, it is work undertaken that will make a contribution to someone's life. The idea that work is about self-interest cheapens the notion of work, robs it of its mentally sustaining qualities, and predisposes us to a kind of emptiness that accompanies acts of selfishness. In fact, the idea that work ought to be somehow connected to one's financial self-interest is a kind of cultural fiction advanced by those who understand that the end result of a policy context premised on this fiction can be a source of enormous wealth to the relatively few who have the power and the resources required to take advantage of it.

Some Possibilities for Creating
Community-Oriented Economics

We Americans like to think of ourselves as citizens of a moral nation—born out of a rejection of tyranny, we stand for freedom everywhere for everyone. For many, of course, our recent military misadventures have shattered that vision of altruistic American motives, though some still cling to it. But either way, doesn't it seem advantageous to demonstrate to the world that we can envision and act to create a future wherein citizens consume in ways such that no one becomes hostage to their comfort?[10]

Now, what does that entail? The best account of that, in my estimation, came from the pen of John Ruskin. Recall his admonition relayed in Chapter 2: "In all buying, consider, first, what condition of existence you cause the producers of what you buy."[11] Now this is sometimes tough to know, and the entire panoply of products for sale represents an inexhaustible source of research projects for schoolchildren. Short of such a contribution made by public school students, however, individuals can do some of their own research. There are a few wonderful consumer "guides" out there intended to help citizens become ethical consumers. Leslie Garrett's *The Virtuous Consumer* is excellent, as is Ellis Jones's *The Better World Shopping Guide*.[12] Some consumer insights are fairly obvious. One would have to be quite isolated, for example, not to be aware of the worker abuse problems within the Wal-Mart organization.[13] Millions avoid shopping there because of this knowledge, and millions more should. But beyond this act of personal boycott, citizens who are aware of what Wal-Mart does to its employees and to the communities where it puts up stores should strive to become policy advocates to fight back. Inventory taxes, for instance, could level the playing field in the retail sales arena such that small businesses could compete with corporate giants.

In general, seek to consume goods produced according to the standard of workmanship, eschewing cheap goods manufactured according to the standard of efficiency, for that standard will inevitably drive down labor costs—wages and benefits—and take shortcuts on quality. Buying goods produced according to the standard of efficiency will dramatically increase the likelihood that lives will be held hostage to your comfort.

The nation's wealthiest, those staunch advocates of the status quo, will quickly call this kind of advice "elitist": fine for those with money, an enormous hardship for those without it. It presents an excellent opportunity for the rich to demonstrate forthright concern for the poor who need low-priced toothpaste and shampoo, and they are quick to make the most of it. But the argument is foolishness and nothing more, as the more intelligent among the wealthy well know. You cannot eliminate the handicap of poverty by providing cheap goods and services. You cannot eliminate poverty itself without first eliminating the mechanisms that create it. Besides, there are many ways that good work, decently compensated, can be inserted into America's economic picture. But this will take changes in the economic policy arena—which will require changes in the political arena, which will require changes in the educational arena. It is important to remember that these efforts must occur across all three realms.

Curricular and instructional liberation in schools will allow students to study traditional school subjects through the lens of the immediate community. Through this process, students growing up in impoverished central cities will come to understand the role played by General Motors in closing down mass transit options, a process that isolated inner cities and enabled employers to take work to the suburbs.[14] Equipped with understandings such as these, they can become informed policy advocates in concerted efforts to revitalize their neighborhoods. Students in rural schools will study the effects of farm policy that worked to flush out small farmers and subsequently the array of local businesses, churches, and schools that once made small-town America thrive.

Both urban and rural students will come to understand that the demise of farming as an occupation, especially during the last half of the twentieth century, was partially aided by the advent of what may fairly be called a second round of enclosure: the removal of farm animals from pastures into concentrated animal feeding operations. Just as with the first round of enclosure in eighteenth- and nineteenth-century England, this one has generated a cityward population drift. In addition to losing people, however, depopulating rural communities have also witnessed the loss of newspapers, hospitals, health clinics, schools, businesses of all kinds, and perhaps most significant, the loss of a sense of pride in their places. Osha Gray Davidson chronicled the demise of the rural Midwest in the wake of the 1980s farm crisis in a book called *Broken Heartland: The Rise of America's Rural Ghetto.* He demonstrated that a variety of business types have moved quickly to rural communities to take advantage of (1) unemployed or underemployed rural residents or non-English speaking immigrants willing to move to rural locales, and, (2) incentives offered by increasingly desperate municipalities, for example, "Build a plant in our town (or move into one of our unused buildings) and you'll be exempt from paying taxes or utilities for ten years." Meatpacking operations have moved into the countryside away from the old large meatpacking centers and the threat of unionized labor. Telecommunications operations have also taken advantage of the desperate conditions in rural America, quickly refurbishing existing buildings and plugging in phone lines. Sadly, meatpacking businesses, telecommunications companies, and many light manufacturing operations are quickly shut down when rumors spread about unionizing efforts, or when the tax breaks and incentives period has lapsed, ending the ten, fifteen, or twenty-year free ride. It is at that point that many of these businesses will simply pull up stakes and move to a new rural community desperate for jobs.

The enclosure process began with poultry production. During the 1940s, feed companies created production contracts with farmers who invested in large structures capable of housing hundreds, and later thousands, of birds confined to small individual cages—so small that the animals could scarcely turn around. The grain companies supplied the baby chicks, feed, and veterinary supplies, and the farmers supplied the labor. In time, the terms of these contracts were rearranged in favor of the large grain companies, meaning that increasingly farmers had to shoulder the burden of supplying feed and veterinary supplies. Tyson Feed and Hatchery was incorporated in 1947, and its owner, John Tyson, quickly became a leader in company-owned chicken farms. Ten years later, Tyson Feed and Hatchery created its own processing plant. The company went public in 1963 after being renamed Tyson Foods. As of 2003, Tyson produced seven billion pounds of chicken annually, the result of some 6,500 production contracts.[15] It is now the clear leader in meat production in the United States, having expanded into pork and beef production. Michaels Foods, a leading egg and egg product producer, has dramatically increased its level of concentrated animal production, with millions of animals confined to a series of buildings in a small space no larger than an acre or two. Tyson, Michaels Foods, and other large poultry producers have notoriously utilized non-English-speaking immigrant labor—paying low wages with few benefits. In fact, in 2001 Tyson was indicted for conspiracy to violate United States immigration laws in a scheme to reduce labor costs.[16]

By the 1970s, the enclosure trend begun in the poultry industry was successfully replicated in the pork industry. The overwhelming majority of hogs produced in the United States are now raised in cemented confinement barns on production contracts. Since the 1980s, concentrated feeding operations have become the norm in dairy and beef production as well. Here, though, the animals are concentrated in small feedlots. Being natural grazers, so many cattle—thousands—in very small lots quickly eat or trample any vegetation that might have been on the ground at the start. The animals thereafter live out their lives on dirt that turns to mud with rain and snowfall. The animals become horrifically dirty from the mud and from the fecal matter of thousands of animals.

Large concentrations of animals—chickens, hogs, or cattle—produce enormous amounts of waste products.[17] Much of this is applied to nearby fields as fertilizer, but often in amounts that are well beyond the ability of natural processes to handle. And the manure itself can carry disease rendering it dangerous. Salmonella outbreaks are frequently traced back to vegetable fields that received manure treatments, as in 2008 when thousands became ill from salmonella-laden tomatoes and peppers. The smells from the manuring process can become overwhelming, doing significant damage to the local quality of life, as well as to property values. Water quality is now a concern all across the country as manure-born nitrates and phosphorus from concentrated animal feeding operations make their way into the nation's groundwater supplies. Overly high nitrate levels can turn lakes into almost solid stands of underwater vegetation—ruining fish habitat and seriously impairing recreational activities.

The largest health concerns stem from the risk involved in concentrated animal feeding operations. One sick animal can quickly become thousands of sick animals. As a consequence, most confined animals are kept on antibiotics throughout their entire lives. Approximately 26.6 million pounds of antibiotics are given to farm animals each year, compared with about 8 million pounds administered to humans. Of the 26.6 million pounds, roughly 8 percent was administered to animals to treat an actual infection or illness.[18] Of course, drugs administered to livestock can easily be transferred to humans. Many scientists believe that due to the ever-present development of antimicrobial resistance, the widespread use of antibiotics in farm animals may spur the growth of such resistance in human pathogens. It could well be that resistant strains of organisms, such as *E. coli* and salmonella, causing disease in humans are linked to the use of antibiotics in animals.[19]

A particularly deadly disease, popularly called "mad cow," technically, Bovine Spongiform Encephalopathy (BSE), is easily transferred from animals to humans. There has been, ostensibly at least, only one case of mad cow disease in a farm animal in this country, yet mysteriously, the number of human deaths due to CJD, or Creutzfeldt-Jakob Disease, has increased dramatically. We can't say by how much, because it is not a reportable disease in this country—unlike in England and Switzerland, for example, where the incidence of CJD doubled during the 1990s. We do know that CJD leaves a molecular signature that is indistinguishable from mad cow disease. We know, too, that it is very frequently misdiagnosed as Alzheimer's in older patients, as a severe viral infection, or even as multiple sclerosis in younger victims.

The disease spreads in animals because in an attempt to maximize profits via the standard of efficiency, livestock are fed slaughterhouse scraps—those parts of animals, like intestines, that are not packaged for human consumption.[20] And in the United States, unlike in Japan, for example, where 100 percent of animals butchered for consumption are tested for the disease, only 1 percent of all animals slaughtered in the United States are tested. Consequently, we may very well have large amounts of infected meat for sale in this country, resulting in the climbing rates of CJD. For the record, the British Health Minister called CJD "the worst form of death imaginable." It literally eats holes in the brain, prolonging an inevitable death for months. The prions that make up the disease are practically impervious to attempts to kill them. They will live through temperatures that would melt lead. As a consequence, it is nearly impossible to find a research center that will perform an autopsy on its victims—since the disease is so deadly and the likelihood of contamination so high.

None of this will reach the "liberal" news media, of course, because the cattle industry would be temporarily destroyed if it did. In a matter of years, most likely, the number of deaths and further research will make the connection indisputable—at which point major changes will take place in the industry. For the time being, though, there are huge profits to be made, and the multinational corporations that control the news media will not interfere with their right to make them.[21]

All of this strongly suggests that by slow strides Americans need to reorder the manner in which food is produced in this country. They can do this via knowledgeable consumption of the sort Ruskin prescribed. For example, to the extent that it is possible, Americans must come to view the terms and conditions in which a food item is produced as every bit as important as its price. Americans have a right to know if the milk they purchase comes from a family-sized operation in their home state, or a gigantic milk factory in a state halfway across the continent. Seek ways to demand this knowledge. Encourage local schools to conduct the necessary research.

Above all, grow something for your own consumption, even if it is nothing more than a potted tomato plant. Garden if you can. Preserve and consume what you grow.[22] Become a catalyst for the creation and maintenance of community gardens. Patronize community-oriented farming ventures by purchasing produce direct from such farms. Organize efforts to take down abandoned and dilapidated buildings in order to create room for small urban farms. Lobby municipal governments to allow urban "chicken cooperatives," small-scale chicken and egg production ventures staffed by volunteers. Such enterprises could put healthy food into the diets of the poorest and most helpless among us.

The idea that a democracy can flourish with food or energy production in the hands of a few corporations constitutes a kind of cruel joke on the American people. But there is much that ordinary citizens can do to prevent further movement in that direction and in the process reclaim food, water, and energy safety and security. While it is a tall order to produce one's own energy needs, there is much that can be done to limit energy consumption. Utilizing public transportation is a good start, as is walking and bicycling. We have access to impressive technologies now for weatherizing homes and thereby decreasing fuel consumption. Something as simple as using energy-efficient light bulbs, or turning down the water heater, would be small steps in the right direction.

We have to collectively face facts that didn't trouble the first generation of classical economists and are only now making a dent in the worldview of present-day economists. The earth is full of people and getting more and more crowded. The economic activity of six to seven billion individuals has heated the earth's atmosphere to levels that will inevitably create climatic change—already have, in fact. Conservatives who profit from the status quo may ridicule global warming as a liberal plot, but the self-interest in such behavior is becoming increasingly transparent. The economy cannot grow forever. It is a biophysical impossibility. Still, it is easy to suppose that a new technology—something we haven't yet seen nor thought of—will emerge and give us several more decades or even centuries of growth. And as Wendell Berry reminds us, "anything supposable can be endlessly supposed," a circumstance that reveals the magnitude of our dilemma.[23] We have to consciously reduce our energy consumption or hasten ecological disaster. John Stuart Mill saw this day coming as early as the 1840s: "It must always have been seen, more or less distinctly, by political economists, that the increase of wealth is not boundless; that at the end of what they term the progressive state lies the stationary state, that all progress in wealth is but a postponement of this, and that each step in advance is an approach to it."[24] He went on to express his heartfelt desire that humankind would recognize the "impossibility of ultimately avoiding the stationary state" and acquiesce to it before exigencies applied it by force. This might still happen, but we are running out of time.

What is required is the creation of a culture that prizes frugality and thrift of the civic republican and agrarian traditions; that is, we need to reembrace the M-stream. While such a cultural shift represents a formidable challenge today, when corporate media, claiming objectivity, regale the assumptions undergirding the L-stream, it was once a fundamental part of American culture and could be so again. Put simply, we need to praise those who find new uses for cast-off "stuff," of which the world is all too full. We need to avoid elevating "shopping" into a form of entertainment. We need to avoid extravagant purchases and, to the extent possible, organize boycotts of ostentatiousness. The wealthy in this country think nothing of spending $1 million or more on a mere party. Such events need to be met with the force of cultural shame (again, schools could play an invaluable role here). We need to patronize merchants who sell second-hand products. We need to avoid debt like the plague. We need to find new idols, new heroes, and snub the world of movie stars, rock stars, and super-athletes. This, too, can be done.

I don't mean to suggest that music, dance, theater, or sports are culturally inappropriate—far from it. They are vital dimensions to the human condition. It is a rare individual who is not moved by artistic expression in one of these realms. A song, a theatrical performance, even a well-executed pick and roll or double play reveals a kind of beauty that generates positive human emotions. But to make big business of these things, to enrich owners and producers and performers with astronomical salaries, is a disastrous mistake from a cultural standpoint. It elevates the wealth-getting and subordinates the artistry. It gives freedom to human impulses that require restraint, especially among the young and impressionable. We will only correct this mistake by boycotting the concert, the theater, and the sports arena. But once again, this is well within our ability to accomplish.

What Can Be Done About Corporate Behavior?

Corporations and the American government are so interlocked that the tightly connected church and state of the feudal era pales in comparison. It will require political efforts discussed in the next chapter to make the necessary separation. Interestingly, the globalizing efforts of huge multinational corporations leaves large "passed over" areas—generally, rural areas and inner cities. By the terms of the global economy, of course, these areas are where the unemployed and poor reside—and statistics confirm this. But these areas represent places where communities can come together and begin to build a local economy based on the standard of workmanship. These areas are places that can reinsert the value of community into economic reckoning.

The most effective tool for accomplishing this is through a process called import substitution. Jane Jacobs explicated this concept in her 1984 book, *Cities and the Wealth of Nations.* The title is actually a bit deceptive, for Jacobs claims that economies are best built *around* cities, that is, a local economy includes a city and its hinterland, the rural regions that surround it. For an economy to grow in such an area, local genius is required. The locality must be innovative enough to develop a product that meets a local need previously met by importation. And virtue is required. Allegiance to one's community will keep the venture strong, even if large distant companies attempt to undersell local operations.

Currently both inner cities and rural areas have a tendency to try to lure in businesses from the outside—a practice that always brings mixed, if not undesirable, results. This must change. Even if citizens of rural areas and those in central cities are not convinced that we must reject a growth economy in the interest of planetary survival, it is in their present economic self-interest to "buy local." I would add to that, eat and heat local, as well.

There is one effective way for some citizens to change corporate behaviors. A little less than half of all Americans have some funds invested in pension plans over which they have very little control. But very little is not the same as none at all. Pension funds control 60 percent of the shares in the nation's 1,000 largest corporations.[25] That's a very significant amount. If more and more Americans move their pension funds to "social choice" plans, corporations will be forced to reduce investments that hinge on worker abuse or environmental degradation. They will be forced to pass a kind of social screening process and amend their anticommunity ways. Every American with a pension plan and the ability to select from plan options should redirect investments into a social choice fund. The relatively short history of socially conscious investing has demonstrated that it can produce return results that are least competitive, and most often more competitive, than antisocial investing options.[26]

What is more, increasingly investment firms are looking at the possibility of tailoring investments by institution.[27] This means a company that allows worker voices in decisions related to pension investing could create its own locally relevant investment strategy—so that one's pension dollars could be used to support business in one's locality, contributing to greater community vitality. Be vocal about this possibility and about socially conscious investing in general. Move your money to it whenever possible. Beyond that, of course, if you should have the opportunity to patronize a community bank, one organized around the idea of community reinvigoration, don't hesitate to do so. There are not many such institutions, but the number is growing.

If there is a phrase that holds more terror for America's power elite than import substitution, it is likely the maximum wage. In 2009, the idea of a maximum wage seems as unlikely to American citizens as space travel to Mars. We no longer possess any memory of when it was a well-considered and often-debated policy option. The idea is so dangerous to the status quo, in fact, that you will *never* hear it uttered on the nightly news, not even to ridicule it.

A maximum wage law, however, is merely a way for society to prevent great extremes between wealth and poverty. It was a decidedly American value at the point of our nation's founding, a piece of wisdom garnered from civic republican theorists from Cicero to Montesquieu. Even the modern liberal Mill recognized the importance of a moderate gap between the nation's poorest and richest citizens, insisting that the matter of distributing a nation's wealth was the prerogative of society and not a matter governed by lawlike strictures. "I know not why it should be a matter of congratulation that persons who are already richer than anyone needs to be, should have doubled their means of consuming things which give little or no pleasure except as representative of wealth; or that numbers of individuals should pass over, every year, from the middle classes into a richer class, or from the class of the occupied rich to that of the unoccupied."[28] In this regard, Mill echoed a long-held tenet of civic republican agrarian theory: extremes in wealth and poverty were to be avoided at all costs.

The mechanism for achieving this was of course taxation, a policy option that could in effect establish a maximum wage. Although the number of Americans who are aware that such a concept exists is small, and those who actively support policy changes to create a maximum wage is still smaller, the movement is nevertheless gaining momentum largely due to the pace at which America's super-wealthy are distancing themselves from the vast majority of the population. Americans have never adopted a maximum wage law, though we have come close from time to time. As noted earlier, during the twenty-year period between 1935 and 1955, billionaires were completely eliminated and the number of millionaires in the country was dramatically reduced. As we saw in Chapter 2,

President Franklin Roosevelt, during his last term in office, openly lobbied for a law that would tax 100 percent of all income over $25,000 per year ($320,000 in 2008 dollars)—a reform measure that never came to be.

The post–World War II graduated income tax scales were nevertheless progressive enough to create a predominantly middle-class society, albeit one that has been completely dismantled in the years since Ronald Reagan's 1981 Economic Recovery Act was passed. The lopsided nature of America's economic distribution cannot go on indefinitely without creating enormous societal instability, and, as a consequence, there are those who have earnestly reproposed the establishment of a maximum wage.

Proponents of a maximum wage use either a ten- or twenty-times rule as a guide for legislation. In other words, laws could be written to ensure that the wealthiest make no more than ten times the amount made by those working for the minimum wage—a guideline with longstanding classical roots.[29] Others contend that a twenty-times rule would be appropriate. In 1940, American CEOs made roughly fourteen times more than the average salaries in their companies. By 2004 that figure had ballooned to 531 times more.[30] The top 1 percent of the American population is now so wealthy that it is virtually impossible for its members to spend their money in their own lifetimes. Making a case for such extravagance is, of course, impossible, though there are many who would try until their last breath to do so. But whether a maximum wage law locked in at ten or twenty times the minimum wage, we would be talking about a massive infusion into the nation's cultural infrastructure, as enormous sums could be utilized to outfit and staff the nation's schools, hospitals, childcare centers, and so on—generating a much healthier sort of economic activity. We could easily become the kind of altruistic and moral nation most Americans thought we were, and would like to be again.[31]

The assumptions about humankind that drove economic theory from Smith to Friedman were wrong, plain and simple. Still, an empty world could accommodate economies driven by passion and greed—but only for a time. As Herman Daly put it, "When the economy's expansion encroaches too much on its surrounding ecosystem, we will begin to sacrifice natural capital (such as fish, minerals, and fossil fuels) that is worth more than the man-made capital (such as roads, factories and appliances) added by growth.[32] When this happens, and one could easily argue that it has already happened at countless locations across the globe, we have begun to produce "bads" at a faster rate than we produce "goods." These bads include war, poverty, starvation, disease, super-storms, coastal flooding, and human misery on a scale that exceeds any prior moment in world history.

We need to build a culture around values emanating from the M-stream, from the agrarian middle way, from economic theory premised on different, more accurate assumptions about the human condition. We need to celebrate genius and virtue as engines for economic well-being. Humans are not economic actors *essentially,* but rather (as agrarian theorists down through the ages have tried to tell us) they are social beings who thrive in community and take fulfillment from leading lives in the service of others. You can help build a culture on that assumption by walking to work, by volunteering for a community project, by turning down your water heater, by growing some of your own food, by encouraging the development of cooperative neighborhood enterprises, by boycotting and marshaling cultural shame on ostentatiousness and indiscriminate spending whenever possible, by insisting that you be allowed to know the terms and conditions under which the products you buy were produced, by being an advocate for inventory taxes or whatever economic policies will give individuals a fair chance to compete with global companies, by moving your money into social choice funds, and, above all, by talking about the possibility of a maximum wage law whenever the opportunity presents itself.

CHAPTER 6

Publius Reawakened

At last we come to the point where most reform advocates choose to begin. That is, it is time to take a look at how the business of American government might look if it were premised on different assumptions. I want to reiterate my steadfast belief once again, however, that what follows has virtually no chance of coming to fruition fast enough to ward off impending social and ecological crises without an education system geared toward preparing politically awake and active citizens, a system capable of delivering what Montesquieu called "the full power of education." Lobby for the curricular and instructional liberation of your neighborhood school first; grow some of your own food, walk to work, and take steps to be as sure as you can that what you consume causes no life to be held hostage to your comfort; and then select from any of the efforts relayed in this chapter to alter the political landscape of the nation. By the grace of God, humans possess an intellect through which to will a better world.

Let's go back to that Philadelphia summer in 1787. There we were, a collection of thirteen semiautonomous republics with a collective population of about 3.9 million, not a single republic boasting a city with a population of more than 36,000. The various states had differing opinions related to war debts and other issues germane to federal revenue, a circumstance that caused more than a little turmoil. Still, a legitimate government under the Articles of Confederation was functioning, though it could hardly be described as smooth sailing. And then there was the frightening rebellion led by Daniel Shays. Was the government so weak that it might fall to a larger and better organized insurrection? Was "faction" capable of ruining the American experiment? Hadn't David Hume warned of such a circumstance? In the minds of men like Hamilton and Madison, this freedom thing was a conundrum. So what was to be done?

The very question exposes the insidious beauty of L-stream logic: humans are *essentially* economic creatures so, according to Hamilton, Madison, and other Federalists, the solution is to tie freedom to the economic arena in an attempt to legitimate the creation of a political system unencumbered by human freedom, and thus very nearly impervious to the threat of faction. Utilizing Hume's argument about the wisdom of large republics, Madison and Hamilton argued that greater power in a central government will diffuse the intensity of aroused communities. Jefferson and other Anti-Federalists, in contrast, insisted that human freedom be tied to the political sphere, since humans were *essentially* social beings. Pulitzer Prize–winning historian Gordon Wood described the circumstances this way:

> The Anti-Federalists thus came to oppose the new national government for the same reason the Federalists favored it: because its very structure and detachment from the people would work to exclude any kind of actual and local interest representation and prevent those who were not rich, well-born, or prominent from exercising political power. Both sides fully appreciated the central issue the Constitution posed and grappled with it throughout the debates: whether a professedly popular government should actually be in the hands of, rather than simply derived from, common ordinary people.[1]

We know the answer. With a great distance between the people and the federal government, with members of the House of Representatives representing tens of thousands of constituents (hundreds of thousands today), it cannot be said with a straight face that there was a "popular" legislative body to inhibit the accumulation of power and the corruption that inevitably accompanies governmental arrangements. Corruption and scandal are therefore commonplace today, and our government is dominated by millionaires who can't be said to represent average citizens. The "death tax" fiasco is as good an example as any. Here's a policy that benefits the wealthiest 2 percent of the population *at the expense of the bottom 98 percent.* Only a government far removed from the people could get away with passing such a law, one buttressed by the complicity of the Big Five media corporations.

Here's where we stand. Our embrace of the L-stream interpretation of economics, that is, empty world economics with no accounting for the finite nature of natural resources, has brought us to the brink of ecological disaster. When the logic of the L-stream was applied to the political sphere, it gave us a government insulated from the direct participation of citizens, robbing them of a crucial source of fulfillment, not to mention the ability to rein in unwise economic activity, outrageously immoral attempts at money-grabbing, corruption, scandal, and abuses of every sort. When the L-stream logic was applied to education, it gave us a sorting machine that put students on waiting lists to enter "evident and probable" occupational tracks. In so doing it decontextualized curriculum and reduced the definition of an education to a test score. A very sad state of affairs all around.

It's past time to stop and say, okay, maybe the assumptions of Locke and Company were wrong. Maybe the agrarian traditions were right, maybe the health of societies does depend on vital community life, on an engaged and fully educated citizenry, on popular participation in life's political sphere. Our present societal trajectory is untenable, unless you choose to put your faith in a technological discovery that has not yet materialized. A Marxist trajectory toward a centrally planned economy is unacceptable, having revealed its inherent inefficiencies and its weakness under certain cultural conditions as a facilitator of tyranny. Where does that leave us? It leaves us with one option—the middle, or agrarian, way—the way of Winstanley, Montesquieu, Paine, Ogilvie, Jefferson, Sismondi, Ruskin, Ward, Dewey, Berry, and countless other ignored spokespersons. But what does a political shift to the M-stream look like in the twenty-first century?

A Good Place to Start

For starters, M-stream political theory suggests that individuals ought to have opportunities to play a political role with their lives. Montesquieu's *corps intermediare,* intermediate bodies, provided this to a degree in America's past. But as Robert Putnam so ably demonstrated, this kind of participation is declining rapidly. Why bother to join a neighborhood small business association when there's nothing to point to that would suggest the group's effort might produce some results? Our representatives are focused on the needs of corporations that provide the resources to put them in office, not the needs of voters. The intrusion of corporations into the governmental sphere has been perhaps the largest single unforeseen development that has taken place while Publius has been asleep, despite the fact that practically every president between Lincoln and Eisenhower warned the public of this growing antidemocratic development.

It appears to me, and I think this sentiment is shared by a great many political observers in this country, that we cannot, at least at this point in our history, rely on rhetorical appeals urging citizens to join local associations. We have to seek new structural means for putting the public into the political sphere. Won't this require constitutional change, one might reasonably ask? My best answer is, probably. But there are some ideas out there that stop short of that. I have proposed one in this book. I believe that every public school must be watched and guided by a Board of Assessors chosen by lot from the community that surrounds the school. If each school selected a ten-member board, we would be inserting a most valuable kind of civic engagement into the lives of nearly a million Americans.[2] These individuals would be entrusted with ensuring that the education professionals within the school were vigorously pursuing the "full power of education" and making it a gift to every child.

The Board of Assessors would operate independently of the more distant district School Board and would engage in substantive discussions with teachers about their curricular and instructional choices, curricular articulation between grades, and how the education being delivered might be well used in the world. This group would be charged with making sure no child was left behind, that all could read, write, speak, listen, and utilize a working knowledge of mathematics, science, geography, literature, and history to demonstrate an ability to discern how the larger world has treated one's home, one's family and neighbors. This group would be responsible for assessing the sophistication teachers bring to the integration of art, music, theater, and sports into the larger educational program. And while the group might choose to occasionally check standardized test scores, their work would put us much closer to weaning ourselves from the tyranny of such devices.[3]

Most Americans, and virtually all politicians, have incredibly simplistic ideas related to what an education is, and how it ought to happen. Witness our current federal policy, or the amazing chorus of approval for "standards" in education.[4] As noted earlier, here's the logic behind this: "Let's decide what students should know so we can test them to see if they know it." I don't mean to be too critical of this logic for I have used it myself. I have often decided, for example, that I want my dog to be able to catch a Frisbee. I do this by repeatedly testing him to see that he's learned how and that he doesn't thereafter forget. There's something troubling, however, about using the same logic as the basis for the nation's educational philosophy—as a basis for interacting with young human beings. One can certainly see, though, how well such a philosophy separates education from anything that might be helpful in the political arena. And that is a part of the L-stream project: keep the focus of schools on the economic arena and you increase the likelihood that government won't be burdened by any sort of sophisticated and widespread public surveillance.

A Board of Assessors system would crystallize another kind of civic engagement, one stemming from the nation's colleges and universities. It is probably not too controversial to say, at least speaking generally, that most institutions of higher education long ago left behind any sense of obligation to citizens by way of intellectual leadership.[5] The elite and well-born who dominated American higher education at the start had no particular inclination in this direction; however, at the height of the M-stream in America, the mid-nineteenth century, this was not the case. In fact, it was at that time that entirely new genres of universities were created—land grant universities with a mission for pursuing practical knowledge of the sort that would be helpful to average citizens, and normal schools (which evolved into teacher colleges), designed to prepare educators for the nation's schools.

Today land grant universities pursue grants to advance the product development or research needs of corporations, and former teacher colleges struggle with the decision to maintain their initial connection to local life or try to emulate the research universities and put themselves in the service of corporate America. These are sweeping generalizations, of course, but my guess is that most of the American professoriate would agree that they hit all too close to home.

Those selected to serve on a school's Board of Assessors would need some preparation for the job as well as some conduit for ongoing professional consultation. This can be provided by colleges and universities all across the country, a convenient way to reinsert a public dimension into the lives of America's professors. Both professors and board members, if selected for this work, would have the right to turn it down. While it may be that local districts could provide a modest stipend for their efforts, we're looking at a task that might just as well be labeled voluntary. Terms should be relatively short as a result, perhaps two years. The entire effort would be much like striking a bargain with the community's teachers: we will give you the freedom to decide how best to teach our children, but we will closely monitor your decisions and your work and we will be involved in the process to the greatest extent possible.

Comparing the potential for curricular and instructional excitement generated by liberated teachers—teachers entrusted to make their own pedagogical decisions—against the current state of affairs where teachers are increasingly told what to teach and how to teach it, the entire matter begins to look like a grand comedy. How could a nation of nearly 300 million people create and support policies that render schools deadening places for children, places where teachers, stripped of anything that brings a sense of fulfillment to their jobs, become technicians going through the motions—reading the script provided by a for-profit textbook company that managed to convince a school board to buy its product and watch test scores rise. If it weren't so tragic, it would be funny.

The late journalist Walter Karp once wrote that it wasn't ignorance that created this state of affairs, but rather a kind of cool, self-interested calculus. Said Karp, "The public schools we have today are what the powerful and the considerable have made of them. They won't be redeemed by trifling reforms. They are not meant to." He went on to argue that "only ordinary citizens can rescue schools from their stifling corruption, for nobody else wants ordinary children to become questioning citizens at all. If we wait for the mighty to teach America's youth what secures or endangers their freedom, we will wait until the crack of doom."[6]

This is why schools are so critical to the larger cause of democratic reform. This is why Americans who care deeply about our political and economic circumstances need to put their energies first into educational reform—pushing for a Board of Assessors system represents a good start. It would not only dramatically increase the number of Americans who enter into a crucial form of civic engagement but would also ultimately improve the educational fortunes of our youth and in the process better equip our society for the tough choices it will inevitably face.

A Well-Considered Plan

Karp's reference to the "powerful and considerable" in American society was just as much a reference to the "mighty" who sit in the nation's board rooms as it was to those who sit in the halls of Congress or the halls of justice. Thanks to Supreme Court decisions that have imbued corporations with the rights of an individual, with the status of personhood, they are free to participate in a kind of bribery that is legal and called a campaign contribution. The obvious problem here is that corporations, ever focused on the bottom line, want a fair return on that investment. Specifically, they want congresspeople to propose legislation crafted by their own corporate lawyers or, short of that, they want a certain kind of vote on key legislation. If this were the only problem with corporate campaign giving, we might actually be able to live with it. But here's what puts this circumstance over the top: the huge sums that go into getting individuals elected has meant that only the relatively wealthy in American society have a shot at playing a political role at the state or federal level. The *New York Times* announced in November 2007 that "Republican Party officials" were "aggressively recruiting wealthy candidates who can spend large sums of their own money to finance their Congressional races."[7]

At its most elemental, this exposes the sheer brilliance of Madison, Hamilton, and other constitutional architects. They set up a system that has managed to keep the elites in power for centuries, if one is willing to overlook the brief period of log cabin presidents and the M-stream ascendancy during the nineteenth century. Of course they can't take credit for the incredible shot in the arm their vision of proper government received by the advent of Darwinian theory, by the advent of the notion that some are more evolved than others, that some rightly deserve to sit in the halls of power. But it is remarkable nonetheless.

A simple measure of household income reveals the crisis of representation that currently defines the United States. Our leaders are overwhelmingly chosen from among the nation's wealthiest citizens. Given the conditions created by elections in this country, they have to be. But political philosophers as far back as Plato have noted the folly in believing that a ruling group composed of the wealthy will have any inclination whatsoever to concern itself with ordinary citizens. As an example, the 109th Congress gave itself several raises while refusing to raise the minimum wage, to say nothing of refusing to do anything to make health care available for the fifty million Americans without it.

The rich and powerful stand to gain nothing by changing the status quo, and so it is foolish to believe that they will seriously consider alternatives to growth economics or to ever more centralized agricultural and energy production, or to schools in curricular and instructional lock-down. Fortunately, however, they are not completely immune to the actions of "the people." If enough citizens force the issue, we can change the standards of representation in this country. There are two ways that this might be done "within the system," so to speak. And there's a third option that may come into play that most would consider a total rejection of the system. We'll examine that shortly. As far as the two *system* options are concerned, one requires a constitutional convention, the other does not. We'll consider the one that does not first.

I am indebted to Kevin O'Leary, a University of California–Irvine political scientist, for what I am about to share, and interested readers should pick up a copy of his fascinating book, *Saving Democracy: A Plan for Real Representation in America,* to learn about it in greater detail. What O'Leary proposes is a 100-person assembly below each of the nation's 435 congressional districts. Each assembly member would be selected by lot and given a choice of whether or not he or she wishes to participate—much like a Board of Assessors might be chosen from the community surrounding each public school. In this way, 43,500 Americans would be given a significant role to play in the political life of our country. These individuals would come from all strata of American society, from the rich and the poor, from the gifted and the disabled, minority and majority groups, men and women, pretty much in equal measure.

To start, the 435 assemblies would play an advisory role only. They would be given the space and time to study and discuss the major issues of the day and thereafter render opinions to their congressional representative. It is easy to see how such assemblies would very quickly replace various polls as a vehicle for getting a feel for public opinion. Polls ask carefully crafted questions that are intended to narrow the range of possible responses—producing statistics that have little validity in terms of measuring how Americans "feel" about various topics.

Media would be forced to attend to what these citizen assemblies say, which would mean that congressional representatives would be hard-pressed to ignore, or certainly consistently ignore, the advice of the assemblies. Granted, without changing the system, Congress would still have to answer to their corporate campaign donors, but O'Leary's assembly system would put an effective counterweight into their reckoning. Without the assemblies, congresspeople can deliver the old stand-by argument that "tax cuts for the rich will stimulate investment, creating a trickle-down" and not worry about who buys it and who doesn't. With an assembly recommendation to the contrary, congressional representatives would be forced to produce real answers.

O'Leary proposed two-year terms for assembly delegates, beginning with a "crash course" in political deliberation—and while he doesn't make this a specific recommendation, this represents, once again, a perfect opportunity for America's professors and other experts and educators to become critically involved in the social and political life of the nation. They could ably direct such crash courses in ways that would maximize the positive benefit of such assemblies.

Recall that Lester Frank Ward called for a kind of Legislative Academy as a first stop for newly elected leaders. It's certainly possible to legislate such a thing, though it is doubtful that seated congressmen and women would do so. It is likely something that would need to await a constitutional convention to become a reality, but this nation could produce a powerful Congressional Academy. Instructors could be chosen by America's tenured professors, so that only the nation's most brilliant scholars of all political ideologies would work with those selected to make political decisions on behalf of the people. Following Plato, it is not difficult to imagine that newly elected congresspeople could follow three months in a Congressional Academy with three months living on nothing more than a minimum wage job with no access to other resources.[8]

Our political system has gradually become so plutocratic that individuals without the slightest clue of what it is like to try to live on the minimum wage are routinely elected to Congress. Such an experience could heighten their awareness of the trials and tribulations of the poor, a perfect follow-up to lessons learned in the Congressional Academy concerning the symbiotic relationship between the existence of the wealthy and the poor. All of this would go a long way toward redirecting America's government away from service to corporate America and back to service to the people—a long way toward creating a kind of separation of corporation and state.

But back to O'Leary's plan. He goes on to describe how his advisory assembly, if successful, could move into the realm of decision-making:

> Adding formal power to the equation, the People's House is the Assembly with a vote. In the People's House, the number of American citizens having an actual vote on federal legislation would expand from a tiny 535 (100 senators and 435 House members) to a larger cross section of nearly 45,000 (44,035 to be exact). In our new multicameral legislature, the face-to-face interaction taking place in the People's House, the House of Representatives, and the Senate would combine with the internet to create a unique form of face-to-face and digital democracy.[9]

The 43,500 members of the assembly would continue to meet physically in each of their 435 home districts, but they would additionally meet virtually via the Internet. Here O'Leary is proposing something that would have frightened Madison and Hamilton but delighted Thomas Jefferson. In other words, he is here proposing an M-stream redirection in the political affairs of the nation.

Of course, realistically, there's very little reason to believe that O'Leary's citizen assembly will materialize based on the merits of the proposal itself. It is certainly not in the self-interest of those who currently control the political system to insert a popular body that will force them to share that control. This fact underscores a central theme of this book. Start with the local school. Shift the ends of education to enculturation into a social and political democracy, and you are gradually building a citizenry capable of creating such a popular assembly.

It seems to me that this assembly, or People's House, may have its best chance of becoming a reality if it is an option selected over an otherwise imminent constitutional convention. To most readers this will sound egregiously radical. We've all been socialized to revere the U.S. Constitution. We've all been taught that it is the world's shining example of how to do democracy. The reality is that since the dawn of the twentieth century, it has been equally, and likely more so, an example to the world of what *not* to do in the name of democracy. In short, the rest of the world has moved ahead, acknowledging that the world has changed while Publius has slept. The most democratic nations by practically any measure utilize proportional systems of representation to maximize the number of voices involved in political deliberation.

Of course that wasn't a goal at the time the Constitution was created, nor is it a goal now, at least among those who currently hold power. But imagine a world with continually diminishing resources, and thus an ever-widening gap between the wealthy and poor. Or consider a world so outraged at America's dramatically disproportionate consumption of the world's resources that terrorist attacks become commonplace. Or consider a world defined by our worst fears related to climate change, a world where states like Florida become submerged, where refugees are everywhere hungry and out of work. In a world like that, a constitutional convention, far from being radical, becomes an imminently predictable conservative measure.

It is not inconceivable that a convention could be called well prior to any of the possible developments described above. Our growing recognition of the connection between community and democratic well-being is creating renewed interest in the civic republican political tradition—that is, in the M-stream. It is not unreasonable to believe that a twenty-first-century Thomas Paine can convince Americans of the need for a constitutional convention, or that groups of concerned citizens will pool their resources and sponsor billboards demanding such a convention now—using public mechanisms of that sort to get around efforts by the Big Five media to ignore a grassroots call for a constitutional convention.

It really isn't a far-off dream. I would wager that if every literate American picked up a copy of University of Texas law professor Sanford Levinson's book, *Our Undemocratic Constitution: Where the Constitution Goes Wrong and How We the People Can Correct It,* and read it thoroughly, a significant majority of Americans would be persuaded by his arguments that we do indeed stand in dire need of a constitutional convention. If all literate Americans read this book, it is reasonable to assume that there may even be a grassroots response, a coordinated campaign to get such a convention to take place (it is possible that such a grassroots campaign may emerge from the tiny fraction of all Americans who really do read the book).

But here's the problem. Sanford Levinson will be dutifully ignored by the Big Five media corporations. That's a certainty. On top of this, the comfortable academics who read the book will tell themselves things aren't really that bad—if we really need a change we can use the amendment process, overlooking the fact that amending the U.S. Constitution is much tougher than amending the constitutions of any of the West's other leading democracies.[10] It is going to take many books like Levinson's, and then courageous leaders willing to brave ridicule, shame, or worse, in the interest of reawakening Publius to the problems that beset us here in the twenty-first century.

As noted earlier, there is one small, "outside the system" political movement underway in several states—a movement that could ultimately serve as a powerful catalyst to an "inside the system" solution in the not-too-distant future. This movement involves the reawakening of the concept of secession. One result of the undemocratic trajectory that has come to define the United States in the twenty-first century is a kind of grassroots desire to leave it. The idea of seceding from the United States is becoming increasingly popular and seems to enjoy its greatest level of support in the state of Vermont, where there is currently a "200 by 2012" campaign under way, an attempt to get the majority of those living in 200 Vermont towns to vote to leave the Union by the year 2012.[11] Such a development is entirely possible in small states, a fact that might make a constitutional convention seem like a middle-of-the-road option.

What a Constitutional Convention Might Consider

What matters ought to be taken up in a constitutional convention? Levinson, like O'Leary, is concerned about the question of representation in America. Clearly it is America's biggest problem, our largest obstacle to functioning as a legitimate democracy. Levinson focuses a large part of his argument for a convention, however, as many others have, on the discrepancy created by the possession of two senators in each state.[12] In North Dakota, for example, each senator represents approximately 350,000 people. In California, each senator represents approximately 35 million. In fact, 25 percent of the nation's senators represent a mere 5 percent of the population.[13] This circumstance exists for one reason only. Had small states not received equal representation in the Senate, the Constitution never would have been ratified back in 1789. The entire Philadelphia convention would have been a waste of time.

It was a necessary concession back in 1789, but is it today? A constitutional convention could be the vehicle for creating more equitable representation, rendering O'Leary's popular assembly less necessary. But there are other less-than-democratic features, shall we say, in our Constitution that need immediate attention—features that represent examples to the rest of the world with respect to what *not* to do when creating or redesigning a government. The electoral college is probably the worst antidemocratic feature of the amended Constitution, a mechanism that makes it possible, as in 2000, for an individual who loses the election to become the president. There is no defense for the electoral college other than the fact that it is constitutionally mandated. If a constitutional convention were called today, no one would dream of defending it as a feature of a new Constitution. It would be among the first things thrown out.

Hard on the heels of that action, of course, would be abolishing life-time appointments to the Supreme Court—both the term of office and the nonelected nature of the office. In theory, from an eighteenth-century perspective, this was not as bad an idea as it has turned out to be in practice. Madison and Hamilton clearly believed that the kind of individual who would ascend to the presidency would be the sort who could dispassionately select the very brightest legal minds for the nation's highest court. And there have been presidents who have attempted to make such selections, but precious few. More often, the opportunity to select a justice becomes a direct way to strike down a law or an indirect way to create desired legislation.

As a consequence, given life terms, the makeup of the Supreme Court is a constant juggling act. Presidents with one set of ideological perspectives hope to replace individuals appointed by an earlier president with different ideological perspectives. In this way we have had Supreme Courts that have rendered utterly racist verdicts, such as *Plessy V. Ferguson* (1896), or antidemocratic verdicts locking the interests of corporations and state, such as *Buckley v. Valeo* (1976).[14] If the manner of selecting justices had worked as it was designed in theory, it is likely that the United States would not have been saddled with the democratic handicaps decisions like these created.

It turns out that forming a supreme judicial body not subject to the "whims of the people" leaves us with one subject to the "whims of a president" who in many cases has not been elected by a majority of the nation's voters. While it is true that the worst selections can be vetoed by the Senate, this all too frequently depends on the strength of something called "party loyalty," a curious expression in its own right, and not one that should have much currency at all in a government of, for, and by the people.

In the twenty-first century it is likely that the people are the best judge of who may be categorized among the nation's most brilliant legal minds—but this would depend on how elections are conducted. It may be that election procedures in this country stand in need of just as much concerted attention as do problems with representation, but we will return to this question shortly.

There is still much more to be said about the question of representation. For instance, there are four interacting circumstances or conditions that have tended to make America's federal government a fairly homogeneous entity: gender, race, wealth, and occupation. Gender and race require little explanation. Congress is now and has always been dominated by white men. The same can be said of the presidency and the Supreme Court (though the level of white male domination in the latter has fallen off some in recent decades). This represents a representation problem.

It may not be as serious as the next one, however. America's government has increasingly become dominated by the nation's wealthiest citizens. Millionaires dominate Congress, for example, which is to say that, overwhelmingly, members of the federal government come from the top 5 percent of American households as measured by income, and even considerably more elite if total wealth is considered. Heeding Plato, once again, we must acknowledge that the interests of the wealthy are categorically different from the interests of average citizens. Or, heeding Ruskin, we ought to remind ourselves that "the art of making yourself rich is equally and necessarily the art of keeping your neighbor poor." While the 109th Congress was likely the most egregiously self-interested in recognizing and acting on this fact, it has had plenty of company.

The last dimension of homogeneity among those who make up the federal government is probably the least recognized, and that is occupation. Lawyers are dramatically overrepresented in the federal government, and they tend to be overrepresented at other levels of government as well (over half of all presidents have been lawyers; almost half of all current representatives and well over half of all current senators are lawyers). One might argue that there is a predictability here, given that lawyers deal with the law for a living. But anyone who has heard the expression "to a carpenter, everything looks like a nail," has a feel for the problem with any one occupational group dominating a nation's political sphere. It is no accident that America is the "nation under lawyers" and also far and away the most litigious society in the world.[15]

Let me share one quick example of what I mean. In the fall of 2006, the Aspen Institute created a "blue-ribbon" panel charged with making recommendations for the signature education law of the George W. Bush administration, No Child Left Behind, prior to its reauthorization by Congress in 2007. The panel was chaired by ex-Wisconsin governor and ex-U.S. cabinet member, and attorney, Tommy Thompson. Thompson's panel came up with seventy-five recommended alterations—most designed to make an altogether unworkable law workable. But some were clearly designed to put their own stamp on the reauthorization, including the recommendation to allow parents to sue their local district, or even their state, if each is not "faithfully" implementing the law. Make no mistake about it: as long as lawyers dominate the law-making institutions in society, there will always be plenty of work for lawyers.

The ramifications or fallout of this circumstance is a serious problem. In the wake of lawyer-made laws we have gradually created a culture that turns first to the court system to settle all manner of disputes. This inclination seems to have increased markedly since courts pronounced lawyer advertising legal, and the American Bar Association, in undeniably self-interested fashion, dubbed it ethical. Now it is impossible for Americans to move through their daily lives without receiving near-constant television, radio, and billboard messages reminding them that they can be richly rewarded if they have been involved in an accident. Our cultural propensity to look first to the courts has meant that genuine public deliberation is rare, and when it does occur it is very often contentious, quickly devolving into a kind of contest to produce what the court would produce, a verdict declaring who wins and who loses.[16] Lost is any kind of cultural inclination to seek consensually derived compromise. The result has further cemented a kind of political ineptness among the American public—an ineptness first cultivated in a school system geared toward the economic dimension of life, at the price of any attention to its political dimension. In short, we get no practice at being political beings—either in school or in the larger society that comprises the "adult world" or the "world of work."

A constitutional convention would no doubt be forced to deal with some of these representation problems. As noted earlier, the fact that the concept of race has virtually no meaning in terms of separating one group of people from another, any attempt to build a representation system that would guarantee the participation of all races would be way too cumbersome to operationalize. The same could be said for the question of occupation—since the huge number of occupation options renders it useless as a source for considering representation levels. In contrast, gender and wealth are simple and straightforward matters. We could very easily guarantee that males and females are equally represented in the federal government (e.g., through rotating and perhaps even periodic random assignment of political districts), and we could just as easily guarantee that all of our politicians come from the middle 80 or 90 percent of the population with respect to wealth. That way the extremes—the very wealthy and the very poor—would be structurally left out of political offices and we could be reasonably sure, therefore, that policies won't be formulated for the benefit of the few at the expense of the many. In this manner we could constitutionally assure ourselves that the average politician will indeed be an average American. An added benefit to gender and income restrictions is that they would virtually guarantee a greater degree of occupational diversity—and perhaps be an aid to greater racial diversity as well.

To deny the wisdom of these constitutional modifications is one and the same as saying you believe that a government dominated by wealthy white men would be better than one that is far more diverse. Granted, you could try to make the argument sound a bit more intelligent by saying that these restrictions would be an infringement on the freedom of wealthy white men, but where's the freedom for a public school teacher making $35,000 per year to run for Congress? To argue that it's there in theory doesn't change the fact that there are no teachers in Congress.[17] It would be better to simply write the rules down in a Constitution than to rig the game and then say that all can participate. It is not asking too much of citizens in a democracy to make a decision about what's most important to them. If pursuing an ever-larger fortune is the goal, swear off of the political arena. If you want to represent your fellow citizens in a political office, make sure your income falls into the middle range of all American incomes. All are free to do so.

The Jack Abramoff scandals of 2003–2005 for a brief period alerted the American public to the incredible phenomenon of corporate lobbying in this country.[18] From time to time while the scandal was hot, in fact, journalists asked politicians whether lobbying might be outlawed. In each instance that I can think of, the politicians responded by saying they didn't think that could be done—always being careful to sound sympathetic with the sentiment. But the truth is that lobbying is part of the unofficial congressional retirement system—representatives and senators, once beaten by an opponent from their home state or district, rush to take appointments with America's largest corporations, lobbying their former colleagues for legislation that will benefit their new employers. Congress has even been forced to pass laws forbidding a too-quick transition from congressperson to lobbyist in the hope that public outrage might be diffused or avoided altogether.

Corporate campaign donations, corporate lobbying—these are the tools used to tie the interests of the government of the United States to the interests of the largest and most powerful American corporations. Those corporations that control the media, the Big Five, do their part to make this corporation-state connection as invisible as it possibly can be. If one believes that the nightly news will eventually expose the depth of this connection, one will wait, as Walter Karp would have said, until the crack of doom. It won't happen. Ordinary citizens will have to generate the momentum required to separate the power of corporation and state, the same way ordinary citizens effected the separation of church and state that put an end to an egregiously undemocratic feudal era.

The fact that we are left to our own devices with respect to moving forward with this burden should expose the centrality of the educational endeavor with respect to our overall prospects for success. As Montesquieu warned us a couple of centuries ago, republics need a school system capable of delivering the "full power of education." Going back further, Gerrard Winstanley described a school system that could balance preparation for economic life with preparation for political life. And John Dewey, a few decades ago, insisted that we need a school system that will focus on the immediate circumstances surrounding the lives of the students attending each school, meaning we need a school system that frees teachers to make curricular and instructional decisions that make sense given their circumstances, but holds them accountable for fully educating each child in their charge. Make this happen today, and our students will make a constitutional convention happen tomorrow.

Short of mandating a system with gender and income restrictions, delegates to a constitutional convention could take up the question of moving the United States to a proportional system. What this would mean is that in each election seats would be assigned on the basis of the percentage showing among voters—if Minnesota was entitled to eight seats in the House, those seats would be divided according to percentage of votes cast for each party. Democrats might receive four, Republicans three, and the Green Party one, for instance. And while third parties would likely always have few seats, at least they would have seats. Their voices would be heard; they could propose legislation, which does not happen in the current system.

Prospects for Proportionalism

In the 2006 congressional elections, Virginia Senator George Allen was challenged by a Vietnam War veteran Democrat named James Webb. The election was too close for corporate news media to call on the day of the election. Always searching for something to talk about, however, several news commentators noted that 26,000 Virginia votes went to the Independent-Green candidate, Gail Parker. "You have to figure most of those votes would have gone to the Democrat," the analysts said, "meaning Webb could have won this thing handily."[19] As it happens, Allen still lost. But the 26,000 Virginians who voted for Parker were left with no voice in the way government happens in this country. The reason for this is that the authors of our Constitution adopted a "first past the post" or "winner take all" philosophy for elections. In a given district (or state, as is the case for senators), whoever gets the most votes gets the seat in the halls of power. Given differing dynamics in different districts and states, our winner-take-all system lends itself pretty well to a two-party system. Third parties are rarely successful.

Unbeknownst to our founders, of course, the winner-take-all system makes it much easier for corporations to lobby effectively. If Congress was constituted by multiple parties there would be many more bases to cover and a much greater likelihood that the behind-closed-doors work of lobbyists would be noted and reported to the public. For this reason and others, most modern democracies have rejected the winner-take-all philosophy and have opted for proportional systems, with the lone exceptions of the United States, Canada, and the United Kingdom. In this last instance, change is clearly on the horizon. For instance, when Scotland and Wales created new legislative bodies in 1999, they chose to adopt proportional systems. All of the United Kingdom is likely headed in that direction, a circumstance that may soon leave Canada and United States alone among the top twenty-five democracies of the world.[20]

Literally millions of Americans are frequently chastised for not voting in the elections of this country without the slightest recognition that nonvoting may be a demonstration of keen intelligence regarding the way the system works. Or it may be merely a tacit understanding, but most nonvoters recognize that the system was created to ignore them as far as possible, so why participate? What good was it to cast one's vote for Parker in Virginia? Why bother to vote for John Kerry in Nebraska? Or George W. Bush in New York? You can make the argument that politicians will then have some kind of generalized understanding of where public sentiment is at, but American politicians are scarcely concerned about the views of those who voted for them, let alone those who voted against them. It may sound cynical, but realistically we know that money puts our politicians in power and they are therefore answerable to those who wield it. In many instances all across the country, therefore, voting is quite literally a waste of time. By contrast, a proportional system renders a vote of some value and would likely therefore dramatically increase citizen participation in the political process.

Moving to a proportional system could come with a turn toward a parliamentary form of government, where we would cash in a winner-take-all president for a prime minister selected from a proportionately determined Congress.[21] The entire system would push American politicians into a mode of give and take, of concession-making and coalition-building. As a consequence, the stakes tied to various elections would not seem so crucial in any given election—meaning the elections would be less likely to generate heavy spending, especially from corporate America as the purchase of party-line voting would be rendered nearly impossible. A move to a proportional system would allow us to rid ourselves of the international comedy represented by current American elections. Thirty- and sixty-second ads that say absolutely nothing of consequence except to try to impugn the integrity or judgment of the opponent—it is a disgraceful and embarrassing phenomenon—would have considerably less utility in a proportional system.

In fact, the entire election campaign process could be cleaned up considerably, allowing voters to make their decisions on the basis of arguments written by the candidates themselves and printed in the nation's newspapers. We could do away with the circus atmosphere, the ridiculous advertisements, two-year election "seasons," and so on, with a simple policy like "nothing purchased, nothing donated." It may even be possible to stop for-profit news corporations from weighing in on America's elections. This would put the deliberative burden back on voters, giving them a chance to examine the merits of candidates via what they are able to articulate in speeches and in written essays. It would drive another effective wedge between corporation and state.

Utilizing rules such as these, we could create an elected Supreme Court and do away with our current entity, which is nothing more than a vehicle for increasing the odds of a president's preferred policies. The "makeup" of the court, ghastly as the expression sounds and reprehensible as it is, is nothing more than a kind of interpresidential tug of war, complete with old men (and now, women) trying to hang on long enough to retire under an ideologically compatible president. Practically every dimension of the Supreme Court is dramatically undemocratic and undesirable. One could make a persuasive case for a constitutional convention on the basis of correcting the flaws connected to this entity alone.

People Versus Corporations

When William Ogilivie argued that it was hypocritical to allow each child born into this world access to the air they breathe, to food and water, but not to a piece of the earth, not to a space to inhabit, his contemporaries quickly condemned his corrective plan as impractical. But as the late Paul Gruchow once noted, reform, at the outset, is impractical by definition. Seven billion people, fast declining stores of Paleolithic sunlight, an overheated atmosphere, super-storms, and a growing global divide between the haves and have-nots creating unstable conditions of which acts of terrorism are but one example—all of these circumstances demand reform now, impractical though it may well seem. The problem is that right now we are in the midst of a veritable free-for-all in terms of wealth getting.[22] American elites are protected by the Big Five media corporations, who will not do so much as mention to the American public how much federal revenue could be gained by increasing the top tax bracket by a single percentage point, let alone what could be done if it were returned to 1950 levels.

As noted earlier, media corporations are able to play this protective role because they work so hard at maintaining the fiction that they are, in fact, liberal. And lest anything be left up to chance, the media have a small army of television and radio "personalities" whose job it is to keep America's poorest and least educated believing that the system is on their side—this is the role played by the Bill O'Reillys, the Rush Limbaughs, and others of that ilk. Between the lines they insinuate to their listeners and watchers that the reason they are poor is because minorities and gays get government handouts. It is not much different from the approach taken by Hitler to convince Germans that the Jews were to blame for their lot in life. It's effective, and there is no use in denying it.

Learned men and women from the academy can bring these issues to light, but they can't compete with the corporate curriculum, given its ubiquitous nature, its constant presence in the lives of all citizens. The media will ignore books such as O'Leary's, Levinson's, this one, and countless others. They can do this because they know that a huge, overwhelming majority of Americans will never see these books, let alone attempt to read them. And they have a small army of fast-track scholars employed in "think tanks" who will produce books of their own—counterarguments that appeal to emotion rather than evidence.[23] All the bases are covered. The control of the power elite, which C. Wright Mills first exposed in 1959, is now greater and more powerful than ever.

But the feudal elite were once very powerful too, and that world collapsed when men and women in seventeenth-century England, and Americans in the eighteenth century, were able to drive a wedge between church and state. Our twenty-first-century feudal era will collapse when men and women are able to drive a wedge between corporation and state. I believe that the fastest way to get there is through a shift that will balance the ends of American public education and liberate teachers so that they can prepare citizens to play a political role with their lives—so they can, in fact, decide for themselves what secures or endangers their freedom. Such a move will have the effect of creating citizens inclined to live in greater harmony with the earth's natural systems and who will work to decentralize America's food and energy production systems. Such a move will produce citizens capable of seeing the humor in the ranting of television and radio pit-bulls, and who will demand either greater levels of real representation in the system we now possess or a constitutional convention that will throw out our undemocratic system and replace it with one not only derived from the people, but truly of, for, and by the people.

Notes

Notes for Chapter 1

1. This is slightly overstated, as the Renaissance era Italian city-states were also possible "examples." On top of this, there has been more than a little speculation about the degree to which our founders "borrowed" from the political organizations of various Native groups, especially the Iroquois Confederacy. See, for example, Jerry Mander, *In the Absence of the Sacred: The Failure of Technology and the Survival of the Indian Nations* (San Francisco: Sierra Club Books, 1991), 230–235. While the arguments are not devoid of evidence, the written records of the founders themselves betray almost no attention to Native governance. In any event, whether Native influences were a part of the equation or not, the end result is our current circumstances.

2. See David A. Kay, "The Illegality of the Constitution," *Constitutional Commentary* 4 (1987): 57–80. Some historians have tried to create arguments absolving the convention of any wrong-doing in this respect, but given the fact that Madison spoke forthrightly of the unauthorized nature of what was done, these arguments appear to have little merit. In speaking of the decision to require the acceptance of nine states rather than all thirteen for ratification, Madison admitted that "in one particular it is admitted that the convention have departed from the tenor of their commission." And he went on to say that "since it is impossible for the people spontaneously and universally to move in concert towards their object," it is "therefore essential that such change be instituted by some *informal and unauthorized propositions* (Madison's emphasis), made by some patriotic and respectable citizen or number of citizens." Benjamin F. Wright, ed., *The Federalist* (New York: Barnes and Noble Books, 1996), 290–292. Kay, in reference to the Constitution, states bluntly that "this foundation of American legality was itself the product of a blatant and conscious illegality" (p. 57).

3. Charles W. Hendel, ed., *David Hume's Political Essays* (Indianapolis: Bobbs-Merrill, 1953), 145–158.

4. Wright, *The Federalist*, 135.

5. It is worth noting here that we are currently witnessing a phenomenon that in many ways constitutes another era of enclosure—one that takes livestock away from

pastures and puts them into enclosed barns or "feedlots." We will examine this development in greater detail in the next chapter.

6. For example, see Brian Donahue, *Reclaiming the Commons* (New Haven: Yale University Press, 2001); Chet A. Bowers, *Revitalizing the Commons* (New York: Rowman and Littlefield, 2006); and my own, *Teaching the Commons* (Boulder, CO: Westview Press, 1997).

7. While there was significant franchise reform under Lord Grey in the 1830s, extending the vote to the industrial workers of England was a part of what has been called "Tory democracy," the political agenda of Benjamin Disraeli during the 1870s and 1880s.

8. Robert L. Heilbroner, *The Worldly Philosophers: The Lives, Times, and Ideas of the Great Economic Thinkers* (New York: Simon and Schuster, 1961), 19.

9. The period immediately before and during the Civil War, 1620–1650, has been called the worst economic period in English history. See Joan Thirsk, ed., *The Agrarian History of England and Wales,* vol. 4 (Cambridge: Cambridge University Press, 1967), 620–621.

10. Paul Slack, *The English Poor Law, 1531–1742* (New York: Macmillan, 1990).

11. Quoted in Christopher Hill, *The World Turned Upside Down: Radical Ideas During the English Revolution* (New York: Penguin Books, 1972), 23.

12. See Alastair Dunn, *The Peasant Revolt of 1381: The Peasants' Revolt and England's Failed Revolution* (Charleston, SC: Tempus Publishing, 2002).)

13. Quoted in Hill, *The World Turned Upside Down,* 31.

14. R. H. Tawney, *Religion and the Rise of Capitalism* (London: John Murray, 1926).

15. A key component of Reformation theology is that individuals could have a relationship with God unmediated by a priest. Protestants encouraged daily Bible reading—provided it was done with the "right" translation. For instance, a Protestant translation of a key Biblical phrase held that "the Kingdom of God is within you" whereas Catholic translations, generally, held that the Kingdom is "among" you—a very different sort of idea. See R. William Franklin and Joseph M. Shaw, *The Case for Christian Humanism* (Grand Rapids, MI: William B. Erdmans Publishing, 1991), 68–69. The issue of using the "right" Biblical translation was a source of serious, sometimes violent, protest when it came to the use of the Bible in America's nineteenth-century common schools. Witness the New York and Philadelphia Bible Riots of the 1840s and the Cincinnati Bible War of 1851. For more on these events, see Lloyd P. Jorgenson, *The State and the Nonpublic School, 1825–1925* (Columbia: University of Missouri Press, 1987). John Rawls argued that "something like the modern understanding of liberty of conscience and freedom of thought" began with the Reformation. See *Political Liberalism* (New York: Columbia University Press, 1993), xxiv. Religious freedom as an idea was not easily separated from connected ideas relating to human autonomy—the freedom to choose from among options about how one's future would unfold. John Milton expressly condemned the prepublication religious censorship of seventeenth-century England, calling it residual "popery." In his view, what made the classical republics great was the complete absence of this "tyranny over learning." God's gift of reason, according to Milton, enabled man "to be his own chooser." See Warren Cherniak's analysis of Milton's views in "Civil Liberty in Milton,

the Levellers and Winstanley," in Andrew Bradstock, ed., *Winstanley and the Diggers, 1649–1999* (London: Frank Cass, 2000), 101–120. The road from religious freedom to political freedom was short.

16. Smith's *Discourse* was edited by Mary Dewar and published by the University Press of Virginia in 1969. Smith's primary focus is on revealing the causes of inflation that so wracked England in this time period and identifying the kinds of governmental interventions that could ameliorate its effects. Dewar also edited Smith's second book, *De Republica Anglorum,* for Cambridge University Press in 1982.

17. Jean Bodin, *Six Books of the Commonwealth,* ed. and trans. by M. J. Tooley, (Oxford: Blackwell Publishers, 1967), 97.

18. Thomas Hobbes, *De Cive* (Indianapolis: Hackett Publishing, 1991), 112–113, 118.

19. Wright, ed., *The Federalist,* 356, 160.

20. John Locke, *Second Treatise of Government* (Indianapolis: Hackett Publishing, 1980), 5.

21. John Locke, *An Essay Concerning Human Understanding,* book 1, chap. 3, sec. 13. From John Locke, *The Works of John Locke in Ten Volumes* (London: W. Otride and Son, 1812), vol. 1, p. 43.

22. J. G. A. Pocock, ed., *The Political Works of James Harrington* (Cambridge: Cambridge University Press, 1977), 158–159.

23. There is considerable debate about Harrington's wishes with regard to more widely distributed land ownership in England. Using 1650s monetary values, for instance, C. B. Macpherson has shown that Harrington's figures would not have dramatically altered the then current distribution. See C. B. Macpherson, *The Political Theory of Possessive Individualism* (Oxford: Clarendon Press, 1962), 185.

24. Unlike Harrington's *Oceana,* which continued to be studied and debated in England and in the North American colonies throughout the eighteenth century, the writings of Gerrard Winstanley were largely forgotten. But the radical nature of his actions, the statement he and others made by digging the commons, remained a part of eighteenth-century political thought either as a reminder of what can happen in the absence of effective authority or as a glimpse of what is possible with the acquisition of sufficient liberty.

25. See, for instance, Winthrop Hudson, "The Economic and Social Thought of Gerrard Winstanley: Was He a Seventeenth-Century Marxist?" *Journal of Modern History* 18 (1946): 1–21; and "Communism, George Hill, and the *Mir*: Was Marx a Nineteenth-Century Winstanleyan?" in Bradstock, *Winstanley and the Diggers,* 121–148.

26. George Sabine, ed., *The Works of Gerrard Winstanley* (New York: Russell and Russell, 1965), 315.

27. See James D. Alsop, "Gerrard Winstanley: What Do We Know of His Life?" in Bradstock, *Winstanley and the Diggers,* 28.

28. Sabine, *The Works of Gerrard Winstanley,* 194.

29. Hill, *The World Turned Upside Down,* 125.

30. Sabine, *The Works of Gerrard Winstanley,* 434.

31. See James D. Alsop, "Gerrard Winstanley's Later Life," *Past and Present* 82 (1979): 73–81.

32. Sabine, *The Works of Gerrard Winstanley,* 501. John Locke would later argue the exact opposite. According to Locke, the advent of the money economy allowed the fruits of the labor one employs to become the property of the employer.

33. Ibid., 511–512.

34. See Dale T. Snauwaert and Paul Theobald, "Two Trajectories of Civic Education: The Political and Educational Thought of Hobbes and Winstanley," *Journal of Educational Thought* 28 (1994): 179–197; and Richard L. Greaves, "Gerrard Winstanley and Educational Reform in Puritan England," *British Journal of Educational Studies* 17 (1969): 166–176.

35. Locke, *Second Treatise,* chap. II, para. 4; chap. II, para. 26; and chap. V, para. 34.

36. Ibid., chap. V, para. 28.

37. Ibid. Locke's emphasis.

38. Ibid., para. 36.

39. Ibid., para. 37.

40. Ibid., para. 45; and chap. XI, para. 134. Locke's emphasis.

41. Charles Taylor, *Philosophical Arguments* (Cambridge, MA: Harvard University Press, 1995), 222–224.

42. Locke, *Second Treatise,* chap. XII, para. 147.

43. See Anne Cohler, Basia Miller, and Harold Stone, eds., *Montesquieu: The Spirit of the Laws* (Cambridge: Cambridge University Press, 1989), 157.

44. Ibid., 6.

45. Ibid., 6–7. Rousseau would later criticize Montesquieu's conception of the state of nature, asking why presocial men feared one another if they were not aggressive. In his lifetime, Montesquieu was apparently never asked to address this ostensible contradiction. However, it is likely that if he had, he would have suggested that the very earliest human interactions would have triggered survival fears in the same way man's first encounter with large animals might—though subsequent interactions would trigger the sense of pleasure an animal receives "at the approach of an animal of its own kind" (p. 7). For Montesquieu, presocial society was indeed an animal-like existence. He noted that animals of the same species do not kill one another, further evidence in his mind that a presocial state of war is misplaced.

46. Burke is quoted by John Wingate Thornton in his edited volume titled *The Pulpit of the American Revolution* (Boston: Gould and Lincoln, 1860), xxvii. Burke's emphasis. As a side note related to Blackstone's *Commentaries,* many scholars have claimed that Blackstone plagiarized Montesquieu extensively. One remarked that it "would be nauseating if it were not comic." F. T. H. Fletcher, *Montesquieu and English Politics* (London: Edward Arnold, 1939), 121. Fletcher also cites a French lawyer who in 1824 published the various plagiarized passages side by side.

47. Hyneman and Lutz, *American Political Writing,* vol. 2, 795. See Rush's comments in Frederick Rudolph, ed., *Essays on Education in the Early Republic* (Cambridge: Harvard University Press, 1965), 3–40.

48. See Merrill Jensen, *The Articles of Confederation: An Interpretation of the Social-Constitutional History of the American Revolution, 1774–1781* (Madison: University of Wisconsin Press, 1970), 263–270. Also see Paul H. Mattingly and Edward W. Stevens Jr.,

eds., *Schools and the Means of Education Shall Forever Be Encouraged: A History of Education in the Old Northwest, 1787–1880* (Athens: Ohio University Libraries, 1987).

49. There were many factors that came to bear upon the creation of free school systems, including heavy Irish immigration, growing urban centers, and the unprecedented growth of popular religious denominations. But the heavily democratic spirit of Jacksonian America played a role as well. See Michael B. Katz, *The Irony of Early School Reform: Educational Innovation in Mid-Nineteenth Century Massachusetts* (Cambridge: Harvard University Press, 1968); and Paul Theobald, *Call School: Rural Education in the Midwest to 1918* (Carbondale: Southern Illinois University Press, 1995).

50. Montesquieu, *The Spirit of the Laws,* 43.

51. Hyneman and Lutz, *American Political Writing,* vol. 1, 111.

52. Ibid., 269.

53. Coram is quoted in Hyneman and Lutz, *American Political Writing,* vol. 2, 760; West is quoted in Thornton, *The Pulpit and the American Revolution,* 280; and Stone is quoted in Hyneman and Lutz, vol. 2, 842.

54. It is possible that no other history text published in the United States has generated as much controversy as this one. And while Beard has had a small army of defenders over the years, eventually what came to be called "consensus history" won the day on this argument. Simplified, the argument runs something like this: All Americans, elite and nonelite, were working on a liberal trajectory together, doing the best they could to build an equitable society. Louis Hartz, in *The Liberal Tradition in America* (New York: Harcourt Brace, 1955) argued that, generally speaking, some elite writers in Philadelphia notwithstanding, the American experiment has been about social freedom and social equality, and this interpretation was widely accepted. By the 1970s, however, there were signs of renewed disagreements, and a full-fledged critique of the consensus view came from the hands of historians who in the 1980s were dubbed "new rural historians"—John Mack Faragher, James Henretta, Timothy Breen, and others. Their arguments suggested this social equality argument was a myth, that there have been deep divisions throughout American history, and that the idea that American institutions moved toward liberal capitalism along a Lockean trajectory is misplaced. The new rural historians demonstrated that there was far greater concern for community in the lives of most eighteenth- and nineteenth-century Americans, meaning the M-stream was a much larger part of the American experience then we previously understood.

55. Wright, *The Federalist,* 136, 358–359.

56. Ibid., 131.

57. Charles de Secondat Montesquieu, *Considerations on the Causes of the Greatness of the Romans and Their Decline* (Indianapolis: Hackett Publishing, 1999), 93–94.

58. Wright, *The Federalist,* 132.

59. Alexis de Tocqueville, *Democracy in America,* ed. Richard D. Heffner (New York: Mentor Books, 1956), 198.

60. Christopher Clark, *The Communitarian Moment: The Radical Challenge of the Northhampton Association* (Ithaca, NY: Cornell University Press, 1995).

61. See Robert Dahl, *How Democratic Is the United States Constitution?* (New Haven, CT: Yale University Press, 2002), 117, 164–169.

62. Montesquieu, *The Spirit of the Laws,* xliv–xlv.

63. Thomas Jefferson to James Madison, December 20, 1787, in *The Papers of Thomas Jefferson,* vol. 12 (Princeton, NJ: Princeton University Press, 1955), 478.

64. Such an amendment would free living persons from, as he put it, "rule by the dead." See Thomas Jefferson, "Letter to Samuel Kercheval," July 12, 1816, in *The Portable Jefferson,* edited by Merrill D. Peterson (New York: Penguin Books, 1979), 1399.

Notes for Chapter 2

1. Reference here is to such examples as the drudgery of fourteen-, even sixteen-hour work days for children in the factories of England and New England; the genocide of millions of indigenous people all across the globe; and the millions who became victims of holocausts at various places throughout the twentieth century.

2. G. D. H. Cole, *The Life of William Cobbett* (London: Home and Van Thal, 1947), 5. The same dynamic, the same tension, exists in the United States today as the second great era of enclosure unfolds. This time, of course, livestock are being removed from pastures and enclosed inside feedlots or barns. The result creates an uneven playing field in farming circles, not to mention environmental hazards and aesthetic concerns ranging from spoiled landscapes to horrific smells. As communities quickly attempt to enact zoning ordinances, the present-day enclosers lobby in state legislatures and in Congress for proenclosure, anticommunity legislation.

3. I need to reiterate the phrase "speaking generally" here, for there were French intellectuals who made significant contributions to the classical economics of Smith, Malthus, and Ricardo—notably Jean Baptiste Say—and there were English intellectuals who contributed views closer to the physiocratic school of Quesnay, Turgot, and Mirabeau—notably William Ogilivie and William Cobbett.

4. No medieval scholar was more prominent in this regard than Aquinas: "To take usury for money lent is unjust in itself, because this is to sell what does not exist, and this evidently leads to inequality which is contrary to justice." St. Thomas Aquinas, *Summa Theologica,* vol. 3 (Westminster, MD: Christian Classics, 1948), 1512.

5. These remarks from Cobbett are quoted in J. L. Hammond and Barbara Hammond, *The Village Labourer, 1760–1832* (London: Longmans, Green, and Co., 1912), 211.

6. Karl Marx, "Manifesto of the Communist Party," in Eugene Kamenka, ed., *The Portable Karl Marx* (New York: Penguin Books, 1983), 208.

7. Jean Bodin, "Aux Paradoxes de Malestroit Touchant L'Encherissement De Toutes Chases and Le Moyen D'y Remedier." In Arthur E. Monroe, ed., *Early Economic Thought: Selections from Economic Literature Prior to Adam Smith* (Cambridge, MA: Harvard University Press, 1924), 127.

8. Thomas Mun, "England's Treasure by Forraign Trade," in Monroe, *Early Economic Thought,* 171.

9. Adam Smith, *An Inquiry into the Nature and Causes of the Wealth of Nations* (Indianapolis, IN: Hackett Publishing, 1993), 121.

10. Bernard Mandeville, *The Fable of the Bees* (New York: Penguin Classics, 1989), 68.

11. Ibid., 142.

12. Here the British finance journalist, Martin Wolf, serves as a good example. One would be hard-pressed to find a more adamant defender of market laws and growth economics. See his *Why Globalization Works* (New Haven, CT: Yale University Press, 2004). Wolf, when speaking about the poor in high-income nations, shifts to the use of the term *unskilled,* without the slightest indication that there may be a connection between a societal embrace of progrowth policy and the extent to which citizens become skilled or unskilled (pp. 168–169). Further, he cites numerous World Bank studies to conclude that people are better off as a result of globalization, with the possible exception of sub-Saharan Africa, "partially because of disease and partly because of the continent's failure to grow" (p. 171). Wolf proves nothing quite so well as the fact that it is possible to blame the victim at a societal, indeed, even a continental, level. Doing business as it does and in the manner it employs, of course, renders the studies commissioned and published by the World Bank susceptible to charges of conflict of interest, a fact that renders most of Wolf's arguments seriously weakened. An ostensibly independent evaluation of World Bank efforts in 2006 noted that only one in five nations receiving World Bank loans witnessed reductions in poverty. The independent evaluation, however, defended the myth that the World Bank's "overarching objective is poverty reduction," and the flawed assumption that "economic growth is essential for poverty reduction." The reality is just the opposite. See "Annual Review of Development Effectiveness: 2006," available online at http://www.worldbank.org. For a related discussion, see also David Wessel, "As Rich-Poor Gap Widens in the U.S., Class Mobility Stalls," *Wall Street Journal*, May 13, 2005, A1–A7.

13. Smith, *The Wealth of Nations*, 9–10.

14. James Scott argues that the grand schemes intended to improve the human condition in the Third World consistently have failed largely because they operate from the same simplistic assumption—that material acquisition is what motivates all people. See his *Seeing Like a State: How Certain Schemes to Improve the Human Condition Have Failed* (New Haven, CT: Yale University Press, 1998). Jane Jacobs observed that Third World development strategies between 1950 and 1980 were merely efforts to replicate the success of the Marshall Plan to rebuild Europe after World War II. These efforts were undertaken without recognizing that "fixing" an economy and changing the assumptions upon which one is built are two totally different tasks. See her *Cities and the Wealth of Nations: Principles of Economic Life* (New York: Random House, 1984), 7–8.

15. Wendell Berry, *The Hidden Wound* (San Francisco: North Point Press, 1989), 119. Berry wrote about blacks in the South who lived very poorly but nevertheless developed great competence in the complex tasks associated with nineteenth- and early twentieth-century agriculture. The same can be said for the peasants of eighteenth- and nineteenth-century England who, dispossessed by enclosure and technological innovations, migrated to cities to take up jobs so defined by Smith's "division of labour" as to be totally devoid of any skilled dimensions. One significant arena for taking pride in one's life and exhibiting the dignity that goes with a sense of accomplishment was removed from peasant lives just as it was removed from the lives of blacks who made the northward migration to the Midwest industrial cities.

16. Smith, *The Wealth of Nations,* 5.

17. England's workhouses for the poor were dreadful and deeply despised. Crabbe's 1783 poetic description holds up to historical verification:

Theirs is yon House that holds the Parish-Poor,
Whose walls of mud scarce bear the broken door;
There, where the putrid vapours, flagging, play,
And the dull wheel hums doleful through the day—
Parents, who know no children's love, dwell there!
Heart-broken Matrons on their joyless bed,
Forsaken wives and mothers never wed;
Dejected widows with unheeded tears,
And crippled age with more than childhood fears;
The lame, the blind, and, far the happiest they!
The moping idiot and the madman gay.

Here too the sick their final doom receive,
Here brought amid the scenes of grief, to grieve,
Where the loud groans from some sad chamber flow,
mix'd with the clamours of the crowd below;
Here, sorrowing, they each kindred sorrow scan,
And the cold charities of man to man:
Whose laws indeed for ruin'd age provide,
And strong compulsion plucks the scrap from pride;
But still that scrap is bought with many a sigh,
And pride embitters what it can't deny.

There is much more, but this reveals a glimpse of the horror of the work-
house. A. J. Carlyle and R. M Carlyle, eds., *The Poetical Works of George Crabbe*
(London: Oxford University Press, 1932), 37.

18. The ballad was titled "Past, Present, and Future" and is quoted in Alun Howkins,
Reshaping Rural England: A Social History, 1850–1925 (New York: Harper Collins, 1991),
62–63.

19. Smith, *The Wealth of Nations*, 129–130.

20. See Elhanan Helpman, *The Mystery of Economic Growth* (Cambridge, MA:
Harvard University Press, 1994); and Wolf, *Why Globalization Works*, 45.

21. Margaret Eisenhart and Robert L. DeHaan, "Doctoral Preparation of Scientifically Based Education Researchers," *Educational Researcher* 34 (May 2005): 3–13. The
authors suggest a variety of ways to socialize graduate students into a "culture of science,"
suggesting, indirectly, that in education (and this holds true in mainstream thought about
economics as well) we should strive to come to know what we can with certainty, and then
act on that certain knowledge. I believe this is precisely the wrong kind of socialization,
be it in education or economics. In both arenas, history suggests such quests are folly
and, as a consequence, to the contrary, we ought to act with full knowledge of what we
do not know for certain.

22. Said Smith regarding the economic views of Quesnay and his followers (called
physiocrats), "This system, with all of its imperfections, is, perhaps, the nearest approxi-
mation to the truth that has yet been published upon the subject of political economy, and
is upon that account well worth the consideration of every man who wishes to examine
with attention the principles of that very important science." *The Wealth of Nations*, 157.

23. Ferdinando Galiani's *Dialogues sur le Commerce des Bles,* published in 1769, is an excellent example. For a detailed account of this work and the quick and virulent reaction of the physiocrats, see Dena Goodman, *The Republic of Letters: A Cultural History of the French Enlightenment* (Ithaca, NY: Cornell University Press, 1994), 187–204.

24. Witness Paul Erhlich's *The Population Bomb,* published in 1968.

25. Said Malthus, "To those who know me personally, I feel that I have no occasion to defend my character from the imputation of hardness of heart; and to those who do not, I can only express my confidence that when they have attended to the subject as much as I have, they will be convinced that I have not admitted a single proposition which appears to detract from the present comforts and gratifications of the poor, without very strong grounds for believing that it would be more than compensated to them by the general and permanent improvement of their condition." See Thomas Robert Malthus, *The Pamphlets of Thomas Robert Malthus* (New York: Augustus M. Kelley Publishers, 1970), 36.

26. Piero Sraffa, ed., *The Works and Correspondence of David Ricardo,* vol. 1 (Cambridge, UK: Cambridge University Press, 1953), 94. It should be noted that many claim Ricardo was not as hardhearted as Malthus; that he believed wages should include room for "conveniences" above mere subsistence. While this much is true, he nevertheless betrayed little optimism about the ability of the working class to marshal self-restraint. He in fact saw this inability as a fixed or lawlike tendency that could reliably be worked into economic calculation, thus the phrase "the iron law of wages."

27. There are many contemporary accounts that one could turn to for verification of the inordinately miserable circumstances. Frederic Morton Eden's *The State of the Poor* is a classic study that dates back to 1797 and is available in several reprinted editions, as late as 2001. Friedrich Engels's *The Condition of the Working Class in England,* first published in 1844, is also available in many subsequent editions. Engels's book draws on countless contemporary reports and commissioned studies in addition to detailed personal observations.

28. Jean Baptiste Say, *A Treatise on Political Economy or the Production, Distribution, and Consumption of Wealth* (Philadelphia: Grig and Elliot, 1836), 133–134.

29. Sismondi was actually Swiss, though he spoke and wrote in the French language.

30. A collection of Say's letters to Thomas Malthus was published in 1936. In this volume are various letters defending his "law" against Malthus's objections. See Jean Baptiste Say, *Letters to Thomas Robert Malthus on Political Economy and Stagnation of Commerce* (London: George Harding's Bookshop Ltd., 1936).

31. Sraffa, *The Works and Correspondence of David Ricardo,* vol. 4, 21.

32. The Corn Laws were one of many issues on which Malthus and Ricardo respectively disagreed. Malthus tended to evaluate the legislation in an objective fashion, delineating the pros and cons without taking a stand; see his "Observations on the Effects of the Corn Laws," in Thomas Robert Malthus, *The Pamphlets of Thomas Robert Malthus* (New York: Augustus M. Kelley Publishers, 1970), 94–131. In response, Ricardo carried on a long correspondence with Malthus, steadfastly urging Malthus to support his position. Wrote Ricardo, "I never was more convinced of any proposition in Political Economy than that restrictions on importation of corn in an importing country have a tendency to lower profits." See various letters on the subject in James Bonar, ed., *Letters*

of David Ricardo to Thomas Robert Malthus, 1810–1823 (Oxford, UK: Clarendon Press, 1887), 35.

33. John Stuart Mill, *The Principles of Political Economy*, vol. 1 (London: Colonial Press, 1900), 357, 245. Later in the first volume, Mill picks up the Malthusian argument contending that if you feed the poor and give them work, they will never learn to muster the necessary restraint (p. 447).

34. Henry George, *Progress and Poverty* (New York: Modern Library, 1938), 140–150. George delivered a death blow to Malthusian theory by asking a simple question: "Does the relative power of producing wealth decrease with the increase of population?" (p. 143). To this, Malthus, Ricardo, and Mill, had they been around to answer (Mill died in 1873; *Progress and Poverty* was first published in 1879), must all have said yes if they wished to maintain their belief that the poor are to blame for poverty. But the answer is clearly and unequivocally no, as George so persuasively demonstrated.

35. See Jeremy Bentham, *The Principles of Morals and Legislation* (New York: Prometheus Books, 1988), 1. It is worth noting that the Mill/Bentham thesis concerning humans as pleasure maximizers considerably stepped up the already quite strong liberal vision of life as an *individual* undertaking. Said Bentham, "the community is a *fictitious body*" and the interest of community is merely "the sum of the interests of the several members who compose it" (p. 3, Bentham's emphasis). In other words, society's focus ought to be on preserving the right of individuals to maximize pleasure and minimize pain. Society ought not concern itself with the well-being of community, a concept Bentham believed to be "fictitious" in any event. I should note here, too, that Mill and Bentham believed public schools should heighten the competitive impulses of the nation's youth in the interest of creating a nation of accomplished self-interest maximizers.

36. John Stuart Mill, *The Collected Works of John Stuart Mill*, vol. 1, 252.

37. Joseph Schumpeter, *Capitalism, Socialism, and Democracy* (New York: Harper and Brothers, 1942), 21.

38. See Thorstein Veblen, *The Theory of the Leisure Class* (Norwalk, CT: Easton Press, 1994).

39. Otohiko Okugawa, "Annotated List of Communal and Utopian Societies, 1787–1919," in Robert S. Fogarty, ed., *Dictionary of American Communal and Utopian History* (Westport, CT: Greenview, 1980), 173–233. Also see Christopher Clark, *The Communitarian Moment: The Radical Challenge of the Northampton Association* (Ithaca, NY: Cornell University Press, 1995), 2.

40. William Ogilivie, *Birthright in Land: An Essay on the Right of Property in Land* (New York: Augustus Kelley, 1970), 7.

41. Ibid., 24–25n.

42. Ibid., 10.

43. Thomas Paine, "Agrarian Justice," in William M. Van der Weyde, ed., *The Life and Works of Thomas Paine*, vol. 10 (New Rochelle, NY: Thomas Paine National Historical Association, 1925, 9.

44. Ibid., 11.

45. Ibid., 15.

46. J. C. L. Simonde de Sismondi, *Political Economy and the Philosophy of Government*, M. Mignet, trans. (New York: Augustus Kelley, 1966), 15.

47. J. C. L. Simonde de Sismondi, *New Principles of Political Economy,* Richard Hyse, trans. (New Brunswick, NJ: Transaction Publishers, 1991), xxviii.

48. Ibid., 131.

49. Ibid., 138.

50. In fact, Sismondi is the only economist quoted in *The Communist Manifesto,* and he received more citations than any other in the first volume of *Capital* (the only volume written by Marx alone).

51. Leon Walras, *Elements of Pure Economics, or The Theory of Social Wealth,* William Jaffe, trans. (London: George Allen and Unwin, 1954), 48.

52. The translator of Sismondi's *New Principles,* Richard Hyse, seems to doubt that Mill really believed distribution was a social issue, noting that "Robert L. Heilbroner ascribes this thought to John Stuart Mill" (p. xxxiv) in his classic *The Worldly Philosophers* (New York: Simon and Schuster, 1961), suggesting, perhaps, that he and others don't. As it happens, Heilbroner labels Walras "an agrarian socialist" in that book (p. 150), wrongly, I believe, but because Walras insists that "the distribution of social wealth must be equitable." See Walras, *Elements of Pure Economics,* 75.

53. Ibid., 77.

54. Ibid.

55. Ibid., 79.

56. John Ruskin, *Unto This Last and Other Writings* (New York: Penguin Books, 1985), 219–220.

57. Ibid., 170.

58. Ibid., 209.

59. Ibid., 213.

60. Ibid., 180–181.

61. Ibid., 200n.

62. Ibid., 218.

63. Ibid., 227–228.

64. Sean Wilentz, *The Rise of American Democracy: Jefferson to Lincoln* (New York: W. W. Norton, 2005), xvii.

65. Ibid., xxvii.

66. Herbert Spencer, *The Study of Sociology* (New York: D. Appleton, 1882), 418.

67. William Graham Sumner, *The Challenge of Facts and Other Essays* (New Haven, CT: Yale University Press, 1914), 90.

68. The 1894 income tax law was the nation's second such law. The first came in 1862 as a revenue-raising measure intended to help finance the Civil War. The nation's first inheritance tax was passed at that time, too. For more on tax history, see John F. Witte, *The Politics and Development of the Federal Income Tax* (Madison: University of Wisconsin Press, 1985).

69. Grant McConnell, *The Decline of Agrarian Democracy* (Berkeley: University of California Press, 1953), 20.

70. Heilbroner, *The Worldly Philosophers,* 217.

71. Though my father never spoke of it, my mother told me that as a boy my father was given pennies by his parents and told to use them to purchase cracked eggs, if they could be had, behind the local produce company.

72. Ronald A. Mulder, *The Insurgent Progressives in the United States Senate and the New Deal, 1933–1939* (New York: Garland Publishing, 1979), 67.

73. Huey Long, *Every Man a King: The Autobiography of Huey P. Long* (New Orleans: National Book Co., 1933), 295.

74. David H. Bennett, *Demagogues in the Depression* (New Brunswick, NJ: Rutgers University Press, 1969), 125.

75. Randolph E. Paul, *Taxation in the United States* (Boston: Little, Brown, 1954), 301.

76. Mark Blyth, *Great Transformations: Economic Ideas and Institutional Change in the Twentieth Century* (Cambridge, UK: Cambridge University Press, 2002).

77. Herbert I. Schiller, *Culture, Inc.: The Corporate Takeover of Public Expression* (New York: Oxford University Press, 1989), 29.

Notes for Chapter 3

1. Ben H. Bagdikian, *The New Media Monopoly* (Boston: Beacon Press, 2004), 3.

2. See Gerrard Winstanley, *The Law of Freedom,* in George H. Sabine, ed., *The Works of Gerrard Winstanley* (New York: Russell and Russell, 1965), 576–579.

3. The first quote is from chapter 1, book 2, paragraph 15; the second is from chapter 2, book 2, paragraph 2. See John Locke, *John Locke in Ten Volumes* (London: Otride and Sons, 1812), 1, 20, 77.

4. Cremin wrote the forward to Peter Gay, ed., *John Locke on Education* (New York: Teachers College Press, 1964), vi.

5. Ibid., 13.

6. I hope the reader will forgive the extensive use of the male pronoun—I use it because of the emphasis given to the expression "economic man" throughout history.

7. Alexis de Tocqueville, *Democracy in America,* vol. 1 (New York: Century, 1898), 395n.

8. See Lloyd Jorgenson, *The State and the Nonpublic School* (Columbia: University of Missouri Press, 1987), 119.

9. Mills's emphasis. He is quoted in Paul Theobald, *Call School: Rural Education in the Midwest to 1918* (Carbondale: Southern Illinois University Press, 1995), 19.

10. Horace Mann is sometimes called an advocate of the five R's—reading, [w]riting, [a]rithmetic, republicanism, and religion. Through instruction in all of these areas Mann believed that citizens would be prepared to become responsible community members and contributors to the overall vitality of American society.

11. Reference here, of course, is to America's curricular response to the Cold War and to the Russian launching of Sputnik. Contemporary literature is replete with pleas to beef up the American school experience so that we might produce the scientists needed to beat the Russians to the moon and to stay one step ahead of them in terms of sophisticated military weaponry. *The Big Red Schoolhouse,* a book-length treatment of Soviet educational efforts, by Fred M. Hechinger (Garden City, NJ: Doubleday, 1959), provides an excellent example. A few decades later schools were called on once again, this time to be America's economic savior, as the popular perception of the 1980s was that

the United States was being out-engineered by the Germans and Japanese. This type of analysis continues to this day. See Mark Gradstein, Moshe Justman, and Volker Meier, *The Political Economy of Education: Implications for Growth and Inequality* (Cambridge, MA: MIT Press, 2005).

12. This is usually done by pointing to poets like William Blake and their references to such phrases as "satanic mills," claiming that these individuals obviously pined romantically—which is to say foolishly—for a past that could never be again. Lewis Mumford observed some fifty years ago that the term romantic "became a mere escapist dream, not a serious alternative to the existing order." To this day we are quick to call anyone a "hopeless romantic" for merely asking whether circumstances might have been better in the past.

13. Clarence J. Karier, "Testing for Order and Control in the Corporate State," *Educational Theory* 11 (Spring 1971): 159–180.

14. See Clarence J. Karier, *Scientists of the Mind: Intellectual Founders of Modern Psychology* (Urbana: University of Illinois Press, 1986).

15. To be fair, not all IQ test creators sought to use their instruments to divide and sort those with considerable intelligence from those with less. The instrument's initial creator, Alfred Binet of France, certainly was not among them. Like Binet, there were Americans who believed that the IQ test could be a valuable instrument for diagnosing learning problems and for suggesting instructional interventions—though this group was a significant minority throughout the first half of the twentieth century.

16. Merle Curti, *Social Ideas of American Educators* (New York: Charles Scribner and Sons, 1935), 209.

17. Stephen Preskill, "Charles Eliot and Differentiated Curricula," *Educational Theory* 39 (Fall 1989): 353–356.

18. President Reagan's Commission on Excellence in Education published its high-profile report in 1983. Given the flamboyant title *A Nation at Risk,* it claimed that America's schools had become overwhelmingly mediocre and, further, that if a foreign power would have inflicted this condition on our schools, we would have considered it an act of war. There has probably never been another presidential commission that contributed such a baseless, and totally useless, report. But its authors weren't about to let the facts get in the way of the message they intended to send. Thereafter, politicians of both parties had found a convenient political "whipping boy" and a good public diversion from more pressing issues. Everywhere there were politicians claiming that they would be the "education president" or the "education governor" if elected. And everywhere those promises became the punch-lines of postelection jokes. Readers interested in learning more about the inanity of the *Nation at Risk* report should consult Gerald Bracey's critique in *Phi Delta Kappan* 84 (April 2003): 616–621.

19. Nell Painter, *Standing at Armageddon: The United States, 1877–1919* (New York: W. W. Norton, 1989).

20. Joseph Mayer Rice, *Scientific Management in Education* (New York: Noble and Elredge, 1912), xiv, 20–24.

21. There was one last attempt, one last twentieth-century effort, to generate proof of racially determined intellectual inferiority. Richard J. Herrnstein and Charles Murray's *The Bell Curve: Intelligence and Class Structure in American Life* (New York: Free Press) was published in 1994. Predictably, it made media headlines, but this time even

staunch conservatives kept their distance. The work was decimated through reviews by the mainstream scientific community, and in fewer than ten years it became a work of historical interest only.

22. Sumner is quoted in Henry Steele Commager, *The American Mind: An Interpretation of American Thought and Character Since the 1880s* (New Haven, CT: Yale University Press, 1950), 202.

23. Israel Gerver, ed., *Lester Frank Ward: Selections from His Work* (New York: Thomas Crowell, 1963), 87.

24. Quoted in Commager, *The American Mind*, 213.

25. Ibid., 210.

26. Quoted in Herbert M. Kliebard, *The Struggle for the American Curriculum, 1893–1958* (New York: Routledge and Kegan Paul, 1987), 54.

27. John Dewey, *The School and Society* (Chicago: University of Chicago Press, 1943), 7.

28. John Dewy, *Democracy and Education* (New York: Free Press, 1966), 60.

29. Butler is quoted in George S. Counts, *Dare the School Build a New Social Order?* (Carbondale: Southern Illinois University Press, 1978), 29. Economists, of course, tend to praise the cultural shift that put economic life at the center of human concern, with little apparent recognition that this might, at some level or another, be a serious problem for humankind. Witness Liah Greenfield's exhaustive account titled *The Spirit of Capitalism: Nationalism and Economic Growth* (Cambridge, MA: Harvard University Press, 2001). According to Greenfield, "Where it developed, the new economic consciousness—the competitive and forward oriented collective spirit of capitalism—followed closely upon the heels of nascent nationalism. In the twentieth century, the economic consciousness has reigned supreme" (p. 107).

30. Dewey, *Democracy and Education*, 54.

31. Ibid., 183, 195, 169.

32. Counts, *Dare the School*, 29–30.

33. Ibid., 38.

34. Ibid., 46–47. Fifty years later actor/singer Kris Kristofferson would capture the same notion, in a song made famous by Janis Joplin, whose lyrics include the line "freedom's just another word for nothing left to lose."

35. Kliebard, *The Struggle for the American Curriculum*, 206.

36. National Education Association of the United States, *Education and Economic Well-Being in American Democracy* (Washington, DC: NEA, 1940).

37. National Commission on Excellence in Education, *A Nation at Risk: The Imperative for Educational Reform*, 5.

38. Gerald Bracey, "April Foolishness: The 20th Anniversary of *A Nation at Risk*," *Phi Delta Kappan* 84 (April 2003): 616–621.

39. David Gardner, the one-time president of the University of California system, chaired the commission that produced the *Nation at Risk* report. Ten years later, when *Newsweek* ran a story titled "A Nation Still at Risk," Gardner was quoted as saying, "What I see is a slow, steady erosion of public regard for public schools." See Barbara Kantrowitz and Pat Wingert, "A Nation Still at Risk," *Newsweek*, April 19, 1993, 121. These remarks prompted Stanley Elam, who at the time coordinated education polls for Phi Delta Kappa, to solicit the data from Gardner that was used to support *A Nation at Risk* and on which

his sentiments expressed in *Newsweek* were based. Said Elam, "Many weeks later, and only after resorting to genteel blackmail, I received a response that cited no research but suggested that evidence of the erosion of public schools was ubiquitous." See Stanley Elam, *How America Views Its Schools: The PDK/Gallup Polls, 1969–1994* (Bloomington, IN: Phi Delta Kappa Educational Foundation, 1994), 8.

40. National Commission on Excellence in Education, *A Nation at Risk*, 7.

41. Lawrence J. Cremin, *Popular Education and Its Discontents* (New York: Harper and Row, 1989), 102. Emphasis added to highlight the acknowledgement that there are other "educational" institutions in society, most prominently, the corporate-controlled media.

42. Louis V. Gerstner, "Our Schools Are Failing: Do We Care?" *New York Times*, May 27, 1994, A27.

43. Debra Viadero, "Study Questions Role Math, Science Scores Play in Nation's GDP," *Education Week*, December 13, 2006, 9.

44. *America 2000: An Education Strategy* (Washington, DC: U.S. Department of Education, 1991).

45. Ernest L. Boyer, *Selected Speeches, 1979–1995* (Princeton, NJ: Carnegie Foundation for the Advancement of Teaching, 1997), 89–90.

46. Bracey, "April Foolishness," 621.

47. Laurie Mifflin, "Nielson to Research Channel One's Audience," *New York Times*, December 28, 1998, C6.

48. Ben H. Bagdikian, *The Media Monopoly* (Boston: Beacon Press, 1983), xv.

49. Robert W. McChesney, *Rich Media, Poor Democracy: Communication Politics in Dubious Times* (Urbana: University of Illinois Press, 1999), 297.

50. Ibid., 275.

51. Bagdikian, *The Media Monopoly*, xiv.

52. John Jay and John Adams are cited as frequent users of this phrase in McChesney, *Rich Media, Poor Democracy*, 6.

53. Ibid., 266.

54. Donald Schorr, "Confessions of a Newsman," *World Monitor* 5 (May 1992): 39.

55. Ibid., 40.

56. Michael J. Graetz and Ian Shapiro, *Death by a Thousand Cuts: The Fight over Taxing Inherited Wealth* (Princeton, NJ: Princeton University Press, 2005).

57. Ibid., 85.

58. Ibid., 6.

59. Ibid., 95.

60. Ibid., 66.

61. Ibid., 65.

62. Ibid., 6.

63. Writing the sentence contending that almost nothing liberal makes it to the airwaves reminded me of one of the early sentences in Thomas Jefferson's autobiography: "During the regal government, nothing liberal could expect success." Beyond the issue of different definitions for the word *liberal* there's a remarkable coincidence between Jefferson's words and what I just wrote. The elite of the feudal era would suffer nothing liberal that might make its way into daily conversation. The elite today are of the same

mind. The first circumstance necessitated the separation of church and state; the second one necessitates the separation of corporation and state. Merrill D. Peterson, ed., *Thomas Jefferson: Writings* (New York: Library of America, 1984), 5.

64. Gregg Toppo, "Education Department Paid Commentator to Promote Law," *USA Today,* January 7, 2005.

65. Marvin Harris, *Cannibals and Kings: The Origin of Cultures* (New York: Random House, 1977), 196.

Notes for Chapter 4

1. See, for example, "America's Creaking Infrastructure," *The Economist,* August 11, 2007, 23–24.

2. Paul S. Mead, Laurence Slutsker, Vance Dietz, Linda F. McCaig, Joseph Bresee, Craig Shapiro, Patricia M. Griffin, and Robert V. Tauxe, "Food-Related Illness and Death in the United States," *Emerging Infectious Diseases* 5, no. 5 (September-October 1999): 607–625.

3. Herman E. Daly, "Economics in a Full World," *Scientific American* (September 2005): 102.

4. Herbert M. Kliebard, *The Struggle for the American Curriculum, 1893–1958* (New York: Routledge and Kegan Paul, 1987), 159. Readers interested in the fate of twentieth-century progressive education should take particular note of Kliebard's account of a massive educational research project that became known as the "eight year study"—an attempt to compare traditional pedagogy versus progressive pedagogy in a selected group of American high schools. While the "verdict" tended to favor progressive pedagogy slightly, there was considerable debate over the results and the methodology used.

5. John I. Goodlad, *A Place Called School: Prospects for the Future* (New York: McGraw-Hill, 1984), 329.

6. Robert Sternberg, "Creativity Is a Habit," *Education Week,* February 22, 2006.

7. See, for example, Michele McNeil, "NGA Kicks Off Push for 'Innovative' Agenda: Effort Stresses Math, Science Education to Keep Economic Edge," *Education Week,* December 13, 2006: 15.

8. Antonio R. Damasio, *Descartes' Error: Emotion, Reason, and the Human Brain* (New York: G. P. Putnam's Sons, 1994).

9. See, for example, Myron Lieberman, "School Board Weakness: The Reform Issue that Can't Be Faced," *Education Week,* September 19, 2007: 24–25. While arguments such as this might be dismissed as ideological ranting, it is nevertheless telling that their publication produces no groundswell of indignation—meaning, apparently, that we have reached a point where it is permissible to assail the very concept of democracy itself.

10. Over the past couple of decades there have been strides made in many states toward including the surrounding public on site-based councils of one sort or another, and the idea behind the creation of a Board of Assessors for each school is in part an outgrowth of this trend. But the Board of Assessors concept is based upon the belief that (1) if selected by lot, such boards would insert a political dimension into the lives of hundreds of thousands of citizens; (2) schools could then be free to turn curriculum

and instructional decisions over to teachers (monitored and negotiated with the Board), revitalizing their professional lives in the process; and (3) the question of accountability would be answered by individuals with something at stake in the question and with the greatest access to the results of educational efforts.

11. It should be noted that while Chicago has experimented with the extension of greater control at the local level, as have countless communities across the country, some large urban centers have worked in the opposite direction. Touting "mayoral control" as the only solution to vexing underperformance in urban schools, proponents of privatization have found a new way to try to make it happen. New York's Mayor Michael Bloomberg represents the most dramatic example. Having pushed through state-level legislation that gave him complete control of the nation's largest school district, Bloomberg has since decreased public school expenditures in all but two areas: (1) the number of multi-million-dollar no-bid contracts given to private consulting firms charged with grading, testing, and inspecting New York City schools; and, (2) the price tag for administering the district (up nearly 25 percent), which Bloomberg and Chancellor Joel Klein have turned over to a small army of lawyers and business school graduates with no educational background whatsoever. Bloomberg has almost completely eliminated popular, democratic input into the functioning of the district. He has created a colossal mess, which the *New York Times* dutifully fails to reveal to the public.

12. A sampling of literature related to constructivist theory includes Catherine Twomey Fosnot's *Constructivism: Theory, Perspectives, and Practice* (New York: Teachers College Press, 1996); Eleanor Duckworth's *The Having of Wonderful Ideas and Other Essays on Teaching and Learning* (New York: Teachers College Press, 1996); Jacqueline Grennon Brooks and Martin G. Brooks, *In Search of Understanding: The Case for Constructivist Classrooms* (Washington, DC: Association for Supervision and Curriculum Development, Revised Edition, 1999); and Maryellen Weimer, *Learner-Centered Teaching: Five Key Changes to Practice* (San Francisco: Jossey-Bass, 2002).

13. For more on this, see David A. Gruenewald and Gregory A. Smith, eds., *Place-Based Education in the Global Age: Local Diversity* (New York: Lawrence Erlbaum Associates, 2008).

14. Neil Postman, *The End of Education: Redefining the Value of School* (New York: Vintage Books, 1995), 27.

15. Wendell Berry, *What Are People For?* (San Francisco: North Point Press, 1990), 164.

Notes for Chapter 5

1. Wendell Berry, *The Hidden Wound* (San Francisco: North Point Press, 1989), 134.

2. The Democrat-controlled 110th Congress moved quickly in 2007 to amend the work habits of the infamously corrupt 109th Congress by calling for five-day congressional work weeks (a move that would approximately double the work hours of the prior Congress). The outcry over this was that congressional representatives would not then be able to fly back to their districts and "connect with their constituents," as if they ever did, or ever could, with such an enormous represented-representative ratio. The

corporate-controlled media, of course, rather than pointing out the ludicrous nature of such claims, merely reported the outcry as if it were a legitimate argument.

3. John Maynard Keynes, *Essays in Persuasion* (New York: W. W. Norton, 1963), 319.

4. Thorstein Veblen, *The Instinct of Workmanship* (New York: W. W. Norton, 1964), 352.

5. Ibid., 36–37. Emphasis added to differentiate the selfless dispositions attached to work, in Veblen's reckoning, from the selfishness that ostensibly guides work, in the reckoning of the classical economics tradition.

6. Ibid., 36.

7. Keynes, *Essays in Persuasion,* 366–367.

8. Robert D. Putnam, *Bowling Alone: The Collapse and Revival of American Community* (New York: Simon and Schuster, 2000), 332.

9. Martin E. P. Segilman, "Boomer Blues," *Psychology Today,* October 1988: 50–55.

10. I won't go into detail about America's complicity in the proliferation of Third World sweat shops. For those who would like to know more about this sordid, yet official, behavior, see, for example, James Brooke and Kate Zernike, "In Pacific Islands, Mixed Feelings About a Lobbyist's Work," *New York Times,* May 6, 2005, A1; and Walter F. Roche Jr. and Chuck Neubauer, "Two Former Aides to DeLay Paved Way for Lobbyist Deal: Their Work on Saipan Helped Get a Contract for a Lawyer Now the Target of a Corruption Probe," *Los Angeles Times,* May 6, 2005, 1. I am indebted to Wendell Berry, who first broached this concept—hostages to one's comfort—in poetic form. See his book of poetry titled *Clearing* (New York: Harcourt, Brace, Jovanovich, 1977), 36.

11. Ruskin, *Unto This Last,* 227.

12. Leslie Garrett, *The Virtuous Consumer: Your Essential Guide for a Better, Kinder, and Healthier World* (Novato, CA: New World Library, 2007); and Ellis Jones, *The Better World Shopping Guide: Every Dollar Makes a Difference* (Gabriola Island, BC: New Society Publishers, 2006).

13. It is difficult to know where to begin to try to relay the ghastly practices of this corporate giant. Despite periodic inspections resulting in multiple violations of child labor laws, the George W. Bush Labor Department agreed to allow Wal-Mart to continue to deny any wrongdoing after paying a small fine. Further, the Labor Department agreed to give Wal-Mart stores a fifteen-day notice before further inspections occur. And, of course, Wal-Mart was a multi-million-dollar contributor to George W. Bush and other Republican candidates during the Bush era. Money well spent, obviously. To get a glimpse at the magnitude of worker abuse, perhaps one needs to look no further than the fact that Sam Walton's widow and their four children are among the wealthiest eleven Americans. Each has a net worth in the vicinity of $15.5 billion. In contrast, fewer than half of Wal-Mart employees receive health benefits, and those that do must pay for almost half of a miserable plan that includes a $3,000 family deductible, a $300 pharmacy deductible, and a $1,000 in-patient hospital deductible. As a result of this ill-treatment, Wal-Mart is in a constant search mode for new employees. The great majority of those hired stay for less than a year. By the time this book is published, Wal-Mart will have no doubt made improvements on its parsimonious health insurance plans—as there is considerable public outrage over the issue. Wal-Mart typically responds with deceptive television

advertisements designed to convince the public that it does indeed provide "affordable health insurance" to employees despite the fact that most get none, many get a plan that scarcely deserves to be called a plan, and the relatively few at the management end of the business are well compensated with lucrative salary and benefits.

14. Jacobs, *Dark Age Ahead,* 38–39.

15. David R. Moeller, "The Problem of Agricultural Concentration: The Case of the Tyson-IBP Merger," *Journal of Agricultural Law* 8 (2003): 8.

16. Ibid., 9.

17. Animals in confinement operations in this country produce thirteen times the amount of fecal waste as humans do. Environmental Protection Agency, *Preliminary Data Summary: Feedlots Point Source Category Study,* EPA–821-R–99–002 (Washington, DC: Office of Water, 1999), 14.

18. J. E. Brody, "Studies Find Resistant Bacteria in Meats," *New York Times,* October 18, 2001, A12.

19. Terence J. Centner, *Empty Pastures: Confined Animals and the Transformation of the Rural Landscape* (Champaign: University of Illinois Press, 2004), 39.

20. In 1997 laws were enacted to prevent "ruminants from eating ruminants"— ending the legal feeding of dead cattle to live cattle. Some contend, however, that the practice has not stopped and that, in addition, it is alive and well in the poultry and pork industries.

21. Howard Lyman, a former Montana cattleman, has become a spokesperson of sorts for the BSE-CJD connection, doing his best to alert the country to this huge breach in the safety of our food production system. He told the story on the *Oprah* show and was immediately sued, as was Oprah Winfrey, by the Texas Cattleman's Association. After six years in the court system, Lyman and Winfrey prevailed. Still, the case prompted powerful lobbyists in thirteen states to create and push through "food disparagement laws," making it illegal to criticize or question food or how it is produced.

22. There is a discernible trend in this direction, as the proliferation of "voluntary simplicity" organizations attests. With the establishment of these organizations has come websites and publications that share guidance and practical knowledge necessary to, as one organization maintains, "live outwardly simple and inwardly rich."

23. Wendell Berry, *Entries* (New York: Pantheon Books, 1994), 37.

24. John Stuart Mill, *The Principles of Political Economy* (New York: Penguin Classics, 1988), 111.

25. William Greider, *The Soul of Capitalism: Opening Paths to a Moral Economy* (New York: Simon and Schuster, 2003), 104.

26. Ibid., 117.

27. See, for example, a report titled "Socially Responsible Investing Comes of Age," available at http://www.tiaa-cref.org.

28. Ibid., 114.

29. Said Plato, for example, "The lower limit of poverty must be that value of the holding.... The legislator will use the holding as his unit of measure and allow a man to possess twice, thrice, and up to four times its value. If anyone acquires more than this ... he should hand over the surplus to the state." *The Laws,* V, 744 in Edith Hamilton and Huntington Cairns, eds., *Plato: The Collected Dialogues* (Princeton, NJ: Princeton University Press, 1961), 1328–1329. Aristotle largely agreed with Plato on the question

of wealth disparities, though he allowed for the richest to acquire five times as much as the poorest.

30. Ibid., 125.

31. Readers should consult the work of Sam Pizzigati for persuasive accounts related to how maximum wage legislation could be implemented equitably. See his *The Maximum Wage: A Common Sense Prescription for Revitalizing America by Taxing the Very Rich* (New York: Apex Press, 1992); also see his *Greed and Good* (Washington, DC: Council on International and Public Affairs, 2004). Pizzigati demonstrates that far from being "impractical," when compared to weaning America from a reliance on fossil fuels, maximum wage legislation could be easily operationalized—a fact that legitimates the complete and total censorship of even the phrase "maximum wage" in the nation's corporate media.

32. Herman E. Daly, "Economics in a Full World," *Scientific American,* September 2005: 100.

Notes for Chapter 6

1. Gordon S. Wood, *The Creation of the American Republic, 1776–1787* (Chapel Hill: University of North Carolina Press, 1969), 516.

2. As one might expect, it is difficult to get a firm figure when it comes to counting the nation's public schools. Old schools are closed and new ones are opened every year. Plus, there is the complication of charter schools, residential schools, etc. Somewhere between 85,000 and 90,000 is probably a reasonable estimate, meaning institutionalizing a Board of Assessors concept could bring 850,000 to 900,000 Americans into an integral form of civic engagement.

3. Actually, the "tyranny of testing" is the title of a book released in 1962 authored by a well-known American scientist, Banesh Hoffman. It is a devastating critique of the Educational Testing Service and persuasively reveals the inescapable difficulties involved in trying to reduce learning to something that can be captured by a number. Said Hoffman, "Human abilities and potentialities are too complex, too diverse, and too intricately interactive to be measured satisfactorily by present techniques. There is reason to doubt even that they can be meaningfully measured at all in numerical terms." Far from giving us pause, Hoffman's warnings were ignored, and the testing industry has marched on, effectively ignoring all others following Hoffman's lead. Our current educational policy is premised on the very idea Hoffman suggested is largely unattainable. In other words, everything understood today, at least in policy circles, as having to do with education, is also connected to the deployment of a test. Hoffman concluded his book with the following: "All methods of evaluating people have their defects—and grave defects they are. But let us not therefore allow one particular method to play the usurper. *Let us not seek to replace informed judgment* [of the sort teachers possess after nine months working with a child], with all its frailty, by some inexpensive statistical substitute. Let us keep open many diverse and noncompeting channels toward recognition. For high ability is where we find it. It is individual and must be recognized for what it is, not rejected out of hand simply because it does not happen to conform to criteria established by statistical technicians. In seeking high ability, *let us shun overdependence on tests that are blind to*

dedication and creativity, and biased against depth and subtlety. For that way lies testolarty."
The man was nothing if not prophetic: NCLB can be fairly categorized as the very pinnacle
of testolatry. See Banesh Hoffman, *The Tyranny of Testing* (New York: Crowell-Collier,
1962) 30, 216–217.

4. John Dewey decried what he called the "vice of externally imposed ends"
back in 1916. He argued that "the intelligence of the teacher is not free; it is confined to
receiving the aims laid down from above." Consequently, teachers are unable to let their
minds "come to close quarters with the pupil's mind." He noted further that the vice of
externally imposed ends includes "an inclination to propound aims which are so uniform
as to neglect the specific powers and requirements of an individual, forgetting that all
learning is something that happens to an individual at a given time and place." What he
would have thought of the dramatic emphasis on externally imposed standards in the
twenty-first century is anyone's guess. It is likely, however, that he would no longer think
the term "vice" to be adequately descriptive. See his *Democracy and Education* (New York:
Macmillan, 1916), 108–109.

5. See, for example, Richard A. Posner, *Public Intellectuals: A Study of Decline*
(Cambridge, MA: Harvard University Press, 2003).

6. Walter Karp, "Why Johnny Can't Think," *Harpers Magazine,* June 1985. You
can find the full article at http://www.sourcetext.com/grammarian/johnny.html.

7. Raymond Hernandez, "Short of Money, G.O.P. Enlists Rich Candidates," *New
York Times,* November 26, 2007: A1.

8. New congresspersons could get a head start on this requirement by reading
Barbara Ehrenreich's *Nickel and Dimed: On Not Getting By in America* (New York: Met-
ropolitan Books, 2001). Equipped with a college education, a Ph.D., and a small amount
of emergency cash, Ehrenreich made an attempt to work enough minimum wage jobs to
create a life lived within her means. She failed. In the process of recounting her experiences in book form, she busted practically every common myth about minimum-wage
workers and concluded, much the way Ruskin did in nineteenth-century England, that
we live off of *their* generosity.

9. Kevin O'Leary, *Saving Democracy: A Plan for Real Representation in America*
(Stanford, CA: Stanford University Press, 2006), 96–97.

10. Donald Lutz, "Toward a Formal Theory of Constitutional Amendment," in
Sanford Levinson, ed., *Responding to Imperfection: The Theory and Practice of Constitutional Amendment* (Princeton, NJ: Princeton University Press, 1995), 261.

11. Bill Kauffman, "Bye, Bye, Miss American Empire: Or, the Sweet Smell of Secession," *Orion* 26, no. 4 (July/August, 2007): 56–61.

12. See, for example, Robert A. Dahl, *How Democratic Is the American Constitution?*
(New Haven, NJ: Yale University Press, 2002), 17–18.

13. Sanford Levinson, *Our Undemocratic Constitution: Where the Constitution Goes
Wrong and How the People Can Correct It* (New York: Oxford University Press, 2006),
51.

14. *Plessy v. Ferguson* was the infamous case that set the cause of civil rights back
by a half-century or better, creating a judicial precedent with the doctrine of "separate
but equal." *Buckley v. Valeo* declared spending money to influence elections an act of
free speech and, given the legal status of corporate personhood, thereby tied the power
of corporate wealth to the outcome of American elections.

15. Between 1960 and 1990 the number of cases filed in federal courts tripled, while the number of cases in all courts increased steadily, if less dramatically. This increase has come to be called the "litigation explosion." See Mary Ann Glendon, *A Nation Under Lawyers: How the Crisis in the Legal Profession Is Transforming American Society* (Cambridge, MA: Harvard University Press, 1994), 52–54.

16. See Deborah Tannen, *The Argument Culture: Stopping America's War of Words* (New York: Ballantine Books, 1999).

17. Using the 109th Congress at the time of this writing.

18. Jack Abramoff, now serving a five-year sentence for defrauding American Indians and corrupting public officials, was a Republican businessman and lobbyist. As of this writing, the Justice Department still has not sorted through all of the many ways he and his organization worked to alter major pieces of federal legislation. Newspaper articles abound tying Abramoff's activities to the Bush White House.

19. There was a great deal of misinformation surrounding the entire circumstance. Democrats across the country were angry at the Virginia Green Party, not recognizing that Parker was not affiliated with it. She ran as an Independent but called herself an Independent "Green." Because Parker is quite conservative compared to the official Green Party in Virginia, there is a chance that Parker took votes away from Allen, though this will never be known. The larger issue has to do with the fact that these 26,000 people were given no voice in Congress. The same cannot be said for those who cast their votes for Allen, for Republicans remained well represented in Congress after the 2006 elections.

20. Dahl, *How Democratic Is the American Constitution?* 58–59.

21. There would clearly be options in this regard. France, as an example, has a president who serves as "head of state" and a prime minister who manages the affairs of the nation.

22. Between 1995 and 2006 the number of millionaires in the United States more than doubled. We are currently the fastest millionaire-producing country on earth. Two things should be obvious to readers at this point: (1) this development is the result of our current political, economic, and educational arrangements; and (2) it necessarily entails the simultaneous growth in the ranks of the poor, the uninsured, and the pensionless. See Robert Frank, *Richistan: A Journey Through the American Wealth Boom and the Lives of the New Rich* (New York: Crown Publishers, 2007); also Kevin Phillips, *Wealth and Democracy: A Political History of the American Rich* (New York: Broadway Books, 2002).

23. A team of scholars at Arizona State University have created what they call the "Think Tank Review Project," which is merely an attempt to submit the reports of think tanks to something like an academic peer-review process. In other words, they enlist a network of scholars from across the country to do reviews of think-tank reports to assess the methods used, the assumptions made, etc. Readers can check out the project at http://www.thinktankreview.org.

Index

About the Author

Paul Theobald holds the Woods-Beals Chair in Urban and Rural Education at Buffalo State College. He has published widely in the area of community-based and place-based education and is author of *Teaching the Commons: Place, Pride, and the Renewal of Community.*